The way children learn their native language has been the subject of intense and widespread investigation in the last decades, stimulated by advances in theoretical linguistics and the behavioural sciences. For the student, this has meant a bewildering number of research reports, often differing in their theoretical viewpoint and the methodological approach they advocate, and apparently conflicting in their conclusions. *Child Language* provides the student with a cool, clear and concise survey of the most important recent research work, and puts into perspective the contributions made by Chomsky, Piaget and others. The research surveyed, though primarily of English-speaking children, includes studies of children whose first language is not English and bilingual children.

Dr Elliot believes that the study of child language necessarily raises questions about the nature of language – is human language something only humans can learn? – and about learning itself – how does our ability to learn language depend on biological factors, such as our age, and how important is our social and linguistic environment? Little justification is found for the view that language has an independent existence for the young child, and his linguistic achievements are studied within the context of his development in general.

The challenges to research that still have to be faced are made explicit, but Dr Elliot's book clearly shows that the study of child language does have 'its own intrinsic fascination'. Written primarily for students of psychology and linguistics, this stimulating and comprehensive textbook is accessible to anyone with a serious interest in that study.

CAMBRIDGE TEXTBOOKS IN LINGUISTICS

General Editors: W. SIDNEY ALLEN, B. COMRIE,
C. J. FILLMORE, E. J. A. HENDERSON, F. W. HOUSEHOLDER,
R. LASS, J. LYONS, R. B. LE PAGE, P. H. MATTHEWS,
R. POSNER, J. L. M. TRIM

CHILD LANGUAGE

CHILD LANGUAGE

ALISON J. ELLIOT
LECTURER, DEPARTMENT OF PSYCHOLOGY
UNIVERSITY OF EDINBURGH

CAMBRIDGE UNIVERSITY PRESS

CAMBRIDGE
LONDON   NEW YORK   NEW ROCHELLE
MELBOURNE   SYDNEY

Published by the Press Syndicate of the University of Cambridge
The Pitt Building, Trumpington Street, Cambridge CB2 1RP
32 East 57th Street, New York, NY 10022, USA
296 Beaconsfield Parade, Middle Park, Melbourne 3206, Australia

First published 1981

Printed and bound in Great Britain at The Pitman Press, Bath

British Library Cataloguing in Publication Data
Elliot, Alison J
Child language. – (Cambridge textbooks in
linguistics).
1. Children – Language
I. Title   II. Series
401'.9   LB1139.L3   80–41240

ISBN 0 521 22518 3 hard covers
ISBN 0 521 29556 4 paperback

CONTENTS

Contents

I

Introduction

A 2-year-old boy looks up from his toys and says 'Where's Mummy gone?' Suppose that two linguists and two psychologists observe this happening through a one-way screen. We ask them to interpret what the child is doing and how he has come to be able to do it.

The first linguist notices that the child has produced a well-formed question. This linguist has spent considerable effort analysing English questions and has produced a complicated description of them – more complicated, for example, than the one for the corresponding declarative sentence *Mummy has gone into the kitchen*. He is impressed by the child's achievement and wonders whether the child has had the same difficulty in coming to terms with questions as he has had in his linguistic descriptions. Is it only lately that he has managed to produce question forms? More interestingly, was there a time when he was regularly producing statements but never turning them into well-formed questions? This linguist delves back into the records which have been kept of this child's earlier utterances and takes careful note of the grammatical errors he has made.

The other linguist is a functionalist. He sees that the child is using his language competently to enquire for a particular piece of information which he lacks. He therefore has learnt two things about language – it can be used to convey information about the state of the world and it can also be used in an instrumental way to engage other people in the task in hand, that of discovering Mummy's whereabouts. This linguist is impressed by the way in which the child uses language efficiently to demonstrate these two functions simultaneously. He suggests that this is quite a sophisticated accomplishment, probably predated by earlier occasions on which one of the functions of language would have been in evidence but not both, so he decides to examine the records of the way in which the child has previously used language in his interactions with other people.

Our first psychologist is not particularly impressed. The child has uttered a string of words not very unlike others which he hears around him all day long. Doubtless he himself has already uttered similar sentences and has found that people pay attention to him when he does. 'Where's my milk?' has resulted in his milk being placed in front of him by a mother who has previously said things like 'Where's my purse gone?' while looking for her purse. The psychologist does not doubt that if he combs through the mother's earlier utterances he will find support for the obvious fact that the child is simply imitating versions of what he has previously heard because he has been encouraged to do so. How else would he learn to talk?

The second psychologist tries to be interested. The child is giving verbal expression to a very important discovery; although he cannot see where his mother is at present he does realise that she must be somewhere and that it is probably possible to find out where she is. However, the psychologist knows that the child made this discovery long before he was speaking fluently and so, although his language is a useful addition to his intellectual powers, its main advantage is that of giving precision and coherence to knowledge he already possesses. He knows that although the child can talk plausibly about where objects might be, there are still gaps in his knowledge about spatial relations, so he decides to play with the child to probe these deficits further.

Notice that in these caricatures each of our investigators saw the problem in a way that was grounded principally in this theory of language – that language is a set of grammatical sentences, that language is a means of social control, that language is a collection of motor responses, or that language is one example of symbolic functioning. Similarly the kind of data they set out to gather depended partly on the question they were asking but also on their view of human learning – that we have a special skill for discovering the rules of our language from a minimal linguistic input, that each child creates language afresh in response to an increasing need to communicate with others, that we learn language, as we learn everything else, through selective reinforcement of our spontaneous behaviour, or that learning consists in a constant restructuring of our understanding of the working of the world about us. They are not entirely free to pair any model of language with any model of development – for example, the first psychologist would not be so blithely confident about his understanding of human learning if he had a more sensitive account of human language – but it is important to bear both elements in mind when trying to evaluate their perception of the problem.

Can we say of all four accounts that although each is different, each is correct in its own way? Unfortunately, this is not likely. Our characters are basically visitors to the subject of child language with a variety of ultimate destinations in mind. The theoretical luggage they have with them was packed elsewhere and will serve them well in other climes. They are principally interested in the nature of adult language or human intelligence and believe they can find adequate motivation for their theories without looking at children's language. Eventually, they must be able to account for child language but at present they are content to look only for confirmation of their views in such data. As a result some of them tend to accept the language of the child uncritically. On the face of it, the child in our example noticed his mother's absence and enquired about where she had gone, using the linguistic form appropriate to such a request. It may have been, however, that the question form was a partial accident – the result of merging together the two previous forms *Where's Mummy?* and *Mummy gone.* The latter form might have already been used several times simply to comment on the disappearance of an item of interest to him, without implications for its subsequent location. The first, although in the form of a genuine enquiry, is similar to language frequently used in conversation between the child and adults where the adults ask 'Where's your nose?', or similar questions which are not real requests for information but rather ritualised behaviour patterns forming games which both enjoy. If this were the case, this child-centred account would invalidate most of the explanations presented above, since it proposes an analysis of the problem which is qualitatively different from what one would expect had an adult been the actor.

One must be cautious, therefore, about invoking the behaviour of a young child directly in support of a particular theory of language or of development. However, some general questions about the nature of language or of development can be illuminated by carefully watching a child learning his language. In particular we keep returning to debates about the autonomy of language and of the continuity of development. To what extent can language be approached without consideration of other symbolic or communicative systems or other sources of knowledge? To what extent should development be viewed as a gradual, quantitative change in a body of knowledge or of skill, and to what extent should it be viewed as a series of qualitative changes?

It has been a tenet of much twentieth-century linguistics that language can be conceived of as a body of knowledge separable from other aspects of intelligence, and that human speech is qualitatively different from communication in other species. Comparative studies show, for example, that children without overt language perform well in non-linguistic measures of intelligence, that relatively unintelligent children can still acquire a complicated natural language, that parrots cannot use language creatively and that clever chimps cannot be taught to produce vocal language. Not surprisingly, such work has inspired people to refine the concepts of communication, language and intelligence so that the relation of language to those other processes can be investigated at a more interesting level.

Claims about the autonomy of language can also be tested by looking at the development of a child, and at this point we find ourselves beginning to debate the issue about the continuity of development as well. The main point of contention is where language comes from. Does it appear from nowhere, or does it have roots in the child's early, prelinguistic experience that could explain its emergence and development? If language is a trivial extension of the young child's early skill at communicating and if it is only one formulation of his non-linguistic knowledge, then the arguments that language should be accorded a special, autonomous status are considerably weakened. On the other hand, if the emergence of language represents a qualitative change in the child's abilities which has no direct link with his earlier experiences, we may wish to accord it a special compartmentalised treatment in relative isolation from his other skills.

An important consequence of this latter position is that, having

4

allowed that at one point a new ability can appear with no obvious precursor in the child's accumulated experience, one is invited to adopt a discontinuous view of other aspects of development. Thus development could be seen as a series of steps, each one qualitatively different from the one before, rather than a smooth scale of increasing knowledge or ability. One of the consequences of allowing that development may be discontinuous is that on particular points the child may appear to take a step backwards, instead of forwards. To take a famous example, many children appear to unlearn the proper past tense of strong verbs. Having correctly used the forms *came* and *went*, they enter a period of saying *comed* and *goed* instead. The discontinuous view of development would comment that they had got to the stage of imposing the weak past tense ending on all verbs, and so had revised their earlier opinion of what the proper forms should be. This possibility that later experience can restructure the form of earlier knowledge is an important consequence of seeing development as discontinuous and not simply gradually cumulative.

This view then feeds back in an interesting way into the question of the autonomy of language. Language may or may not have identifiable roots in non-linguistic experience, but once the child begins to learn to talk it is still possible that this may modify the rest of his intellectual and social abilities, in such a way as to bring language and thought much closer together at a later period. Since the child is learning more about language, people and objects simultaneously, it is unlikely that these developments do not continually modify each other. Any adequate explanation of language development must therefore take these other developments into account.

Thus we see that the question of the autonomy of language has two prongs to it which are relevant to studies of child language. These are the prongs of origin – where does language come from? – and of development – in what sense does the child make use of his discoveries about language to help his general cognitive and social development, and vice versa? Related to these questions is the debate about the nature of learning – to what extent does the child simply soak up language from what he hears around him (in which case the nature of the environment in which the learning takes place is of crucial importance), and to what extent is he imposing a succession of different organisations on his raw material (in which case the nature of the environment may be of secondary importance to the child's more general information-processing abilities)?

Such is the theoretical background against which many of the more specific debates in child language are set. However, it would be wrong to give the impression that everyone who studies child language is motivated only by these grand considerations. The subject has its own intrinsic fascination, and the number of people working primarily in the area has been increasing steadily for some time. The following pages should give some indication of why this is so.

2

Mechanisms for language acquisition

The study of language acquisition has a long history,[1] but in the last twenty years work on this subject has grown explosively. No one would doubt that the impetus for this was the writing of Noam Chomsky, so in this chapter we shall outline his account of language acquisition,[2] discuss the background and implications of its major claims and assumptions, and introduce criticisms or modifications to the theory which have been indicated by some of the research to be discussed in greater detail in the rest of this book.

2.1 Chomsky's views on language acquisition

As a linguist, Chomsky's central aim is to construct a theory of language, and so one might imagine that his views on language acquisition are only incidental to his overall theory of language. In one sense this is true but in another sense the relation is more complex. The image of the child learning his native language is one to which Chomsky returns repeatedly, emphasising the parallel between child and linguist until it becomes difficult to distinguish his theory of language from his views on language acquisition.[3]

Both child and linguist are faced with a set of primary linguistic data. Both have to construct a grammatical system which accounts for the data. Chomsky proposes as a theoretical construct a language acquisition device (LAD), which accepts as input the primary linguistic data and has as output a grammar of the language

1. For a useful sample of some early studies, see Bar-Adon and Leopold (1971).
2. A certain familiarity with Chomsky's work is assumed. Readers wishing a fuller account of his theory should refer to Lyons (1970).
3. For a discussion of this aspect of Chomsky's work, see Derwing (1973) and the review by Smith (1975).

from which the data have been drawn. He then sees the task of general linguistic theory to be that of specifying the nature of the device. From our point of view, the important idea is that Chomsky sees the activities of the child learning his language as formally equivalent to the workings of the LAD with the input and output specified above. The problem of language acquisition will be solved for him once the characteristics of the LAD have been made explicit.

Notice the way in which Chomsky poses the problem for the child. His aim is to construct a grammar of the language. In other words, Chomsky is outlining an account of the acquisition of linguistic competence – that is, the growth of the body of knowledge about the structure of the language which, Chomsky proposes, underlies a native speaker's ability to speak and understand his language. His reasons for favouring this characterisation of the problem are familiar enough. In his writing he emphasises the central importance of linguistic creativity – that is, the ability of a native speaker to produce and understand sentences of the language which he has never heard before. He can produce novel sentences which are grammatical and which he is assumed to be able to distinguish from ungrammatical ones. This demonstrates that he has access to more than an accumulation of previously heard utterances. Chomsky argues that a native speaker has access to knowledge about the structure of his language which guides him in his language use. Chomsky calls this knowledge linguistic competence. He distinguishes this from language performance, the use of his language by a native speaker in a particular social context. Explanation of competence is the task of the linguist: for Chomsky, acquisition of competence is the goal facing the child.

This defines the central problem. The data out of which the child and linguist have to create the competence model are the data of language performance. Here the child is seen to be in an even worse position than the linguist. The connection between competence and performance is elusive even when the performance data are written sentences. A child, in addition, has to filter out many characteristics of the spoken language – lapses of attention, self-interruptions, hesitations, and changes of plan in mid-sentence, to mention some of the more serious ones for someone trying to use spoken language as evidence of underlying competence. Thus the primary linguistic data which are the input to the LAD are seen as being a particularly degenerate sample of the language to be learned, quite apart from the fact that in principle they are several analytic stages removed from the stuff of competence.

Such considerations constrain the nature of the LAD. Since input and output are qualitatively different, an inactive store of past experience will be inadequate to the task of transforming the one into the other. Even if the more gross deviations from grammaticality are identified as such by a system of reinforcement, such as an operant conditioning account would propose (see section 2.6), the problem of creativity still remains. The standard solution to this problem of creativity is to invoke generalisation by analogy.[4] The child analyses the contexts in which he experiences certain linguistic units and identifies some sets of items as appearing in similar positions in utterances. He then tends to place these items in similar positions in new utterances, so extending his ability to produce acceptable utterances to a class wider than those he has actually heard. This explanation is inadequate for Chomsky's purposes on two accounts. He feels that it attempts to conduct a linguistic analysis purely at the level of surface structure. Since Chomsky argues for the need for a transformational grammar, this account misrepresents the nature of language as he sees it and thus cannot, he believes, work in principle. Secondly, it is an extremely laborious method of learning if it is followed to the letter and has difficulty accounting for the speed with which children learn to use sentence forms which are syntactically quite complex. Thus the available conditioning models of learning – ones which see learning proceeding inductively on experience with minimal contribution made by the subject's own efforts – failed to give a convincing account (in 1959) of the course of language acquisition.

A common alternative to an inductive view of discovery is one which involves the subject in testing hypotheses. Experience is then not directly the source of knowledge about the object of learning but is instead data against which hypotheses about the object of learning are checked. This system is more efficient in terms of the time necessary to learn something and lighter in its demands on the environment of learning. It pays for this efficiency, however, by

4. See, for example, the model of contextual generalisation, proposed by Braine (1963b).

9

increasing the contribution made to the process by the learner himself and requires a more sophisticated account of the individual's capacity for learning. It also raises the question of the source of the hypotheses to be tested.[5]

Since the hypotheses in question are hypotheses about language structure and since Chomsky had already claimed that the categories necessary for linguistic analysis were not identifiable in the surface form of sentences, he could not find a satisfactory account of how children could come to discover the kinds of hypotheses necessary for the task. At this stage he introduced into the argument some observations about language and its acquisition. He stressed the importance of universals of language: despite many superficial differences between them in their surface structure, the languages of the world share many important features at a deeper level. He observed that language was species-specific; only human beings had evolved a communication system with the properties of natural language. There also appears to be a critical period for language acquisition: adults find it far more difficult to learn a second language than primary-school children. He claimed that almost all children by age 5 have learned the basic structures of their language, despite considerable differences in intelligence as measured by IQ scores and differences in the richness of the learning environment. Supported by these observations, he proposed that the LAD should represent an innate capacity for learning a natural language, separate from other learning abilities.[6] Notice that none of his observations necessarily implies that the LAD should be innate, since they could all be explained in other ways. Language universals may be a reflection of some other aspect of the shared human condition; other animals may have the capacity to learn a communicative or symbolic system although for other reasons it has never proved useful for them; and the lack of relation between IQ measures and the course of language development may be more a reflection of the inadequacy of the particular conception

5. The distinction between inductive and hypothesis-testing approaches is probably a matter of degree (Marshall, 1979: 444).

6. It should be noted that everyone must postulate innate learning mechanisms of some kind (cf. Fodor, Bever and Garrett, 1974) if only to explain an organism's capacity to store experience and perform rudimentary inductive processes on it. Chomsky is termed a nativist because of the detail and specificity of the mechanisms he proposes.

of intelligence incorporated in the construction of IQ tests than a testimony to the uniqueness of children's language acquisition skills. However, granted an innate capacity specifically geared to language learning the observations are collectively given an explanation. As to the precise structure of the LAD, Chomsky still sees this as a topic for further research, but he suggests that it should incorporate within it information about universal aspects of language structure. Thus, part of the child's inborn capacity for language is knowledge about the structure of the language he will have to learn, which ever one it may be.[7]

About the development of the specific properties of the language the child is learning, Chomsky is silent. McNeill (1966b) proposed to divide the task into acquisition of the base component and the transformational component of the language. Hypothesising the existence of a universal base, he suggested that knowledge of the universal base is innate, along with sufficient information about the nature of transformations to enable the child to form hypotheses about the form of his particular language. It is unfortunate that details of this process which are, after all, the crux of the problem, are not given, particularly since it is here that the complexity and source of linguistic creativity are most evident. In addition, the linguistic model has now been modified to the point where McNeill's suggestion is no longer reasonable.

In conclusion, then, Chomsky does not provide us with a theory of language acquisition. He has made certain claims about the nature of the problem and pointed out ways in which explanations of the process should be constrained. In so doing, he has also opened up the whole area and directed attention once more to the child and his achievement, consigned by psychologists and linguists of the preceding generation to a general, all-purpose learning mechanism. Before reporting recent findings in the area we shall return to Chomsky's claims and examine them more thoroughly.

2.2 **Competence and creativity**

Chomsky was impressed by the fact of linguistic creativity – the fact that native speakers can make grammatical

---

7. Slobin (1971) proposed that the LAD may be more fruitfully conceived as a general information-processing ability. These two extreme alternatives have become known as the content and process accounts of the LAD (cf. Aitchison, 1976).

judgments on strings of words from the vocabulary of their language whether or not they have heard that particular combination before. This is indeed remarkable if you assume learning is simple storage of experience for future unprocessed regurgitation. Of course, such a view is untenable and introduced as a straw man, preparatory to discussion about the nature of the processing necessary to explain linguistic creativity.

At this point it is important to point out that intelligent understanding of novel experiences is not a capacity restricted to the production and perception of sentences. Most of us can switch on the television on a Saturday evening, turn down the sound, and on the basis of novel visual input alone cheer and groan with the crowd watching the football match being televised. In other words, we can identify fouls, recognise goals and interpret interactions between referee and players although we have never before seen that particular pattern of visual input. This example is instructive in that the explanation of our ability, at least at an initial level, is obvious. We can do this because we know the rules of football and know how to use them to understand the progress of the game, though it may be objected that it is unlike linguistic creativity in that the rules are explicit and can be formulated, whereas no one has been able to give a satisfactory account of the rules of grammar. But consider another example: we can all walk through a room full of furniture which we have never seen before, without bumping into any of it. This time there are no agreed sets of rules to enable us to convert the visual input into information about the distance and location of one object from another, which we then use to guide our movement through the room. Some people have drawn an analogy between similar problems in visual perception and language and have shown that equally complex structural models are required to account for both abilities. It is interesting to note in this connection that nativist explanations for depth perception have been revived recently as well.[8]

Linguistic creativity is thus not as isolated a phenomenon as Chomsky implies. All the time we are coping intelligently with novel experiences. Of course this is no reason to cease wondering at the linguistic skill because explanations for other skills are not

8. See Bower (1977) for discussions of depth perception, and Oatley (1972) for an introduction to the use of structural models in visual perception.

plentiful or satisfactory. It does encourage us, though, to ask whether Chomsky has isolated the most relevant example of linguistic creativity on which to base his theory.

Many people think he has not. Their argument has two prongs to it. In the first place, it is an empirical question at what stage children can make grammatical judgments about isolated sentences. Eventually they can to some extent, so presumably it is still valid to keep grammatical judgments as the output of the LAD. However it is important to consider whether this ability is a fundamental one, necessary for every competent speaker of the language however young or illiterate he may be, or whether it is a relatively specialised ability, widespread among Western adults but none the less a byproduct of our literate culture. It is certainly very difficult to demonstrate that children and adults from non-literate cultures can make isolated linguistic or logical judgments.[9] While it is important not to confuse our failure to elicit such judgments with their validity as theoretical constructs, it is still interesting to bear in mind the possibility that the restricted grammatical competence which Chomsky seeks to explain may be a late development and may develop only in some cultures.

The second prong to the argument consists in drawing attention to what children can do very well. From an early age they appear to communicate very fluently, producing utterances which are not just remarkably well formed according to a linguist's standards but also appropriate to the social context in which the speakers find themselves. Children are thus learning far more about language than rules of grammar and, since there is doubt about the status of grammatical competence for them, it has been proposed that it is more appropriate to identify the child's task as that of acquiring communicative competence (Campbell and Wales, 1970). In other words, the focus should be placed on language in context rather than on a body of rules of the structural well-formedness of system sentences (Lyons, 1977). Remember that the reason for the proposal to alter the object of learning is not simply a reflection of the preferences or interests of the investigators: it concerns the question whether linguistic competence is a legitimate concept for

9. Cole, Gay, Glick and Sharp (1971) describe the frustrations of trying to study logical development with people from a non-literate culture, and Olson (1975) discusses the possible distorting effects on theories of language acquisition of failing to recognise the importance of literacy.

children and the belief that the relation between knowledge of language structure and knowledge of the rules of language use may be quite different for the child than it is for the adult.

This does not mean that communicative competence is to be equated with performance. We still have to contend with creativity, except that now we note the native speaker's (and child's) ability to produce and interpret in appropriate contexts utterances which he has never heard before. We are therefore still a long way from following Bloomfield's characterisation of a natural language as 'the totality of utterances that can be made in a speech-community' (1926). There is still a body of knowledge underlying the ability, but instead of being restricted to knowledge about linguistic form it also includes knowledge about whether something is appropriate in relation to a context in which it is used and evaluated, as in the definition given by Hymes (1971). It is important to note that this is more than the superficial rules of etiquette. It includes at least control of basic linguistic features such as deictic reference, pronouns of address and speech acts. Notice also that while the two criteria of acceptability are, generally, separable for the adult, their relative status for the child is less clear.

In conclusion, many people working with children find Chomsky's characterisation of the object of the child's learning at best restrictive or uninteresting, at worst misleading. This does not involve challenging the importance of creativity or the arguments for separating competence as the object of study rather than performance: instead it involves adopting a more extensive aspect of creativity and consequently a modified view of the specific details of the type of competence.

Such a modification of the notion of competence may, however, have repercussions on the formal properties of the model. It is possible for Chomsky to argue for competence as a generative system which explicitly specifies whether a word string is a sentence of the language or not. As such it attempts to make discrete statements, although not everyone agrees that this aim is reasonable (cf. Hockett, 1968; Lakoff, 1971). It is more difficult to decide for a model of communicative competence whether it will be generative in this sense or simply make probabilistic statements about appropriateness, since no one knows what to expect of a model of social context.

2.3   **Primary linguistic data**

We have seen that Chomsky identifies the input to the LAD as primary linguistic data which, as the material is part of language performance, are supposed to include a degenerate sample of the language in question, full of false starts and ungrammatical utterances, and extremely complex when compared to the child's own linguistic level. We will see in chapter 7 that studies of mothers' speech to children indicate that, far from being complex and ungrammatical, language addressed to young children is usually simple and remarkably free from hesitation and deviation from grammaticality. How else might Chomsky's model have to be modified to make it a better reflection of the problem the child faces?

The major modification has to do with what other aspects of the child's environment might be important for his language learning. Chomsky played down the role of the environment in language learning, claiming that despite wide differences in social background, richness of stimulation or cultural origin, children all master a set of fundamental linguistic structures by roughly the same age. He was interested in telling a universal story, and so did not pursue the differences in rate and smoothness of development which undoubtedly do occur and may depend on features of the external environment. For example, differences can be shown which depend on whether the child has siblings (and if so whether he is first born or a twin), sex of the child, and socio-economic background of the parents.[10] Not many cross-cultural comparisons are available. Some of these differences may be long-lasting, so are important to the individual children involved. In addition they indicate which parameters may be centrally involved in the acquisition process. These factors will be dealt with more fully in chapter 7.

Other aspects of a child's external linguistic environment are less clearly identified but may well be crucially important for the ease with which a child learns his language and even the nature of the final product. In particular, many investigators are currently drawing attention to the quality of the interpersonal relationships which children experience even before they begin to produce

---

10.   Many studies of this kind were done in the psychometric days of the 1930s and 1940s and are summarised in McCarthy (1954).

recognisable verbal utterances themselves. In these relationships, the child himself is certainly an equal partner – in some cases the controlling one – and careful analysis of interactions between children and their mothers or siblings have suggested ways in which children may come to understand some of the rudimentary functions of language at an early age. They may even learn how to segment their experience in ways which will later be useful as a basis for linguistic analysis. It is also apparent that at the preschool stage children are very quick to pick up clues to the intentions of adults, and use this as an aid to making sense of their utterances. It is not yet clear how important variations in the nature of the child's interpersonal experiences are for the course of his language development. However, since social interactions are a major part of the young child's world, many investigators now view early language acquisition within the wider context. Their approach will be discussed in chapter 3.

Just as there is a core and a periphery to a child's social environment, so his cognitive development can be viewed as having a central course, which all normal children follow, and specialised experiences which only some are fortunate enough or unfortunate enough to undergo. As Chomsky had emphasised the relative lack of effect of differences in a child's external social environment on the central features of his language development, so he claimed that IQ did not correlate with progress in language acquisition. Again, he fails to compare like with like. IQ tests are designed to highlight differences in intelligence between individuals, while his key concern is to draw attention to universal processes. This concern he shares with many developmental psychologists and so it is not surprising to find attention drawn to suggestive parallels between linguistic and cognitive development. Not everyone would agree with Piaget in seeing language as simply one aspect of a general symbolic function, but few find they can ignore the question of how the child conceives of the world, social and cognitive, at any stage of his language development if they want to understand the details of their observations. Again, chapter 3 will elaborate on these issues.

It is important to note again that it is not simply a matter of preference which leads some investigators to study language development in its social and cognitive contexts. The input to the

LAD must include information about the meaning of the utterances which constitute the primary linguistic data, or at least about sameness of meaning. This in turn must be the meaning the utterance has for the child, and so immediately one is forced to become involved with the details of social and cognitive development. Chomsky in fact denied that language acquisition should be regarded as a completely separate system, but it is clear that he expected the interaction with other aspects of cognition to be minimal. In view of the comments in the previous section as well as evidence to be discussed in chapter 3, it is unlikely that this will be the case.

2.4 Language in chimpanzees

When it is proposed that children have a specific disposition to learn language, a whole host of subsidiary issues are raised. In particular, is it only human beings who have this specific learning ability or are other species similarly endowed? If so, could they be persuaded to learn a human language just as children do? If not, how sophisticated are their own species-specific systems of communication? The debate which has arisen around these questions has generated more passion than most, because of the atavistic threat to man's distinctiveness which appears to be involved in the answers to the questions.

It is clear that, while a recurrent fantasy in many human cultures is that animals should be able to talk, none do, apart from the imitative displays of parrots and mynah birds, which do not demonstrate any understanding of the content of the utterances they produce. It is not so clear, however, that it would not be possible to teach animals of another species some form of human language, and in the last fifteen years several research projects have been set up which have proposed to do precisely that.

These projects fall into two groups, according to their aims and methods. Premack (1971, 1976) set out to see whether his chimpanzee, Sarah, could be trained to use an artificial language which had in it constructions which were formally equivalent to particular English constructions. (See also the report on Lana's progress given in Rumbaugh (1977).) Premack's concern was therefore to discover whether the chimp could demonstrate adequate cognitive sophistication for handling certain features of language. His method was strictly experimental. Sarah was exposed to the task in a laboratory and was trained, using rigorous operant conditioning techniques (see section 2.6), to follow instructions and answer questions. These instructions were given to her by means of a vertical array of plastic chips of different colours and shapes, which could translate into a few propositions, closer to the notations of logic than the surface form of English. Most of the chips were like words in that they corresponded to object, person or property, such as *pail*, *Sarah*, *red*, but there were a few chips which translated into relations such as *same as*, *not*, *implies*, and one which could be used to pose questions. Sarah was given a pile of chips to use as answers and was rewarded with a piece of fruit when she responded correctly. Sarah could distinguish between the word and its referent – the chip for *red* was, in fact, not red in colour. She could distinguish between strings such as *Randy give apple Sarah* and *Sarah give apple Randy*. She could interpret *Key? pencil* as a request to choose between *same* and *not same* and *?key same pencil* as a choice between *yes* and *no*, these strings translating into the English sentences *What is the relation between key and pencil?* and *Is key the same as pencil?* respectively. She also learned the use of chips corresponding to plural markers, quantifiers and forms of the copula, and could answer questions about the colour, shape or size of objects. She could handle coordinated sentences such as *Sarah insert banana pail apple dish* after carefully graded training, and she could generate novel sequences but only at the level of lexical substitution (i.e. having been trained on *Randy give apple Sarah*, she could produce *Randy give banana Sarah* in an appropriate context).

Many of Sarah's accomplishments are not surprising when seen in the context of other experimental work with chimpanzees which is not specifically oriented towards language (Jolly, 1972). Chimpanzees readily participate in token economy schemes where they are rewarded with tokens which can be exchanged for food, so Sarah's ability to distinguish between 'word' and referent could have been expected. Again, chimpanzees perform well on classification tasks which are similar in principle to the problem of learning modifiers in Sarah's task; and they can solve complicated oddity problems, where the reward is contingent on choosing the 'odd man out' of an array, so Sarah's success with the limited range of negatives employed is not surprising. What is provocative is the way in which Premack has drawn attention to the linguistic potential of these skills.[11]

Fodor, Bever and Garrett (1974) record their scepticism about the syntactic power of the system Sarah has learned. They point out that there is little or no constituent structure about the sentences involved and draw attention to the observation that Sarah had difficulty learning to substitute Modifier + Noun for a noun in her sentences. Having learned *Insert apple dish* she had difficulty dealing with *Insert apple red dish*. On the other hand, Brown (1973) worries about the fact that, when Sarah was given a new trainer who was not familiar with the system, her performance deteriorated. He takes this as suggesting that a lot of Sarah's success might be attributed to the possibility that she was picking up cues to the correct response which her original trainer was emitting unconsciously. Premack (1976) replies in detail to these criticisms.

Brown also points out that Sarah seldom used the chips to initiate conversation, unlike the behaviour of young children with their first words. This underlines the artificiality of the Premack system, a characteristic which other investigators have tried to avoid.

This other group of projects has had a rather more ambitious aim. They set out to see whether a chimp would learn a language when it was immersed in, and included as a partner in, a particular linguistic environment. The most famous of these projects was that carried out by the Gardners with their young female chimp, Washoe. The idea of bringing up a chimp as one of the family was not a new one. Kellog (1968) reported half a dozen studies where a chimp had been included in a family circle, but without much success as far as the development of linguistic skills was concerned. The Hayes had tried to train their chimp Viki to speak but in the end she could produce only four words – *mama, papa, cup* and *up* – and these were produced with considerable strain, using a

11.   The relation between linguistic and non-linguistic skills is not always obvious. Premack and Premack (1974) expected that before understanding the linguistic distinction between *same* and *different* chimpanzees should be able to perform a match-to-sample task – that is, they should be able to pick out from a range of stimuli the one which matched a sample stimulus shown to them. They found that their chimpanzees Peony and Elizabeth could solve the linguistic task only after they had solved both match-to-sample and oddity problems using the materials.

stage whisper instead of proper voiced vowels, and had been taught to her using elaborate and artificial techniques. The Gardners, however, decided to communicate with Washoe, not vocally, but using a form of American Sign Language (ASL), so exploiting the chimp's natural skill at manipulation rather than expecting her to use vocal apparatus which was not suited to the characteristics of human speech.

Washoe came to live with the Gardners when she was 11 months old, by which point they and their assistants had learned how to communicate using ASL. Washoe was welcomed into the family and, while she was present, they did not speak to each other but, instead, communicated with each other and with Washoe by sign language. Washoe began to sign readily and was helped by the Gardners to form the signs. By the time she was 5 years old she had learned a vocabulary of at least 132 signs (Gardner and Gardner, 1975). She did not simply associate a sign with a single exemplar of it but could generalise and restrict the usage of the sign. For example, having been taught the sign for *flower*, Washoe began to use it in the context of a wide range of smells, but when a suitable sign for *smell* had been introduced to her, she then restricted the use of the flower sign. She could generate novel combinations of signs, producing *water bird* in the context of a duck. She could reply to a series of signed *wh*-questions with a sign of the grammatical category appropriate to the question with a fair degree of success. In fact, the Gardners favourably compared Washoe's performance of 84 per cent correct replies to *who*, *what*, *where* and *whose* questions with reports of the Stage III children studied by Brown who were giving 50 per cent correct replies to *who*, *what* and *where* questions. The Gardners note idiosyncratic features of Washoe's signing which have also been noted in the signing of children learning ASL, such as an enlarged signing area, the orientation of signs towards the self instead of towards the receiver and the reduction of certain hand configurations to a single pointing finger. Since the Washoe project, several other chimps have learned to sign (see Fouts 1973; Linden, 1974).

The Gardners' work has captured the imagination of a wide audience. They seem to be confident that Washoe has learned to communicate successfully in ASL. However, several people remain to be convinced that Washoe has in some sense acquired a form of human language (Brown, 1970b, 1973; Fodor, Bever and Garrett, 1974). Many of these criticisms consist of appealing to the design features of language specified by Hockett (1960), such as rapid fading, semanticity, arbitrariness, displacement, productivity, duality of patterning and interchangeability, and trying to determine whether Washoe has demonstrated that her communicative skills have these characteristics.

Brown (1970b) laid great emphasis on the fact that Washoe's early two-word combinations did not appear to have any order constraint on them. However, she did employ the signing equivalent of intonation to mark her utterances, in that she kept her hands in the signing position until the end of a sequence. In addition, Brown (1973) noted that Washoe's early signs expressed the same restricted set of semantic relations as are found in children's early utterances (see chapter 5). In view of the fact that it is not clear how reliable word order is in the two-word stage of child language, Brown concluded that the semantic evidence was a more interesting comparison of early child/chimp language.

Seidenberg and Petitto (1979), however, criticise the work on the ground that it has not been reported sufficiently thoroughly to allow other people to check some of the Gardners' interpretations. In particular, they draw attention to a characteristic of Washoe and of other signing chimps which the Gardners report but do not emphasise, namely, that of frequently repeating signs, so making their communications highly redundant. Early child language, by contrast, is remarkably concise and non-redundant (Greenfield and Zukow, 1978), and this repetition is not reported in the early signing of deaf children. The Gardners edit these repetitions out of their data, making it difficult to know whether Washoe could combine signs according to syntactic rules. Seidenberg and Petitto complain that, on the basis of the evidence which has been presented by the Gardners for public evaluation, much of Washoe's supposedly linguistic skill could be explained away as a direct reflection of the techniques they had used to teach her the signs for certain concepts. Terrace, Petitto, Sanders and Bever (1979) add weight to these criticisms by reporting that when they looked closely at their video-tapes they realised that most of the utterances produced by their signing chimp, Nim, were prompted by a prior utterance by his teacher. In addition, Nim interrupted his teacher more frequently than children do at a corresponding stage of development, and changes in the length of his utterances were quite unlike those produced by children.

Whatever status is eventually given to the content of much of the chimp signing, the Washoe project has demonstrated that chimps can learn, or already know a lot about, the social value of gestures. This has led to a renewed interest in the nature of communication among wild chimpanzees. Plooij (1978) has reported the appearance of gestural patterns among chimp mother–infant pairs similar in form to those observed between human mothers and infants. For example, when a mother lifts up her child, the child has to lift his arms to help her. In time, the child anticipates the lift and raises his arms, and soon the 'arms-high' gesture functions as a request to the mother and, in the chimps studied by Plooij, among adults indicates that no aggression is intended. However much of the communication between chimpanzees in the wild is less obvious to a human observer. Menzel (1973, 1975, 1978) approached the issue of communication between chimps in the wild by first identifying the kind of problem for which the chimps might need to be able to communicate. He then set up the problem for some young chimps in a research station and, from their success in solving the problem, deduced what information had been transmitted. The problem he explored was that of finding food or some other hidden object. He chose one of the chimps and showed him where the target object was hidden, while the rest of the group could not see. He then returned the 'leader' to the rest of the group and noted how successful they were in finding the object. By varying the nature of the object, removing it once the search had begun so that the animals could not be drawn to it simply by sensory means, and occasionally using two leaders and showing them different objects, he concluded that the leaders were retaining and conveying information about the presence or absence of an object, its direction, its distance, whether it was food or some fear-inducing object, such as a dead snake, the relative quantity of food and the type of food which was hidden. However, it was less clear just how this information was conveyed. Menzel reports that early in the study the chimps made greater use of signals such as glances, whimpers, or tapping each other on the shoulder to encourage their companions to follow them than was the case later in the study. He concluded that later on there was very little use of gesture for communication, but probably a lot of information was conveyed by posture and more general body movement.

Intensive study has only just begun into communication in the wild and into the possibilities of training animals to use a form of human language. There is plenty of debate surrounding the question of exactly what has been demonstrated by the studies and one does not need to be very sceptical to decide that the case for chimps using a form of 'our' language is not proven. However, it would be premature to suggest that the case could not be proven. We now see that the natural communication systems of chimpanzees are richer than was previously thought, and the Washoe project has shown that a lot of progress can be made using the Gardners' methods. It is certainly becoming increasingly difficult to propose a list of characteristics of language which would necessarily and interestingly restrict it to a product of human minds.

2.5 Biological factors in language acquisition

Another prong in the argument that the ability to learn language is specific to humans is the claim that there is a close correspondence between the stage of language development demonstrated by a child and biological factors, such as stage of motor development or weight of the brain. The most ambitious claim in support of the biological basis of language capacity is that there is a critical period for language acquisition, namely, between 18 months and early puberty in most people. Within this period, language acquisition is expected to proceed normally, but outside it, language acquisition is difficult, if not impossible.

The evidence for a biological basis for a specifically linguistic ability was most enthusiastically presented by Lenneberg (1967, 1969). He drew a suggestive parallel between the time course of certain features of the maturation of the human brain, and behavioural characteristics of language development under unusual conditions of learning. There are two hemispheres to the brain, connected to each other by a structure known as the corpus callosum. At birth, the hemispheres are not structurally identical, but Lenneberg assumed that they were functionally identical and were each capable in the beginning of supporting language development. Around 18 months he assumed that the hemispheres began to become functionally specialised in that each hemisphere began to control different areas of human activity. In particular, in the normal person, the left hemisphere began to control functions characteristic of language. By puberty, Lenneberg assumed that this functional specialisation had become fixed, so that if a person had not developed language, his left hemisphere would have taken over control of other functions, and language acquisition would be difficult, if not impossible.

Consistent with this account were the following claims: Brain damage to the left hemisphere in adults led to aphasia in 70 per cent of cases surveyed by Lenneberg, while brain damage to children below 18 months had the same effect on their language development, whether damage was to the right or left hemisphere. For children between 2 and 4 years, recovery of the language function was generally possible after a variable period of disruption, during which the child appeared to run swiftly through the stages of development he had passed before the injury. It was claimed that people who have not learned to speak by puberty were unlikely to do so, and learning a foreign language is both harder and follows a different learning pattern after puberty than before. Children who become deaf before they have begun to speak have as great a difficulty in learning a form of language as children born deaf, but those who have learned some language and lose their hearing around the age of 3 or 4 can be trained more quickly and more successfully in language when they start school than congenitally deaf children.

Differences between the hemispheres as regards language function are widely accepted in the case of normal adults, although the details of these differences may not be the same for right-handed men as they are for left-handers or women (Marshall, 1979). Much of the most dramatic evidence for these functional differences come from studies of patients who have had their corpus callosum severed, as a treatment for severe epilepsy (Nebes, 1974). In these people, it is assumed that the two parts of the brain continue to function normally but independently of each other, and it is possible, by controlling the information sent to each half of the brain and observing how the patient carries out various tests, to see how various tasks are affected by this separation of the hemispheres. For example, these patients find it easier to choose from three complete circles the one from which a given arc has come if they have to make the match using their left hand (which is controlled by the right hemisphere) than if they have to use their right. We can then hypothesise that it is the right hemisphere which deals most effectively with part–whole relations and then investigate in more detail how generalisable this claim might be. We can check that the split brain operation does not induce a complete reorganisation of the functioning of each hemisphere by investigating, for example, the performance of normal adults in tests of dichotic listening. In these tests the subject wears earphones and simultaneously hears different material in each ear. We can decide how strongly lateralised different functions are by seeing how accurately subjects can report material from each ear. Using this technique, Kimura found that subjects reported verbal material more accurately from the right ear (associated with the left hemisphere) than the left and melodies more accurately from the left ear (associated with the right hemisphere) (Kimura, 1964, 1967).

There is now evidence that a certain degree of functional specialisation of the hemispheres can be detected long before the child is 18 months old. Molfese (1977) measured the auditory evoked potential from both hemispheres of groups of infants (aged between 1 week and 10 months), children and adults, to speech stimuli and non-speech stimuli (such as a C major piano chord) which came from a loudspeaker placed above the subject. He found that all groups showed differential hemispherical responding to these materials and that, in fact, both speech and non-speech were lateralised more strongly in his infants than in his adults (speech to the left hemisphere, non-speech to the right). Using a different technique, Entus (1977) found evidence of lateralisation of speech and of non-speech in the case of infants as young as 22-days-old. She presented stimuli dichotically, and trained the infants to suck rapidly to ensure the continuation of the stimulation (cf. section 4.1). In time, the rate of sucking dropped, but increased again when the children detected a change in the stimulus being presented. This increase in sucking rate was more marked for speech stimuli when the change occurred in the right ear and more marked for non-speech stimuli when the change occurred in the left ear, indicating that the hemispheres were differentially efficient in analysing the different kinds of material.

It seems, then, that cerebral specialisation of function may begin long before the onset of language acquisition. There is probably still a complex development of cerebral specialisation awaiting the infant (see Moscovitch, 1977, for a review), but it seems that the strong view, that before 18 months both hemispheres are equally capable of supporting language development, has to be modified. At the other end of the critical period, likewise, the picture is more complicated than Lenneberg would lead us to suppose. Curtiss (1977) reports a recent case where a girl who began to learn her first language after puberty made some progress. In this case, however, the girl appeared to use her right hemisphere for language and the course of development was different in many ways from that of children acquiring language under normal conditions. Curtiss interprets these results as indicating that there are constraints on the nature of language acquisition beyond the critical period. Snow and Hoefnagel-Höhle (1978) have challenged the view that acquisition of a second language is more efficient during the critical period than after it. They tested adults and children from 3 years of age in aspects of their language ability in Dutch during their first year of living in Holland. They found that the adults and 12- to 15-year-old children made fastest progress and that the 3- to 4-year-olds scored lowest on all the tests.

Other evidence which leads to a modification of Lenneberg's claims comes from studies on the effect of brain damage in the preverbal infant. Dennis and Whitaker (1977) survey such studies and find that there is more likely to be language impairment, even in these young children, following brain damage to the left hemisphere than to the right hemisphere. On the other hand, damage to the right hemisphere has a worse effect on language in the case of infants than it does in the case of adults, so an increase in specialisation still seems likely. Dennis and Whitaker also give a detailed analysis of the language abilities of three 9-year-old children who had each had a hemisphere surgically removed before the onset of speech. In the case of two of the children, the left hemisphere had been removed, but in the third it was the right. All three children were of normal and similar intelligence and they also scored similarly on the Illinois Test of Psycholinguistic Abilities. However, there were differences in the pattern of abilities which they displayed in these tests. The children without the left hemisphere did better on test items involving visuo-spatial ability, while the child without the right hemisphere showed a greater proficiency on tests of auditory language.

Finally, the idea that language development during Lenneberg's critical period has fixed characteristics, irrespective of the conditions of acquisition, is too simple. Mentally retarded children show a variety of patterns of language acquisition. For example, Cromer (1974b) showed qualitative differences between the strategies used by mentally retarded adolescents and normal children in understanding sentences of the *Children are nice to understand* paradigm (see section 6.2). The mentally retarded group used the same strategies as an adult group, suggesting that they could not rely on the natural language-learning abilities which most young children use. Menyuk (1977) surveys studies relating to the hypothesis of the critical period for language acquisition and suggests that the normal course of development is determined as much by the developing processing skills of the children as by logical dependencies among the linguistic structures being acquired. Thus the question of whether an individual can learn a particular part of language will depend on the nature of his abnormality, the general processing capacity available to him, and the relation of the linguistic structure under inspection to the rest of his knowledge of language, quite apart from factors of motivation and the teaching methods to which he is exposed. To relate his learning potential simply to his age is inappropriate.

Thus Lenneberg's proposal of a clear critical period for language acquisition has to be considerably modified. A certain degree of functional specialisation of the brain does take place before the onset of language, and so specific brain damage during this period can have effects on later language development (although Marshall (1979) points out that there have been reports of remarkable linguistic ability in patients with considerable abnormality of cerebral development). Acquisition of a second language after the critical period may be quite efficient and acquisition of first language may still be possible. The pattern of development during childhood and adolescence may depend critically on the information-processing skills available to the child. However, we should conclude from these studies, not that biological factors are irrelevant to language-learning ability, but rather that the relation between language acquisition and its biological basis is more elusive and tantalising than earlier accounts indicated.

2.6 **Learning and learning theory**[12]

In 1959, Chomsky wrote a highly critical review of *Verbal Behavior,* by B. F. Skinner, one of this century's most famous experimental psychologists. It is well known that Chomsky believes in a strong innate component to language acquisition. As a result, many people ignore work which is done on learning theory, and appear to think of the LAD as a multilingual fairground toy which will churn out the rules of German, if a Deutsche mark is inserted into it, or those of French if it is started with a franc. Instead of looking for mechanisms whereby a child may learn his language, attention has been focused on patterns of development: characterising the way in which the product of these mechanisms changes over time and trying to determine how much similarity there is across children. Eventually we must produce an account of the processes whereby these changes take place and so it is important to be aware of the contributions learning theory can make to the problem.

Chomsky accorded Skinner a back-handed compliment when his review of *Verbal Behavior* was being reprinted in Jakobovits and Miron (1967) by indicating that he had chosen that book for his attack because it was the most fully articulated account of language learning and use of its time. This does not necessarily make it representative, however. Skinner's enthusiastic belief that his view of learning can and should explain all aspects of man's behaviour is not shared by all those who work in learning theory. Since it was primarily the excesses of the extrapolation from the theory which Chomsky criticised, we must again be careful not to dismiss the whole enterprise out of hand.

In some ways, of course, Skinner was representative of his time. American psychology and linguistics had been dominated since at least the 1930s by what are thought of as the doctrines of behaviourism (Mackenzie, 1977). One of these doctrines was the

12. By 'learning theory' we refer to attempts to predict in mathematical detail the course of successes and failures encountered by an animal or a person trying to learn a task under controlled laboratory or educational conditions. It is not possible here to do justice to the richness and variety of work in this area. The reader is referred to Hill (1980) for an introduction.

methodological principle that the raw data on which explanations should be based should be observable, and so neither the introspections of the early Wundtian psychologists nor the linguistic intuitions of modern linguists would have been acceptable to the behaviourists as evidence. Hand in hand with this insistence went the constraint on theory construction, which advised that one should not postulate mentalist constructs as intervening variables. If possible, explanations of observable behaviour should be given entirely in terms of observable conditions obtaining in the organism's environment or in its previous experience. Attention was often deflected away from the contribution made by the learning organism to the point where it was possible to imagine that it was largely irrelevant whether the object of study was a rat, a pigeon or a child. The detail of the behaviour would be different – rats would run, pigeons peck and children cry – but the processes whereby they learned to perform an action, avoid an eventuality or maintain a habit would be the same. This was sometimes elevated (in particular by Skinner) to a principle of universality whereby all behaviour could be explained by considering only the conditions of external stimulation and without paying attention to intervening processes. The organism was reduced to a black box, buttressed on either side by the detailed stimuli of input and responses of output, so characterless as to be normally omitted from the equation. Stimulus–response theories were the order of the day. Notice, however, the sleight of hand which turns an emphasis on external factors into a denial of the necessity of internal ones. There is no reason why a final theory should deny the importance of either kinds of influence.

Skinner believed that language was taught to children according to the principles of operant conditioning, which is the form of learning theory he has pioneered. The theory has two key concepts – the operant and reinforcement. An operant is an action by the organism – an utterance by the child – which achieves a specific outcome which serves to reinforce the operant. If the outcome is favourable to the organism, the probability increases that the operant will occur again and the action is said to be reinforced. It is positively reinforced if the operant is followed by a pleasant stimulus, and is negatively reinforced if the operant is followed by the removal of an aversive (or noxious) stimulus. If the outcome is unfavourable, the probability decreases that the operant will occur again and the action is said to be punished. A true behaviourist, of course, will not describe an outcome as favourable or unfavourable to the organism as this makes reference to an internal state. Instead, reinforcing and punishing events are defined by their results, according to whether they increase or decrease the frequency of the operant. Such *post hoc* identification constitutes a shortcoming of the theory since it is not clear how to predict what events will be reinforcing to an organism. In the laboratory, this is controlled fairly easily: an animal kept at 80 per cent body weight will find food positively reinforcing, while any animal will be deterred by electric shocks. However, no one has yet specified precisely what events are reinforcing to a child learning his language. Brown and Hanlon (1970) looked through their transcripts of mothers' and children's speech to see whether verbal praise such as 'Well done' or 'That's right' would be plausible candidates. They found that, on that basis, mothers reinforced truthful utterances, regardless of grammaticality, which cannot explain why some children grow up into untruthful, grammatical speakers. A much more subtle understanding of reinforcement is required before the theory can be applied to this situation, and Chomsky took Skinner to task for failing to observe his customary caution and strict standards of explicitness in this case.

Identification of the stimulus also creates problems. Once an operant is established, its occurrence is contingent on the presence of a stimulus. It may be that the first occasion on which one says 'Would you like to put your shawl in the bedroom?' is when greeting a new sister-in-law. It will not be the case that the same will be said every time thereafter when these two people meet, nor will the invitation be restricted to new sisters-in-law. Knowing what utterance is appropriate to a particular social situation is a complex skill to acquire and a difficult one to identify. In 1957 the experimentalists hid behind the fact that they could control the material presented to the organism and had done very little to analyse what the organism was attending to in the stimulus and how the stimulus could be identified outside the laboratory. Stimulus identification is a central problem in current learning theory. Within the area of language acquisition, many studies are now directed towards the nature of the environment in which language learning takes place (see chapter 7) and so are addressing this problem.

Finally, definition of the operant itself raises problems. Skinner and Chomsky disagree so fundamentally on the nature of what is being learned that it is difficult to see any reconciliation in this case. An overt verbal operant cannot be made to look like a deep structural description, and it is still far from clear how learning theory can come to account for syntactic development. One aspect of learning theory which would seem to be essential for such an account is that the operant should be treated as a response *class* of functionally equivalent actions (see Lovaas, 1977): for example, the various forms of the past tense inflection may turn out to be a response class. An unsatisfactory aspect of this term is that *a priori* one cannot tell what will or will not constitute a response class. By the same token, once a response class has been identified, because of the lawful nature of the interaction of members of the class with certain reinforcing events, the investigator is not in a position to explain on what basis the original response has been generalised or, to speak in cognitive terms, how the rule has been acquired. In fairness, it should be remembered that the LAD cannot be seen as an explanation of this process either.

On the other hand, if we consider other aspects of the total development we see that conditioning models can shed light on what is happening. It is difficult to avoid adopting something of the kind in explaining the development of reference where a match must be made by the learner between a verbal form and some set of conditions of a non-linguistic nature. Brown's (1958) account of the process shares many characteristics with the stimulus-sampling account of Crothers and Suppes (1967). We find accounts of the process of phonological development which portray the mother shaping the child's initial attempts until they are acceptable forms of the language being learned. This is a means of establishing an operant which Skinner has discussed at length. Initially, any recognisable attempt by the organism is reinforced, but gradually the response has to be increasingly close to the desired response in order to be reinforced. Similarly, parents greet any speech-like sounds enthusiastically from a very young child, but become increasingly particular about what they will accept as the child grows older.

Although there is doubt surrounding the value of behaviourist learning theory as an explanation of language acquisition under normal conditions there is at least one area where its contribution is widely acknowledged – that of the treatment of language disorders in childhood. With their emphasis on external conditions, stimulus–response theorists have considerably advanced our knowledge about how one can teach effectively. They show how conditions can be arranged so that people or animals can be trained to do things. Their theories have been applied successfully by behaviour therapists to help people give up smoking, overcome their fear of spiders, and cope with difficult social encounters. They have also been applied successfully in some language remediation programmes. The practical aims of the clinician require him to be alert to many avenues of help for his patient, and so many different kinds of remediation programmes have been devised. Schiefelbusch and Lloyd (1974) includes reports of several such programmes.

It is rare for children to suffer from language disabilities in isolation from other forms of handicap. In some cases the language disorder is symptomatic of some other abnormality, such as deafness or mental handicap. Whether or not a specific cause for delay can be identified, language delay can create problems of its own for the child, by inducing unusual behaviour from the people surrounding him and, consequently, blocking a major source of information for him. By the time language delay is obvious, it is likely that the child's social and intellectual development have already suffered set-backs from the normal course. For this reason at least, any purely linguistic diagnosis of language retardation is of limited value.

Faced with such a network of overlapping disabilities, the clinician has at least three options. He can concentrate, as far as possible, on the language disability in isolation, basing his training programme on the model of normal development so that the child is first taught those structures which children usually master earliest, saving the later acquisitions for training at a later period. Alternatively, he can bypass the normal acquisition studies altogether, using behaviour modification techniques to train linguistic behaviour in the child, concentrating first on those structures which he considers most useful to the child and most amenable to the techniques being used. Finally, he can look to studies of normal development for indications of what features of the conditions for language development are particularly important and are missing in the environment or abilities of his patient, and then aim to supply some variant of these conditions in the expectation that the normal processes of acquisition can then take over. We shall look at examples of each approach.

Crystal, Fletcher and Garman (1976) adopt the first approach. They emphasise that, from a linguistic point of view, traditional categories such as infantile speech, child aphasia, or expressive disorders are unhelpful as they do not give rise to adequately precise descriptions of the patient's language. Crystal *et al.* therefore bypass such categories and make a fresh survey of the characteristics of the patient's linguistic output. This gives rise to a speech profile which they then compare with similar profiles of the speech of a normally developing child. The aim of the programme is to modify the patient's profile until it matches a particular point in the normal developmental sequence and then proceed to train the patient to master the other features of the language in the order in which they characteristically appear in acquisition. They recommend that the training procedures used in normal second language learning should be used in these remediation programmes, modified to suit the individual needs of the child where necessary.

On the face of it, there is no reason why the developmental sequence which is the output of normal acquisition processes should be a particularly appropriate set of goals for a remediation programme. Crystal *et al.* acknowledge that they chose this developmental sequence as a model for their work in the absence of any coherent alternative. They needed a scale which would predict the complexity of different parts of the target language in order to provide a rationale for the order of training particular constructions in their patients, and the sequence of normal acquisition certainly provides them with such a scale.

However, the patients who are to be exposed to such a remediation programme are those for whom the normal processing which results in this particular sequence has failed to function, and so one need not expect that it will be particularly suited to their needs. This encouraged Guess, Sailor and Baer (1974) to adopt the second approach, to dispense with the acquisition literature and build their own set of goals into the design of their programme. They chose to train a selection of language forms and skills which would be maximally useful to the child in controlling his environment. These fell into the categories of reference, control (which enabled him to make simple requests), self-extended control (to help him acquire information he lacks) and integration of the previously trained skills.

Lovaas (1977) reports a similar training programme for twenty severely autistic children, half of whom were mute and half echolalic, in that they repeated the speech of others: the receptive language of the children was missing or minimal. Lovaas and his colleagues devised several programmes for the children, ranging from ones which trained the child to produce recognisable words, to understand abstract relations, such as spatial terms or time concepts, or to use grammatical relations, such as adjective–noun or subject–verb relationships, to programmes which encouraged the children to carry on conversations or to use language spontaneously. An important part of their design was that they involved the parents in the children's training.

They report quite dramatic improvements in the case of some of the children: after a year of therapy, one 4-year-old child, Linda, showed very small differences from her peers, although at the start she had shown distorted reactions to perceptual events and considerable self-stimulatory behaviour, and her only linguistic skills had consisted in labelling a few objects and following certain commands, when properly motivated. The major difficulty Lovaas and his colleagues encountered was how to maintain verbal behaviour once it had been acquired by their patients within the system of artificial reinforcers used in the clinical sessions.

The attraction of structural approaches of these kinds, where the goals of the programme are clearly specified, is presumably that an end-point is seen as being attainable and, if a patient can be led through to this end, some degree of normal linguistic control will have been achieved. This is often a long process, however, and the therapists have to ensure that the programme does not falter as a result of the various skills becoming imbalanced during the training. One way to avoid this is to work within an 'integrated developmental perspective' (Crystal *et al.* 1976: 20), and it is natural that therapists should look to language acquisition studies for such a perspective.

If they do so, they should find more than a characteristic sequence of linguistic forms to guide them. They should find an indication of what conditions might be important for acquisition to proceed, and some day in the future they should also find a specification of the learning processes employed by the child. Bricker and Bricker (1974) took heed of the Piagetian argument about the importance of developing cognitive structures and they report encouraging results. Similarly, Horton (1974) emphasised the importance of the role of the caretaker in creating an appropriate linguistic and emotional environment of acquisition to take place. In her scheme she trained the parents of the young deaf children she was treating as well as the children themselves, and obtained a good success rate in language growth and impressive long-term results. The disadvantage of such approaches is that they rely on the hope that the information-processing abilities of the child are adequate to the task. In many cases, of course, this assumption may not be valid (Cromer, 1974b; Menyuk, 1977).

For such children, it is important that we improve our understanding of these abilities to the point where they could be the focus of remediation procedures, supplemented by a sequence of linguistic goals.

So a certain amount of success can be achieved in teaching children a first language, in cases where they are unable to learn by the normal processes. One must hope that future work on language acquisition will help to increase this success rate. One must be cautious, however, about interpreting the theoretical significance of these results. Learning something and being trained to do it are not the same thing. Certainly, when one has been trained to drive a car, one has learned to do it, but has one learned because of the training or despite it? In other words, even in situations where training undoubtedly takes place and success is achieved, the key to that success may reside, not in the carefully planned schedule of instructions which constitute the course but, for example, in the fact that the student likes the instructor or is being jeered at by his friends for his lack of driving skill and that this mobilises some natural learning skill which is applied to the minimal material offered by the instructor. This may seem to be a mean comment to make at the end of reports of hard-won success in language training, but it is a point which is commonly made in discussion of the effectiveness of many kinds of therapies. Lovaas (1977:119) considers this possibility in his book and reports, regretfully, that there was no evidence that the children they studied took a sudden step forward, due to the activation of some innate structures which guided their learning.

What, then, about normal language acquisition? Are children taught language in the sense that their conditions of learning are similar to the training schedules devised by learning theorists? If so, does this training explain their learning or do we have to consider other factors? It is a measure of the rapprochement between behaviourist and cognitive approaches to the study of language development, detected and encouraged by Staats (1974), that recently there has been a considerable volume of work which investigates the details of the child's language-learning environment (see chapter 7). Unfortunately, it is also a measure of the antagonism towards the behaviourist tradition still present in the area, that few of these studies are set within a wider, explicit learning theory framework. Perhaps that is no bad thing for the present!

3
Language in the developing child

General linguists of this century are familiar with the contention that language can be studied as an autonomous system. Post-Saussurean linguistics has sought to look inwards for explanation and justification to preserve the internal consistency of the structure being built out of a language. The conviction that this method will succeed begins to crumble as one approaches the edges of the semantic system (cf. Katz and Bever, 1977; Matthews, 1979), but many linguists continue to attempt to treat language as an object separable from other aspects of experience. The assumption is rarely queried that the native speaker also has the ability to treat his language as a separable object of reflection.

Initially, the assumption behind the early work in this recent phase of interest in language development was that child language could be approached in the same way as adult language. It required a different kind of ingenuity to elicit the child's linguistic knowledge but there was little doubt that it would be appropriate to aim to construct successive grammars of child language, similar to those constructed for adult language, and watch the way in which the adult system was built up by the child.

However, it soon became clear that this approach was at best severely limiting and at worst completely invalid. A child learning language is developing on all fronts, not just the linguistic one, and is trying to make sense of his social environment and the world of objects around him as well as of his linguistic input. At the very least this creates considerable methodological difficulties for anyone trying to isolate his linguistic development from his immaturity in other directions. From a more extreme point of view, it becomes theoretically invalid to try to do so, as there is little justification for assuming that language has an independent existence for the young child.

37

The central theme of this chapter will be the relation of human language to other cognitive and social kinds of knowledge, and how it changes during development. The most influential author in this area is Jean Piaget, whose voluminous writing over the last sixty years constitutes the most fully articulated account of child development that we possess.[1] Much of the discussion centres round the attempt to specify what cognitive and social achievements have been made by children before they begin to produce speech recognisable as being attempts at their mother tongue. From this arises the question of how necessary these developments are for language acquisition, and although it will be argued that certain developments do appear to be prerequisite for language development, either on logical or empirical grounds, the reader should be warned that it is not claimed that these developments are sufficient for language acquisition. The child still has to learn the way in which *his* language expresses certain ideas or performs certain functions. In a famous paper, Slobin (1973) pointed out the way in which particular languages posed special problems for the children learning them. He compared the stage at which children learning different languages managed to express a particular idea, and from this suggested which were the kinds of construction children found difficult to learn. From that he derived strategies which the children appeared to be following in grappling with the language-specific difficulties they were encountering, such as 'pay attention to the ends of words', 'avoid exceptions', 'avoid interruption or rearrangement of linguistic units'.

There will be some discussion of studies of this kind later in the chapter (section 3.3), but most of the work reported here aims, not so much at building up an explanation of how a child masters the constructions in the particular language he is learning, but rather at indicating the kinds of constraints which have to be imposed on any explanation which might succeed. It will render implausible an account which requires the child to reflect consciously on features of his language. It will render unnecessary an account which

1. It is not possible to summarise Piaget's theories here. Flavell (1963) is the best known of several summaries of his work. Piaget and Inhelder (1968) gives a condensed account of the theory. Turner (1975) discusses Piaget's work along with other theories of cognitive development, and Donaldson (1978) adds an appendix on Piaget's theories to her book on some recent findings which call some of his ideas into question.

explains the understanding of the nature of communication as being a postverbal development. It will render unrealistic an account which fails to link semantic development to what the child knows about the way his environment is structured. As such, it still leaves a lot to be done.

3.1   Egocentric speech

Cognitive and social development meet and modify each other in an illuminating way when we look at the function and social nature of speech for the nursery-aged child. In particular, focus will be placed here on what has been called the egocentric speech of these children.[2]

This description is due to Piaget who, in the 1920s, published a study of *The Language and Thought of the Child*. In a preliminary survey of the speech used by children in a Genevan kindergarten he found that, while much of their speech was adapted to the needs of a specific listener, a fair percentage of it was addressed to anyone who happened to be within hearing range and gave no evidence that the child was attempting to take into account the knowledge or interests of a specific listener. This speech he called egocentric speech. He originally included three kinds of speech in this category: repetition of words and syllables serving no obvious social function, monologues where the child talks to himself, as if thinking aloud, and collective monologues where a second person serves as a stimulus for the child's speech but is apparently not expected to understand or even attend to the speech. Later work has concentrated on collective monologues, and indeed the definition of egocentric speech shifts in Piaget's writing (see Hughes, 1975). Piaget emphasised the lack of social adaptation characteristic of egocentric speech. He saw this speech as a reflection of the thought processes of the young child which then, and in subsequent work, he set out to investigate in considerable detail. The feature of the thinking of the preschool child which impressed him most was

2.   The speech is described as egocentric – centred on the self – not because the child is uninterested in considering the views and needs of other people but because, according to Piaget, he does not understand that their views and needs are different from his own. Thus the term is not supposed to carry the smack of moral judgment which would be associated with it if it were applied to adult speech.

the way in which it was centred on the child's own point of view, literally, in perceptual terms, and also figuratively, in terms of the knowledge he assumed the second person possessed. Time and again Piaget claimed, on the basis of ingenious experiments, that preschool children were often not aware that a second person's point of view could be different from their own, far less what it might be. This cognitive egocentrism he took as indicating that the child was still imperfectly adapted socially. Thus, in the interpretation of egocentric speech, two characteristics of Piaget's views on child development meet: the view that language primarily reflects thought and does not shape it and the view that the child has to develop into a social being from a stage of being imperfectly socialised.

A different interpretation was accorded to egocentric speech by Vygotsky. He agreed with Piaget about the existence of the phenomenon and elaborated on it by demonstrating that the proportion of egocentric speech relative to total output by a preschool child was heavily dependent on the conditions under which it was measured. In particular, if some obstacle was introduced which caused the child frustration, the proportion of egocentric speech increased dramatically. Vygotsky agreed that egocentric speech was a transitional phenomenon, but, while Piaget saw it as characteristic of an imperfectly social phase of the child's development, soon to disappear, Vygotsky saw it as being a precursor to verbal thought. For him, it was 'speech on its way inward' (1962:46). He saw language and thought as having independent origins, both phylogenetically and ontogenetically. He emphasised the existence of prespeech intellect (in apes and babies) and pre-intellectual speech (in parrots and babbling infants), and proposed that in the young child enquiring about the names of objects the two strands meet and 'speech begins to serve intellect and thoughts begin to be spoken' (1962:43). In egocentric speech, the function of the child's speech changes from being social and communicative to being individual and self-regulating. It arises when the child, according to Vygotsky, begins to be capable of organised reasoning. Its function is similar to that of counting on one's fingers – an external manifestation of a process soon to become internalised. In time these new functions are served by inner speech or verbal thought. Vygotsky does not question the social function of the child's early speech and so sees verbal thought as having a social origin, which leads him to propose the 'indisputable fact' that 'Thought development is determined by language, i.e., by the linguistic tools of thought and by the sociocultural experience of the child' (1962:51).

The disagreement between Piaget and Vygotsky appears to rest on the extent to which they believe very young children to be capable of social and intellectual cooperation. Piaget accuses Vygotsky of 'excessive bio-social optimism' (Piaget, 1962:2) in believing that children's early attempts at communication are either well adapted or successful. On the other hand, Piaget's extreme pessimism as regards the egocentric nature of child thought is currently under heavy fire (see Donaldson, 1978). We shall see later that the nature and quality of the interaction between infants and their caretakers is now being minutely studied.

The conclusions drawn by Piaget and Vygotsky are frequently opposed in discussions of the question 'Does language precede thought or thought precede language?' However, even at this stage of the discussion we can see that this question can be given several interpretations. For a start, it divides into the two questions of origin – does thought originate in language or does language build on cognitive achievements – and of development – can a linguistic discovery initiate an intellectual development or does language just give voice to an understanding which has already been established non-verbally? For Vygotsky, we have seen, thought and language have separate roots but once they combine forces they begin to act mutually on each other. In contrast to Piaget, Vygotsky emphasised the importance of language as a means of directing action, and the way in which children learn to use language for planning future action and preparing steps in the solution of a task (Vygotsky, 1978:2). He also pointed out that children's word meanings develop, and that there is a stage of 'naive psychology' where the child sprinkles his speech with logical connectives, such as *if* and *because*, which give a spurious impression of logical thought but which do not guarantee adequate understanding of their semantic implications. He concluded that, as children develop, language can sometimes serve as an impetus to thought, and the child's vocabulary development need not wait upon his cognitive development. Vygotsky then concluded his case for the importance of language for thought by characterising mature thought as being primarily verbal, a restriction which is by no means necessary.

Piaget's views are in no way a photographic negative of Vygotsky's although he is less impressed by the importance of language than Vygotsky. He concentrates more on the content of linguistic development than on language's changing function and he also has a more complex characterisation of thought than Vygotsky. His account is not simple, as we shall see in the following section.

3.2 Piaget's views on language

In his treatment of egocentric speech, Piaget was quick to note a lack of social adaptation manifested by the phenomenon and to look for an explanation for egocentric speech in the child's developing cognitive system. It is characteristic of Piaget that he should dismiss social factors in development, creating a view of the child working single-handedly to master an understanding of the physical world around him, and displaying in his language the partial insights and successes of this developing understanding. Most discussion of the interface between language and cognition by developmental psychologists comes back to Piaget and his theory at some point, and so it is worth emphasising some of the characteristics of Piaget's views of development at this stage. He believes that the child constructs an understanding of the way the world works, largely by his own actions. His intelligence at any time is a product both of his environment and of certain mental structures interacting with each other. In tracing the development of these structures, Piaget concluded that the child passes through a series of stages. Each stage is characterised by certain properties of the child's thought and each child has to pass through the stages in a fixed order, although the rate at which he does so may vary from one child to another. The major stages are the sensorimotor stage (from birth to 18 months), the pre-operational stage (18 months to 7 years), the stage of concrete operations (7 years to 11 years) and the stage of formal operations (11 years and over). The ages given are approximate as some children may take longer than others to pass from one stage to another.

3.2.1 *Piaget as an epistemologist*

Just as a lot of current work on language acquisition is influenced by the Chomskyan theory of language, so Piaget's views on child development cast a powerful shadow over the area. And yet, paradoxically, as in Chomsky's case, the shadow is cast at a considerable slant, for Piaget has never concerned himself directly with a theory of language development. In Chomsky's case, his observations on language development are a byproduct of his efforts to develop a theory of language; in Piaget's case, his comments on language are just as partial and have to be seen in the light of his primary aim, which is to understand the nature of knowledge. Piaget describes himself as a genetic epistemologist, which means that he has a philosopher's desire to specify the way in which we understand the workings of the physical world or of logico-mathematical systems, and that his approach to the problem is to look at the way in which children come to this understanding. For example, by studying the systematic errors children make in learning to make judgments of relative quantity, he hopes to achieve insights into the nature of number which will not be available to an adult mathematician who has a fully mature, working concept of number and has forgotten the partial under-standings of his earlier years, which held elements of truth in them (Piaget, 1952).[3] As a result of his research programme he has provided us with a vast body of information about the way young children behave and, in particular, some of the surprising errors they make in their attempts to understand their environment. He has also developed an impressive interpretation of this behaviour which is easily the most comprehensive and detailed theory of cognitive development available to us. However, to reiterate, his interest in the child is almost exclusively in an intelligent being setting out to understand the workings of his physical environment, and so even as a theory of cognitive development it is limited. A great generality is claimed for the theory and it throws an interest-ing light on other aspects of development to which it is applied, but it should not be expected to give detailed consideration to these other areas.

Piaget has frequently been criticised for underestimating the importance of language in cognitive development. In his writings, language appears largely as a source of data, rather than as an object of development, and mostly its operation is seen in a negative light.

---

3. For an alternative account of the development of number, see Gelman and Gallistel (1978).

It is seen in its role as a channel of communication between the child and the social group, and Piaget appears to be suspicious of it at both ends – as a source of information for the investigator about the child's true understanding of the world and as a source of information for the child about physical and logico-mathematical knowledge. It is useful to separate these two aspects of the verbal channel in considering his views on language.

3.2.2 *Child's expressive language*

Piaget is not alone in his unwillingness to base his assessment of children's knowledge purely on their spontaneous speech. While a child's understanding of a phenomenon is developing, his use of language may well conceal rather than expose this development, unless it is studied extremely carefully. Recent studies of semantic development and many of the earlier diary studies have amply supported this position. Take the simple case of *more*, which is one of the earliest words in a child's repertoire and yet causes errors in understanding for many years after its first appearance (see section 6.4.2). The fact that a child uses a word in his speech in no way guarantees his complete mastery of its wider semantics. To this extent, Piaget's suspicion is justified and shared by other authors.

However, it should be noted at this point that Piaget is not uniformly suspicious of children's expressive use of language. Once a child has shown that he understands a particular phenomenon or has mastered a practical skill, using largely non-verbal means, Piaget sets great store by the child's ability to explain the phenomenon or justify his decisions. For example, if a child can produce the correct answers in a test of conservation (see section 3.2.3), he is classified as an 'intuitive conserver' and becomes a 'conserver' proper only once he can also correctly justify his answers. Recently (Piaget, 1977, 1978), Piaget has been exploring the stages through which a child's explanation of a skill passes, so tracing the construction of a conscious understanding of the phenomenon. He sees this conscious understanding as a more advanced achievement by the child.

3.2.3 *Child's understanding of language*

Turning now to the other end of the verbal channel, the child's receptive understanding of language directed to him, we find Piaget anxious to demonstrate that knowledge is constructed afresh by the child, not simply handed on to him verbally by other members of the community. Writing against a background of logical positivism and linguistic philosophy, he set out to challenge a nominalist interpretation of mathematics which proposed that one could explain logic simply through language. According to this view, the natural explanation for the source of an individual's understanding of logic, and so in Piaget's terms his intelligence, lay in his command of language, an ability transmitted to him by other members of his social group. Piaget believed that the source of intelligence lay not in the social group, but rather in the individual's own actions on his environment. A lot of his early writing traces the development of sensorimotor intelligence, the cognitive understanding of the physical world possessed by the preverbal child. Having first shown that intelligence was evident before the child began to speak, and thus that not all intelligence was dependent on verbal transmission, he then went on to propose and to test the hypothesis that in the child's development language followed thought and did not direct it. In other words, he proposed that even for the verbal child language could not be the source of understanding about the properties of the physical world or of logico-mathematical systems, although it could transmit information about social systems – notions of family, nation, kinship terms, etc. (1928). Unless the child had developed to the point where he understood a particular phenomenon as a result of his own actions, he would not be able to appreciate fully attempts to explain it to him. According to Piaget, verbal transmission of information was not, of itself, sufficient to give the child a true understanding of physical phenomena.

Again, the academic climate has now changed in Piaget's favour, to the extent that children are seen as having an active, constructive role to play in their own development. Few believe that children wait passively to have knowledge of any kind imparted to them. At the same time, many believe that Piaget has misconstrued and underestimated the role of other people in a child's development and that a social interactive model is necessary to explain development in the first two years, whereby child and caretaker explore social and physical phenomena together. The intelligence of the preverbal child is not in doubt, but the conclusion that intelligence cannot have a social origin, just because the child cannot speak, is being challenged.

Similarly, the view that a child can fully understand only those utterances whose semantic interpretations fall within his cognitive capacity appears to be quite acceptable to a psycholinguistic community schooled in the central importance of semantics. Indeed, it runs the risk of being trivially true so long as one considers only utterances to which the child can assign an adult semantic interpretation. However, when one concedes that a child with a developing semantic system assigns partial interpretations to utterances, the question is more open as to how far these partial interpretations may serve as the impetus to further cognitive exploration.

Most of Piaget's evidence about child development comes from the results of experiments he carries out with children. One of the better known series of experiments has to do with the preschool child's understanding of the conditions under which quantity is conserved. A child who passes these tests of conservation is known as a conserver, and one who does not is described as a non-conserver. In a typical test of the conservation of number, the child is shown two rows of counters, with the same number of counters in each row and placed in such a way that the counters in the two rows are in one-to-one correspondence with each other. Thus the two rows are of the same length and the same density. The experimenter asks the child whether there is the same number of counters in each row and the child generally agrees that there is. The experimenter then spreads out the counters in one of the rows, making that row longer and less dense than the other row. He repeats the question about the number of counters in the two rows. A non-conserving child will then usually judge that there are more counters in the longer row. A conserving child will correctly indicate that changing the length of the rows does not change the number of counters in the rows. He realises that number is conserved despite a transformation in the length of the array. Similar tests are designed to test whether the child knows that the length of a piece of string is conserved despite changes in its shape, that the volume of liquid in a glass is conserved despite changes in the shape of the glass and that the weight of a ball of clay is conserved despite changes in its shape from a round ball into a long sausage. Children do not learn to conserve in all these media at once. They tend to learn to conserve number before volume, and volume before weight, for example.

Recently, Piaget's practice of relying heavily on the child's comprehension ability in his experiments has been criticised (Karmiloff-Smith, 1979; Elliot and Donaldson, forthcoming). The clinical interview method, which Piaget devised for conducting his experiments, involves asking the child a prepared set of questions about the experimental materials but also encourages the experimenter to talk freely to the child and follow up interesting leads on the spot. Since Piaget believes that the child's cognitive development is in advance of his language development he is presumably satisfied that his method runs no risk of overestimating the child's understanding of, say, conservation. However, the child's cognitive abilities may be severely underestimated, since this method takes no account of the intralinguistic difficulties the child may be experiencing. Piaget may also be in danger of misinterpreting his data for other reasons. Recently, studies have shown that apparently innocuous changes in the way a question is asked can have strong effects on the child's ability to answer it (Sinha and Walkerdine, 1978). They have also demonstrated that the social dynamics of an experiment are poorly understood, as are the ways in which children interpret an adult's questions in a formal setting. Language and cognition interact extensively in these explanations and so any account, such as Piaget's, which assumes that the two systems are easily separable by the investigator stands in need of revision (Donaldson, 1978; see chapter 6 below).

3.2.4   *Universals and language variation*

Piaget's claim about the primacy of cognitive development over linguistic development has several interesting aspects to it. Since his interest is epistemological, he concerns himself with certain aspects of cognition – the concept of an object, differentiation of the self from the environment, the logical structure of classes of objects, invariant features of quantity, concepts of reversibility and reciprocity and combinatorial properties of classes and objects – which one expects to be largely free from cultural variation. In other words, he concerns himself with potential universals of cognition. Although his own work was all carried out in Geneva, his tests have been applied to children from a variety of cultural groups and impressively similar results have been obtained.[4] Certain tests may be passed earlier by children from a cultural background which affords them greater familiarity with particular materials than is common for children of that age, but the pattern of development outlined by Piaget has not been substantially challenged by cross-cultural studies. His theory of development can therefore claim to capture aspects of cognition which are universal.

It is not surprising that Piaget will have most to say on universals of language and least to say on language-specific features of language development. The area of language he is most interested in is that part which gives expression to these cognitive universals. It is plausible to assume that the semantic structure involved in such linguistic expressions could be a candidate for the status of a linguistic universal, so the primary focus of discussion for Piaget on linguistic matters is the source of linguistic universals and in this he found himself in conflict with Chomsky.

Piaget was just as reluctant to accept the idea of an innate language-learning ability as he had been to accept the idea that intelligence might be verbally transmitted. Both these views ignored the importance, which he sees as paramount, of the activities of the preverbal infant. If it was necessary to propose that before a child began to speak he had to have knowledge of universal aspects of language, then there was no need to rush to nativism for an explanation. A far more interesting and provocative hypothesis would be to propose that these universals were a subset of cognitive universals and that the emergence of language in the second year was the natural outcome of aspects of sensorimotor intelligence (see section 3.2.5), motivated by the need to go beyond the spatio-temporal restrictions characteristic of that stage of development.

3.2.5 *Development of the concept*

Piaget divides the sensorimotor stage into six substages and traces the way in which the child learns to coordinate his actions into intentional sequences, using tools or other people to get

4. Lloyd (1972) and Dasen (1972) report some cross-cultural comparisons of Piagetian tasks. Cole, Gay, Glick and Sharp (1971) point out the difficulties involved in testing the cognitive processes in people from a radically different culture from that of the experimenter.

objects he cannot grasp, for example. He also suggests that the child is learning to separate himself from his environment and analyse his physical environment into separate objects which still exist when they are hidden, which can be walked around and so on.

Piaget traces two particular achievements of the sensorimotor stage of development in detail (Piaget, 1951). These are the development of the symbolic function whereby a signifier can stand for a signified object, and the development of representation, whereby experience can be stored and retrieved. When the two developments come together, the possibility is there for the child to adopt the public symbols of the wider community in place of his personal signifiers: in other words, language becomes possible, as well as other aspects of the general symbolic function, such as drawing.

Although the child is ready to develop language by the end of the sensorimotor period, the task of full symbolic communication has only just begun. The form of representation used by the sensorimotor child is primitive. It is tied to specific instances in the child's experience and Piaget refers to it as an image. As such, the child's early 'verbal schemas' are not true concepts, which Piaget defines as 'systems of classes, sets of objects grouped according to relations between wholes and parts or systems of particular relations grouped according to their symmetrical or asymmetrical nature' (1951:218). The schemas do not exclusively relate to properties even of the specific objects with which they were originally associated in the child's experience, but instead also evoke the activities associated with the object, the child's position, attitude or activity at the time and so on. Thus when the child starts to use words, at the end of the sensorimotor stage, it is much closer to a schema with a verbal component than to a true adult concept. This is the period of the holophrase,[5] and Piaget's approach has been taken up by some in the debate over the proper analysis for this phenomenon (Nelson, 1974). Gradually, the child attends primarily to the properties of the objects in his application of nouns, but Piaget is still reluctant to

5.   The holophrase will be discussed most extensively in section 5.3. The term refers to the earliest one-word utterances that a child produces which, although they are only one word long, appear to have the effect on the listener of a complete sentence. Thus, *biscuit* is interpreted as 'Can I please have a biscuit?', 'Where are the biscuits?', 'The dog's got a biscuit', 'I want a biscuit, not a banana' in different contexts.

accord him full understanding of a concept, characterising the next stage instead as that of the preconcept. He claims that the preconcept is still dominated by an image of a particular exemplar of the class, arising from the child's individual experience. Later, images and prototypes persist, but only as a kind of shorthand for the true concept and not as an integral part of it, and it is not until the child enters the stage of concrete operations, around age 7 or 8, that Piaget credits him with the ability to form truly generalised and operational concepts. In this he is probably at odds with recent linguistic analyses by Lakoff (1972) and experimental studies by Rosch (1973), which indicate that images and prototypes are more central to adult concepts than his analysis would suggest. However, his account of the emergence of language with the beginnings of representation is among the most penetrating of his writing and does constitute a positive contribution to a theoretical analysis of language development.

3.2.6 *Summary*

On the whole, unfortunately, Piaget's contribution to theories of language development is negative. He challenges the need to postulate a learning ability specific to language and claims that language learning can be accommodated within general mechanisms of cognitive adaptation. He says that language development will be constrained by cognitive development in that there will be aspects of language which the child will be able to master only after he has attained a corresponding level of cognitive control. In addition, there is much about language development on which he is silent. By implication he restricts his interest to universals of language and has little to say on the development of language-specific features. Also, just as he denies that language is a sufficient source for cognition, so he denies that cognitive development is sufficient for language development. Although certain achievements in language development have necessary prerequisites in cognitive development, the cognitive achievement does not ensure the linguistic advance: other processes are necessarily at work, which he leaves unspecified. Moreover, the mapping between features of language and their hypothesised cognitive prerequisites is also left unspecified and is largely dependent for clarification on the ingenuity of the investigator. Some Piagetians

have, however, risen to this challenge and we shall now consider
their contribution to the subject.

3.3   The cognition hypothesis

The major Genevan representative on language is Her-
mine Sinclair (de-Zwart), and for at least ten years now she has
been drawing parallels between features of language and cognitive
development. Perhaps her most interesting contribution has been
in the characterisation of language *structure* in cognitive terms. For
example, she draws attention to Piaget's analysis of the very young
baby as unable to differentiate between action and object or self and
others, and points out that a similar analysis has been made of the
holophrase – an unanalysed amalgam of grammatical categories
with the function of a sentence. Gradually, through the processes of
assimilation and accommodation,[6] the sensorimotor child separates
the psychological categories of agent, action and object, so paving
the way for the grammatical categories, subject, verb phrase and
noun phrase. The point of these parallels is to emphasise, not that
cognitive development is sufficient for language development, but
that the proposal of specific linguistic universals or learning
mechanisms may be premature. Other writers have concentrated on
linking the content of one- and two-word utterances with aspects of
sensorimotor intelligence (Edwards, 1973; Nelson, 1974; Corrigan,
1978; Ingram, 1978), and Brown (1973) has used these links as a
means of increasing confidence in the linguistic analysis accorded to
the child's utterances (see section 5.5).

Specific studies with older children have also sought to explain
their difficulties in Piagetian terms. Sinclair (1967) studied the
relation between conservation level and use of comparative adjectives, concluding that conservers and non-conservers used dimensional adjectives differently in their descriptions of objects, and that
training the non-conservers to change their manner of description

---

6. Piaget was originally a biologist and often discusses development in terms of
the adaptation of the child to his environment. This is particularly true of the
sensorimotor period. Adaptation has two parts to it – assimilation of new parts
of the environment (new objects) to schemas which have been established first
with other objects, and accommodation of these schemas to meet the
challenges of the wider environment. Thus schemas can generalise to assimilate different objects and can be restructured to accommodate the particular
demands which these objects make on them.

did not make them conservers. Cambon and Sinclair (1974) invoked egocentrism to explain the developments they observed with the *John is easy to see* construction. Sinclair and Ferreiro (1970) found horizontal décalage[7] at work in the understanding of passive sentences. Beilin (1975) explained children's difficulty in translating active sentences into passives by referring to the operation of reversibility[8] necessary for the transformation. Bronckart and Sinclair (1973) offered a Piagetian explanation for the early attention children give to aspect rather than tense. The list is long and increasing.

The importance of cognitive development for language development became increasingly recognised in the mid-1970s, and several authors, without being Piagetians, subscribed to some form of the cognition hypothesis, which proposed, in its weak form, that 'we are able to understand and productively to use particular linguistic structures only when our cognitive abilities enable us to do so' (Cromer, 1974a:246).[9] In an influential paper, Macnamara (1972) contrasted two possible mechanisms of early language development. According to one model, the child abstracted semantic categories from the language he heard – he tried to work out what the linguistic input meant and would create categories according to his success at doing this. The model Macnamara favoured, however, was one where the child started with an understanding of the world and sought linguistic means to express this understanding – his language proposals (Nelson, 1973) were grounded in his non-linguistic understanding of his environment, his cognition. The evidence in favour of this model centred on the match between the linguistic analysis of the child's early utterances and some other analysis of the kind of understanding or interests the young child is

7. Horizontal décalage refers to the fact that the material to which an operation is applied has an effect on the difficulty of the test. In this case, children understood passives of some verbs before the passives of others.
8. Reversibility refers to the relation between two operations, such as addition and subtraction, which, when applied successively, cancel each other out.
9. Fodor (1976) has recently proposed a particularly strong form of this hypothesis. He argues that we cannot learn a system which is conceptually richer than the one we start with. Consequently, he argues, we must build language on an equally rich conceptual base which cannot be learned and so must be innate. For comments and further discussion, see Campbell (1979, 1980).

expected to have. For example, Macnamara pointed out that words for invariant properties of objects were likely to be late acquisitions for the child, while features which were likely to catch the child's attention appeared early in his vocabulary. Nelson (1974) noted the functional basis for much of the child's early language. His concepts centred on his own experience of and actions on the objects, rather than on the perceptual features which were often criterial for identification of exemplars of the concept in the adult language.

The idea that the generative basis for early child language was cognitive was frequently placed approvingly alongside observations that generative semantics was becoming popular in linguistics, and many people felt that these two developments would merge into an explanation of language learning. In practice, case grammar (Fillmore, 1968) was widely adopted as a linguistic model (cf. Bowerman, 1973a,b; Brown, 1973) and even children's one-word utterances (Greenfield and Smith, 1976) or their preverbal communicative acts (Lock, 1980) were accorded descriptions which used labels taken over from Fillmore's early article (1968). In this work, the distinction between semantic and cognitive descriptions and categories was frequently obscured (Macrae, 1979).

Some authors have distinguished between cognitive and semantic structures by reserving the term semantic for those aspects of the child's understanding that he intends to communicate (Parisi, 1974), or for those aspects which have some kind of linguistic consequence (Schlesinger, 1974). Consideration of this distinction also leads to observations of the ways in which different languages select different cognitive features to assume linguistic significance (Bowerman, 1976). Consequently, more attention is now being devoted to the linguistic developments which are more language-specific and not obviously rooted in cognition.

This interest has recently been displayed by one of Piaget's students, Annette Karmiloff-Smith (1979), who has applied her Genevan training to the question of how French-speaking children learn the various uses of determiners. Her work shows how the child grapples with the problem of trying to sort out the particular way his language expresses these functions, and pinpoints several intralinguistic difficulties which he faces. She explores the basis for the acquisition of the gender distinction between the pairs of articles and concludes that children's early use of them is governed by the intralinguistic principle of phonological marking, rather than the pragmatic basis of the sex of the referent.

A different intralinguistic problem is faced by the child learning German, who has to master the system of plural inflections for nouns, which, in German, has few regularities to guide the young learner. Park (1978) found that the two children he studied acquired the plural inflections (i.e. supplied them in at least 90 per cent of the contexts in which they were necessary, in accordance with Brown's criteria) at a later stage of language development than English-learning children. Children learning Egyptian Arabic apparently have even greater difficulty with plural inflections (Slobin, 1973).

Johnston and Slobin (1979) explored intralinguistic difficulties in language development by taking comparable groups of Italian-, Turkish-, Serbo-Croatian- and English-speaking children, aged between 2 years and 4 years, 8 months and giving them all the same test, designed to elicit locative expressions. They found several interlinguistic differences: for example, children learning Turkish or Italian produced a greater number of different locative notions than those learning English or Serbo-Croatian and also made greater progress over a four-month interval.

The authors relate these results to the relatively simple mapping in Turkish and Italian between locative notion and lexical item. There were also differences between languages as to the order in which the words for the major locative notions appeared. However, the authors did take note of the effect of cognitive complexity in the acquisition patterns: most difficult were expressions such as *in front of / behind* X where X was not a fronted object; next most difficult were similar expressions, where X was a fronted object, and also expressions like *between X and Y*; easiest were expressions containing *in*, *on*, *under* and *beside*, or their equivalents.

An ideal context in which to explore the relative difficulties for language learning posed by cognitive and linguistic factors is the development of bilingual children. Slobin (1973) reports the case of two girls learning both Hungarian and Serbo-Croatian. They quickly learned to express the Hungarian equivalents of the directional prepositions *into*, *out of* and *on to* and of the locative preposition *on top of*. However, it was a long time before they began to produce equivalent expressions in Serbo-Croatian. Slobin relates this delay to the difficulty of the different structures in the two languages: Hungarian expresses these notions by means of case inflections on the noun while Serbo-Croatian requires, in addition to a more complicated system of inflections, a preposition before the noun. Celce-Murcia (1978) draws attention to a similar phenomenon in the vocabulary development of her daughter, who was learning both English and French. There were cases where she had been introduced to both the French and the English names for an object but carefully avoided the word which was more difficult for her phonologically – she would use *couteau* and avoid *knife*, use *spoon* and avoid *cuiller* – even to the extent of constructing the idiosyncratic 'piedball' to avoid the initial fricative in *football*.

It is likely that this phenomenon of delay in the acquisition of an expression in one of the child's languages occurs only where there is a marked difference in difficulty between the languages. Where both languages use expressions of comparable but slightly different complexity, there appears to be delay in the acquisition in both languages. Thus, Celce-Murcia identified as a class of items which her daughter found particularly difficult those where the lexical items in English and French were phonetically similar. For example, she hesitated over and was confused by the pair *école* and *school*, and by the differing pronunciations of *bus* or *Hubert*. On the other hand, she clearly differentiated between *cheval* and *horse*, or *oiseau* and *bird*. At the syntactic level, Imedadze (1978) noted that her son was delayed in his expression of the relation between subject and object in both Russian and Georgian relative to monolinguals in these languages. In this case, Russian uses the nominative and accusative cases to express the relation, while Georgian uses the dative and nominative cases – no more difficult than Russian, just different.

To complete the picture, we would expect that, if both languages express a notion using the same mechanisms, a bilingual child should begin to use the equivalent expressions at roughly the same time. This seems to be the case. Imedadze reports the simultaneous appearance in both Russian and Georgian of the instrumental case, of the genitive of possession and of the instrumental genitive. Burling (1959) found his son beginning to talk about colour in both English and Garo (a language of North India) at the same time.

Parents of bilingual children are frequently concerned about whether learning two languages might adversely affect their children's intellectual development, and so it is important to consider the relation between linguistic and cognitive development in older bilingual children. Early studies in America suggested that bilingual children scored lower on IQ tests than monolingual children, but Lambert (1977) points out that these studies generally failed to consider the social class or educational background of the children they studied and thus failed to demonstrate an effect on IQ of bilingualism alone. On the contrary, Lambert indicates that there are now several studies (for example, Ianco-Worrall (1972) with Afrikaans–English bilinguals, and Ben-Zeev (1977) with Hebrew–English bilinguals) which suggest that bilinguals do better than monolinguals on measures of cognitive flexibility, creativity or divergent thought. For example, they generally find it easier than monolinguals to recognise the arbitrary relation between a word and its referent and are better able to play games which require them to call a cow *dog* or to replace *into* in their speech with the word *clean*. However, Lambert does caution that it may be necessary for the child to reach a particular (as yet, unknown) level of linguistic competence before he can reap the cognitive benefits of speaking two languages. He also points out that the studies he was reviewing all referred to situations of 'additive bilingualism', where the second language is regarded as an added skill which will not overtake the home language. Children who have no choice but to learn a second language and whose home language is devalued in the process ('subtractive bilingualism') may not present such an optimistic picture.

Finally, we can look to studies of language retardation for evidence on the relation between linguistic and cognitive structures. Furth (1966) challenged the view that an active control of a verbal language was necessary for the development of intelligence by investigating the development of cognitive structures in deaf children, following the Piagetian model in the design of his tests. Although development was delayed, he found considerable evidence of operational thinking which suggests that thought can develop to some degree without verbal language. However, it appears that wherever possible children will create a form of language: Feldman, Goldin-Meadow and Gleitman (1978) studied six deaf children, each of whom were being brought up in families where no sign language was being taught. They found that each child had spontaneously constructed a manual gesture system and that there were similarities across the children in the properties of the systems they had constructed. Thus, it is dangerous to assume that deaf children have no language of their own and so to use their performance on cognitive tests as an indication that cognition can develop very far without language of some kind. In addition, certain concepts do need language to give them form. In teaching vocabulary to a 40-year-old deaf man, Wolff (1973) found that, while his subject found it easy to group items into classes such as footwear, cutlery or flowers, he found that the distinction between *touch* and *hold* was difficult to acquire, suggesting that he had developed some conceptual groupings without language but that they sometimes failed to match those of the language he was trying to learn.

3.4 Functional origins of language

When children start to produce vocalisations which are recognisable as words in the target language, they often spend some time in the holophrastic phase of language development. Their output is usually restricted to one word at a time, but these utterances seem to be capable of conveying as much meaning to the adult listener as a complete sentence would have done. There has been much discussion of the most suitable way of analysing the content of these utterances (see chapter 5), but there seems to be little doubt that by the time children begin to learn the lexical content of the language around them, they already have a fairly sound idea of how language can be used for efficient communication. Several investigators have followed this lead back into the prelinguistic stages, and have tried to trace the development of the child's ability to communicate with those around him and to identify preverbal roots for the various functions of language.

The phenomenon of the holophrase does seem remarkable when the child's utterance is described as consisting simply of a single word, but of course the adult who interprets that word as having the same communicative value as a sentence has other sources of information to aid his interpretation. To begin with, he can refer to the intonation pattern produced by the child. Dore (1975) has suggested that intonation may be an important means whereby the child produces a particular illocutionary force[10] with his single-word utterance. He proposes that the most appropriate analysis of the holophrase is in speech-act terms, and that much of the extra interpretation supplied by the adult when he expands the child's utterance into a sentence is the result of his making explicit its illocutionary force. Much of the interpretation is also aided by relating the utterance to characteristics of the objects or people to which the child is attending while speaking. Greenfield (Greenfield and Smith, 1976; Greenfield and Zukow, 1978) has explored the way in which children at this stage make their utterances maximally informative in the context in which they occur. She predicted that, if a child was at the stage where he could use language to refer to several aspects of a situation and had the vocabulary to do so, he would use his single-word utterance to refer to the aspect which held greatest uncertainty or contained the newest information. Thus, if the child wanted to be given a banana, he would be more likely to say 'banana' than 'want'. However, if he did not want a banana which was being offered to him, he would be more likely to say 'no' than 'banana'. These predictions, and several others to cover a variety of situations, were supported in the case of several children when the situations arose naturally, although similar predictions about which features in a series of similar pictures would be commented on by the child were not supported. They were more likely to name the figure than the ground of each picture, even though a series of pictures had the same figure but varying ground. It appears, then, that when they are using language naturally, young children combine language and context in an extremely economical way and so make the most of their limited linguistic resources. Greenfield is anxious to emphasise that the utterance is informative *from the child's point of view*. In other words, he talks about the things which are informative for *him*. Most of the time the adult can identify what is catching the child's attention and so communication proceeds smoothly, without the child needing to take account of what is capturing the other person's attention. In other words Greenfield's claims need not be in conflict

10. In his account of speech acts, Searle (1969) analyses an utterance into a proposition (the conceptual content of the utterance) and an illocutionary force, which indicates, for example, whether the addressee is to take the utterance as an assertion, a question, or a command.

with Piaget's proposal that children of this age are profoundly egocentric (see section 3.1).

Other authors have concentrated on a topic which makes Piaget's egocentric infant less plausible – the development of the ability to draw attention to an object or activity. This ability is in essence social and requires the child to know when the adult is attending to something and when he is not. It is also an extremely important prerequisite for smooth language use – the deictic terms of the language depend on the ability of both speaker and addressee to work out each other's point of view, and successful reference could be described as the act of ensuring that both speaker and addressee can attend to the same referent.

Before the child can use the words of the parent language, attending to an object is the same as looking at it and the earliest means of directing attention is by the use of gaze. Scaife and Bruner (1975) found that infants between 2 and 14 months could follow an adult's gaze. Understanding the function of pointing to direct attention, however, is a later development. Clark (1978a) reports a study which found that it was not until 18 months that children would follow the direction in which an adult was pointing when that conflicted with the direction of gaze, although the ability was beginning to emerge at 12 months.

Children begin to point only after they are able to reach for objects (around 5 months) and there seems to be a continuity to these gestures, even though by 9 or 10 months reaching and pointing have assumed distinct hand configurations and body postures (Lock, 1980). Bates (1976) reports that one child she was studying began pointing at objects around 9 months without using the gesture communicatively in that she did not check that the adult was also looking in the same direction. By 12 months, she would point first at the object, then back at the adult and again at the object, later simply glancing at the adult for confirmation that he was attending to the object.

Why should the child try to direct the adult's attention to an object? Bates outlines the development of two early performatives which include this activity – the proto-imperative and the proto-declarative. The two functions are complementary. In the proto-imperative, the child's goal is to obtain an object and he uses the adult as an agent to bring that object to him. In the proto-declarative, the child's goal is interaction with the adult and he uses the object as a pretext for the communication. The two performatives develop in parallel. Between 6 and 9 months the child develops various complicated means of getting to objects which he cannot immediately grasp, and by 9 months he is able to use tools to bring the object to him. Not until 10 or 11 months does the child begin to invoke the adult's help in these attempts, and by 13 months (in the case of the children Bates was studying) the appeal to the adult has become more ritualised and the child summons the adult, points to the desired object and waits for the adult to get it. The roots of the proto-declarative go back as far, beginning with the efforts by the young infant to establish physical contact with the adult for social reasons. From 9 or 10 months, the child starts to show objects to adults and around 12 months will give the object to the adult or will point to it, to establish joint attention.

Bates emphasises the coincidence between the time when her children could use these performatives as stylised routines and the point at which they entered the fifth stage of Piaget's sensorimotor period. This is the stage at which the child develops the ability to discover new means for achieving his goals and so begins to understand the operations of instrumentality and agency. Shortly afterwards the children begin to accompany these performatives with standard vocalisations, but Bates proposes that these do not yet have any referential function – they are still part of the performative itself. In this, her analysis agrees with that by Greenfield and Smith (1976) of the early utterances of the children they studied. Reference has to await the sixth stage of the sensorimotor period and the development of the symbolic function.

This social discovery of cognitive functions which later assume an importance in linguistic analysis (the categories of agent and instrument) has also been explored by Bruner (1978) who has traced the development of the roles of donor and recipient during games of give and take between the child and adult. During the early games, the mother is concentrating on trying to get the child to take the objects, but around 10 months it is the child who begins to initiate the activity. By 13 months, the child plays the game smoothly, getting pleasure from the exchange itself, rather than possession of the object. Exactly how this achievement is related to the use of case roles later on is not clear.

One thing that the child is doing in this example, however, is showing that he can take turns in a joint activity, timing his contribution to occur in the correct place in the sequence. Turn taking is a characteristic of adult conversation which has been extensively studied, but it seems to be a much more general feature of interaction. Trevarthen (1974) has looked carefully at the timing of exchanges between mothers and infants as young as 2 months, and finds that even then there are interacting cycles of activity as each participant makes his contribution and then retires slightly to allow the other person to make his. Mothers are not surprised when they are asked to talk to children as young as this, and indeed it appears that they are able to carry on a satisfying conversation of a primitive kind with their infants.

Exchanging roles during verbal exchanges appears to be a much later activity, and Halliday (1975) treats the development of dialogue as a major achievement of the period between $16\frac{1}{2}$ and 18 months. He calls this period Phase II, a transitional stage between Phase I and the adult language in his account of the way in which his son, Nigel, laid the foundations for learning the language around him. In Phase I, lasting from 9 to $16\frac{1}{2}$ months, Nigel began to control half a dozen functions in his utterances, with each utterance corresponding to a single function. The first to appear were the instrumental, regulatory, interactional and personal functions, later followed by the heuristic and the imaginative. During Phase II, Nigel's utterances began to be plurifunctional and words from the adult language could be identified in his speech. However, the major characteristic of this period was the separation of his utterances into two principal functions – the pragmatic function, in which language is used to satisfy the child's needs and to interact with others, and what Halliday calls the mathetic function, in which language is used to learn about the child's environment and about the language itself, resulting in a dramatic increase in vocabulary at this time. Nigel marked these two functions with separate intonation patterns, using rising tone for pragmatic utterances and falling tone for mathetic ones. Halliday traces this distinction through to the two major functional components of the adult system, the ideational and the interpersonal, and then leaves Nigel at the point at which he gets to work mastering the adult language with a strong functional foundation already constructed.

4
Development of the child's sound system

As with other parts of language development, the development of the sound system can be divided into three major phases. The central phase is the period during which the child attempts to produce target utterances in the adult language, leading gradually to an approximation to phonemic control of the target language. Prior to this is the period of early vocalisations, during which the child produces various segments of speech-like sounds and discriminates certain features of adult speech. Finally, there may be a period during which the child can be shown to be aware of the phonological rules of his language and use them to distinguish between potential and inadmissible utterances in his language. During all three phases, discussion of receptive and productive processes have to be treated separately and possible relations between them considered.

4.1 Vocal productions and discriminations in infancy

Stark (1979) divides the vocal productions of the first 18 months into five stages as follows:

Stage 1 (0 to 8 weeks): Reflexive crying and vegetative sounds (such as burping, swallowing, sneezing)

Stage 2 (8 to 20 weeks): Cooing and laughter

Stage 3 (16 to 30 weeks): Vocal play (including isolation of primitive segment types)

Stage 4 (25 to 50 weeks): Reduplicated babbling (series of repeated consonant–vowel syllables)

Stage 5 (9 to 18 months):   Non-reduplicated babbling and expressive jargon (in which stress and intonation patterns are imposed on the babbling)

To propose a developmental sequence of this kind is to contradict the popular view that during the 'babbling period' children can produce the full repertoire of sounds used in the languages of the world and do so without any apparent regularity (Jakobson, 1968). While recognising important individual differences between children in the content of the stages, Stark proposes that a developmental sequence can be outlined which may have certain aspects that are universal. In her account, it is possible to see the sources of the alternative view that the period lacks structure and that all possible speech sounds may be produced. She points out that if one looks closely at the crying, sucking and coughing infant, one can identify virtually all the articulatory features of speech in his early productions, such as stops at the start of a crying sequence or bilabial formations during sucking. These features are, moreover, well coordinated for the child's purposes: what changes is the combinations of features produced. During this development, in addition, there are apparent regressions in the child's productions which may give the impression of disorder. When the child begins reduplicated babbling, in which he restricts his vocalisations to repetitions of a single consonant–vowel syllable, his utterances are much less varied than at the end of the stage of vocal play, and initially utilise a restricted repertoire of consonants: labial and alveolar stops and nasals and /y/ glides.

Jakobson (1968) emphasised the discontinuity between the babbling period and the period of the development of the speech sound, with its associated phonemic value. During the latter period, the child's speech lacked sounds which had been produced during the former and, in addition, he discerned a consistent order in the appearance of phonemic contrasts during the latter period, while all orders of acquisition had been reported during the babbling period. Menyuk (1977) has suggested that there may be a closer link between the two periods than Jakobson implies because, although the order of appearance of sounds during babbling may vary, there are changes in the frequency with which consonants containing certain features are produced. She indicates that these proportions are later reflected in the order of acquisition of speech-sound features. Stark's account also helps to establish a continuity between these periods.

One aspect of the development of vocalisations which is obscured by an analysis which emphasises the appearance of phonetic features is the change in the function of these vocalisations. Stage 1 seems to be given over entirely to the expression of discomfort, but the cooing and laughing baby of Stage 2 begins to vocalise responsively; and at this stage one can identify the beginnings of turn-taking sequences between mother and baby which can be seen as elementary conversations (Trevarthen, 1974). Other coordinated actions appear at this time as well (such as lip and tongue movements and gesticulations), not all of them resulting in vocalisations, which alternate with the mother's activity and appear to have a rudimentary communicative function. These activities have been described by Trevarthen as prespeech. Conversely, not all the phonetic developments traced out by Stark have communicative value: she points out that reduplicated babbling is not used communicatively, but that during Stage 4 children are beginning to communicate more effectively by the use of gestures such as reaching, grasping and pointing.

To ask whether preverbal children can perceive phonetic distinctions in adult speech is a question which has to be clarified before it can be answered, and before comparison can be made with later speech-perception data. Perception generally straddles the two extreme processes of discrimination, where some distinction is merely detected, and understanding, where the distinction can be mapped onto a larger stored body of knowledge and interpreted accordingly. Several studies have explored the ability of new-born babies to *detect* linguistic distinctions, without establishing that the distinction has any immediate significance for the child. Evidence that children younger than 18 months *understand* utterances by decoding their phonetic properties, rather than by interpreting other features of the total context of utterance, is extremely difficult to obtain (Clark, Hutcheson and van Buren, 1974). Menyuk (1974) suggests that discrimination of suprasegmental features may precede discrimination of segmental features, but that claim also has to be carefully modified in the light of the evidence.

Three main techniques have been used to establish whether neonates can detect linguistic distinctions in speech sounds (see Mehler and Bertoncini, 1979; Morse, 1979, for summaries). With very young children (of 1 month) the high amplitude sucking (HAS) paradigm has been found to be successful in demonstrating discrimination. The heart rate (HR) technique is less successful with such young children but is widely used with children over 3 months of age. Finally, the head turning (HT) technique has also been used. In the HAS technique, the infant learns that by sucking he can make an interesting sound continue. After a while, the sucking rate drops as the infant loses interest in the sound. However, if a new sound is introduced, the infant begins to suck quickly again. Obviously, this happens only if the child can recognise that the sound has changed and so, if a change in sucking rate occurs when the sound changes, we can conclude that the child can discriminate the sounds concerned. The HR paradigm exploits the child's attention to new sounds in a different way. It rests on the observation that if a stimulus is repeated regularly, it soon becomes uninteresting and the subject stops paying attention to it – he habituates to the stimulus. The subject's attention can be monitored by measuring his heart rate. During habituation, heart rate increases to a steady level. However, if a new stimulus is introduced, and if the child notices the difference, then he may begin to pay attention again. This is referred to as dishabituation and is indicated by a sharp drop in heart rate. In the HT technique, the child learns that if he turns his head when the sound changes, he will see an interesting display. In all of these methods, if dishabituation occurs then one can assume that the child can discriminate the difference of interest. If the child does not dishabituate, however, then the result is more difficult to interpret.

The contrasts which have been explored most extensively in this area are those of place of articulation ([ba] vs. [ga]) and of voicing ([ba] vs. [pa]). All the experiments use synthetic speech stimuli. Using HAS, Morse has shown that children as young as 6 weeks can discriminate place of articulation, and the same result can be found using HR, provided that no delay is introduced between the stimuli (Morse, 1979). In addition, Eimas has shown that infants aged 2–3 months perceive these distinctions categorially, that is

65

they discriminate stimuli which straddle the phonemic boundary but do not discriminate stimuli which are physically just as close together but which adults would categorise as being variants of the same phoneme. Again using HAS, Eimas has shown categorial perception of voicing contrasts in infants as young as 1 month although this time the HR method has not been able to demonstrate discrimination below 10 months of age. Morse (1979) summarises the first decade of research on infant speech perception and concludes that for almost all the discriminations tested, the infant's perception is remarkably like that of adults. Almost the only exceptions are the fricatives /f/ and /θ/ which give trouble up to age 5. Discrimination of vowel contrasts is non-categorial, just as it is with adults. One limitation of the studies, however, is that in general they have kept the phonetic context of the distinctions constant so that it is not clear whether the children would be able to demonstrate perceptual constancy – that is, the ability to identify the same phoneme when it occurs in different phonetic environments. (Kuhl (1979) reports on the beginnings of investigations of this kind.)

The discovery that infants perceive phonemic contrasts categorially is intriguing. Categorial perception is required for normal speech processing. Until recently it was not thought to be a characteristic of human non-speech auditory perception (although it has now been demonstrated that both adults (Cutting and Rosner, 1974; Kuhl, 1979) and children (Jusczyk, Rosner, Cutting, Foard and Smith, 1977) can distinguish categorially various music-like and other sound stimuli). Thus infants had been shown to be sensitive to speech sounds in a particular way which was appropriate for linguistic processing. Might this be a species-specific innate predisposition for an aspect of language processing? Investigation started on the effect of the linguistic environment on the infant's perceptual abilities and on the abilities of non-human animals to discriminate speech sounds.

Kikuyu is a Bantu language which has no voiceless consonants but does distinguish between voiced and prevoiced consonants where voicing precedes articulatory release. In particular, the language has a prevoiced bilabial stop with a voice onset time (VOT) more extreme than −30 msec. This means that, when a spectrographic analysis is produced of a word beginning with this stop, it can be seen that the second formant begins more than 30 msec. after the first formant. For a stop with +30 msec. VOT, the first formant begins 30 msec. after the second. Streeter (1976) synthesised syllables beginning with a bilabial stop which varied in VOT from −30 to +80 msec. and tested discrimination by 2-month-old Kenyan infants, using the HAS paradigm. She found that they could discriminate between VOT of −30 and 0 msec. and also between 10 and 40 msec., the latter being a discrimination which straddles the voiced/voiceless boundary of English (around +30 msec.). There was also some evidence of discrimination within the voiceless category, unlike in the Eimas study, but performance here did not differ significantly from a control condition. Thus the infants who had had some exposure to a linguistic environment different from that for English were able to discriminate both their native prevoiced/voiced boundary, unlike Eimas' American infants, and the English voiced/voiceless boundary, to which they had not been exposed. In addition, Kenyan adults were able to make both discriminations. This indicates that phonemic distinctions may vary in their psycho-acoustic salience and that the English voicing boundary may have exceptional properties compared with other phonemic boundaries. It also indicates that in only two months infants can learn a lot about the phonological characteristics of the language around them. In its turn, the Kikuyu prevoiced/voiced boundary may be more salient than the Spanish voicing boundary, which lies between −20 and +20 msec. of VOT. Lasky, Syrdal-Lasky and Klein (1975), using the HR paradigm, found that Guatemalan infants of monolingual Spanish-speaking parents could not make this Spanish discrimination by 6½ months of age although, like the Kenyan infants, they could make a more extreme prevoiced discrimination and could also discriminate in the area of the English voicing boundary. It appears from these studies that infants are innately sensitive to certain distinctions which some languages use to carry semantic distinctions, while they have to learn to discriminate certain other phonemic distinctions.

The +30 msec. VOT boundary also figures in studies of speech perception by non-human animals. Kuhl found that chinchillas were most sensitive to VOT changes in this region, and Kuhl and Miller (1975) showed that when chinchillas had been trained to discriminate between 0 and +80 msec. VOT, they subsequently classified stimuli intermediate between the training stimuli in such a way that the boundary varied according to place of articulation, as is the case with human speech perception. Morse and Snowdon (1975) found, using HR, that rhesus monkeys could discriminate the place of articulation of voiced consonants. Although they showed discrimination both between and within the English phonemic categories, they showed greater discrimination between categories than within them.[1] Thus the ability to discriminate between phonetic features which among humans carry phonemic contrast is not confined to humans: certain mammals can also demonstrate this ability.

Thus, it appears that infants and other mammals are differentially sensitive to auditory stimuli. Some languages use these areas of special sensitivity for carrying semantic distinctions but there are other phonemic distinctions which the child has to learn.

Finally, it should be noted that these studies do not explore the limits of an infant's auditory discrimination ability. Failure to *show* discrimination need not reflect an inability to detect a difference, given the paradigms used. Snowdon (1979), in discussing the work with animals, points out that evidence of discrimination varies according to which testing technique is used. In its natural habitat, an animal may not necessarily show discrimination of a distinction which he may well be able to demonstrate if he has to do so to avoid an electric shock. Pisoni and Lazarus (1974) found variations in adult speech discrimination when the method of testing was altered. Thus, we know which contrasts infants are specially sensitive to and, perhaps, find interesting, but they may also hear many other differences which do not show up in the results.

4.2 Early perception and production of phonemic distinctions

Despite infants' early proficiency in discriminating voiced and voiceless stops, this distinction is mastered late when it has to bear a semantic burden. The infants in the speech discrimination studies simply had to hear and respond to a change in sound. They did not have to remember the sound and, in fact,

---

1. Kuhl (1979) also reviews several other studies on speech perception by animals.

Morse found that when a delay of 30 seconds was introduced between stimuli, the very young infants failed to make the distinction. To make any headway with learning a language, however, we have to be able to remember the sounds we hear and be able to identify them at a later date.

The development of this ability was investigated by Garnica (1973) as follows. On any trial, the child was shown two little figures who were named by the experimenter, the names being nonsense syllables of the form consonant–vowel–consonant which differed only in the initial consonant. The difference between these consonants was an example of the distinction being tested. The child was then asked to perform an action with one of the figures, such as giving it a ride in a toy car or putting a hat on it. For this, the child had to identify the figure correctly on the basis of the nonsense name it had been given. In order to do this reliably, he had to be able to store the name differently in memory – in other words, he had to be able to perceive the phonetic distinction being tested.[2] Garnica tested children between 1;5 and 1;10 and found that a general pattern of difficulty emerged. For example, distinguishing a sonorant from a fricative or from an affricate, or distinguishing a nasal from a glide was relatively easy for the children. On the other hand, the distinction between stops and affricates or between voiced and voiceless consonants proved extremely difficult for them. However, Garnica noted that there was considerable variation in this pattern, in that some children could make a distinction which was difficult for the group as a whole and yet fail to distinguish some of the easier oppositions.

To extract a single-feature opposition from two syllables and make it carry a semantic distinction may be particularly demanding for children of this age and probably does not reflect the way they go about learning phonological oppositions. Children are seldom faced with minimal pairs to learn in this way. It has been suggested that, in the beginning, they learn words and their meanings as a whole (Ferguson and Farwell, 1975), without analysing them carefully into smaller phonetic units. This leads us to be careful in interpreting Garnica's results. They are extremely

2. Garnica did not vary the vocalic environment of the distinctions systematically and so it is not clear from her data whether these distinctions were phonemic for the children.

important in demonstrating that not all phonological oppositions are perceived equally readily by the child, but we should not be surprised to find that a child who fails to make the voiced/voiceless distinction on her task may not confuse *goat* and *coat* when he encounters these words in a story.[3]

Edwards (1974) took the opportunity to explore some specific hypotheses about phonological development using the same task as Garnica. For example, testing children between 1;8 and 3;11, she asked whether the voice discrimination would appear in stops before it appeared in fricatives, or whether velar spirants, which are non-phonemic in English, would be discriminated at the point in development that would be predicted by a consideration of their complexity relative to other sounds in the language. She found far greater variation than expected both at the level of the performance of individual children and also in terms of the interaction between the distinctions of interest and other phonological distinctions. For example, she found that place and manner of articulation caused the children more difficulty in the development of stops and fricatives than voicing.

The Edwards study is important because she extended the investigation to considering the relation between the perception and production of these contrasts by the children. She encouraged the children to repeat the names of the figures both before and after the perception task and compared their productions with their level of perceptual discrimination. In general, she found that perception of a contrast did precede its mastery in production. However, there were several cases where, individually, children could produce distinctions they failed to discriminate in this task. Eilers and Oller (1976) report a similarly ragged relation between perception and production of phonemic contrasts. The picture becomes even more uncertain, and intriguing, with the report by Macken and Barton (1980) that children may be observing distinctions in their productions which even trained phoneticians cannot hear. They analysed spectrographically some word-initial stop consonants which had been produced by four children between 1;4 and 2;4. They

---

3. Eilers and Oller (1976) tested the ability of children between 1;10 and 2;2 to discriminate between minimal pairs where at least one member of each pair was a word familiar to the children, and Barton (1978) found good discrimination of voicing contrasts by 2-year-olds, using familiar words.

identified a period during which the children were producing a difference in VOT between the initial consonants of words which in the adult language are distinguished by the presence or absence of voicing. However, this difference, although statistically reliable, fell within the adult voiced category and so was imperceptible to those listening to the children. Thus adults may underestimate how much productive control a child is exercising over the distinctions in his language, and this all serves to obscure the relation between perception and production in the child's phonological system.

Theories of phonological development seek to explain why children should produce some sounds before others and why their mispronunciations of adult words should take the form they do. Since they are trying to account for the child's attempts to produce a target in the adult language, they have to consider how the child perceives that target. A major distinction between theories of phonological development rests on the extent to which they treat perceptual difficulties as being contributory to the child's production difficulties.

It would be possible to argue that the child's productions are a faithful reproduction of what he perceives the target to be. Mispronunciations would then have their source in the child's faulty perception. We have seen, however, from the studies by Edwards and by Eilers and Oller that children can frequently make perceptual discriminations which they cannot produce. Dodd (1975) asked children between 2;3 and 4;7 to pick out one of four flash-cards both to an instruction given by an adult with correct pronunciation of the name and to one which incorporated a recording the children had made previously themselves in which they had mispronounced the target name. She found that the children could identify the card more accurately in response to the adult recording than to their own mispronunciation and that the closer their pronunciation was to the adult's, the better they could use it to identify the card. This indicates that the children can hear that their pronunciations deviate from the adult one and they can interpret the adult form more easily. Thus their production does not simply mirror their perception. In addition, children frequently produce sounds which do not occur in the language they are learning, such as the voiceless sonorants produced by Smith's son (Smith, 1973). It would require an elaborate account of the child's perception to explain this phenomenon.

At the other extreme, one might want to argue that the major source of the child's production errors lies in the motor difficulty of producing certain sound sequences which he can perceive successfully. This explanation is inadequate, however, as children may mispronounce a word which in the adult language has the same phonetic form as their mispronunciation of another word. Smith's (1973) example of this phenomenon is now a classic. His son mispronounced the adult word *puddle* as 'puggle' and yet produced the form 'puddle' quite happily as his form of the adult word *puzzle*. Thus there was no reason of a motor kind for him to mispronounce *puddle* in the first instance since he showed on another occasion that he could produce the phonetic sequence required. In some cases, the child may have difficulties in getting his tongue round the words – the widespread reduction of initial consonant clusters may be attributable in part to problems of articulation – but it cannot be more than a contributory factor to the child's difficulties in producing the words of the target language.

Thus an adequate account of phonological development must move away from peripheral explanations based on the child's perceptual or articulatory inadequacies. One of the bravest attempts to characterise the child's phonological development was that by Jakobson (1968). He emphasised that perception was frequently in advance of production, but saw the latter as being constrained into a sequence of development which reflected the phonological complexity of the target phonemes, as outlined in his distinctive feature theory. He predicted that children who mispronounced a sound would do so by substituting one which was phonologically less complex (cf. Edwards, 1974). He also mapped out a parallel between phonological acquisition, language dissolution[4] and the distribution of distinctive features across languages, whereby sounds early in acquisition would be late in disappearance and would be common across languages.

He proposed that the earliest consonant to be produced would be a forward articulated stop and the earliest vowel a wide one. The first consonantal distinction to be acquired would be the nasal/oral

---

4. Jakobson's later work on language dissolution (Jakobson, 1963) concentrates on the variety of types of aphasia, each with distinctive linguistic characteristics, and he denounces the 'unitarian heresy' of earlier writers.

distinction followed by labials and dentals. This constitutes the minimal consonantal system of various languages. Later, for example, children would acquire fricatives after the corresponding stops, back consonants after front ones and affricates after fricatives.

Jakobson is not explicit about the relation between perception and production, talking instead in terms of the acquisition of distinctive features. Interpreting the theory as a set of predictions of perceptual development, Garnica (1973) notes that her data fail to support his predictions, and de Villiers and de Villiers (1978) cite counter-examples from production data. Kiparsky and Menn (1977), on the other hand, criticise Jakobson for being not sufficiently explicit in many of his predictions to make his theory testable. Despite this, his work was valuable as an attempt to propose a coherent set of rules to account for the course and nature of phonological development.

Smith (1973) is frequently criticised for taking too sanguine a view of the young child's perceptual abilities. His approach was interesting. Working from a record of his child's speech between 2;2 and 4;0 he presented two analyses both of the child's system at 2;2 and of its development longitudinally. In one, he assumed that the child's productions were a fair reflection of his perception, and attempted to characterise the data by a system of rules. In the other, he assumed that the child's perception could uncover an accurate phonological representation of the adult form, and he attempted to account for the child's productions by a set of realisation rules taking the adult form as input. He found that the latter account was more satisfactory. He has since acknowledged (Smith, forthcoming) that there may be instances where it is necessary to assume that the child does not represent the lexical item in its adult form, as evidenced by the fact that a realisation rule which should apply to all words of a particular adult form results in some apparently arbitrary exceptions in the child's speech. However, he emphasises that the underlying representation from which the child's production arises must be distinct from that produced form and carry information not present in his production. For example, although his son pronounced the adult singular forms *cat*, *cloth* and *horse* all with similar endings (namely, [kæt], [klɔt], [ɔːt]), he formed their plurals according to a rule which required him to uncover the final coronal continuants characteristic of adult *cloth* and *horse* but not characteristic of adult *cat,* so producing [kæt], [klɔtid] and [ɔːtid] as plural forms.

Other accounts of phonological development propose that the child bases his production on an imperfect representation of the adult form. Ingram (1974) suggests that the child hears the adult word as alternating stretches of identifiable sound and unidentifiable noise, the latter sometimes being analysed as a consonant, vowel or syllable. To this underlying form, various phonological rules apply, including several context-sensitive rules such as reduplication, weak syllable deletion, cluster reduction, voicing and assimilation. Thus two identical utterances of the child may have completely different sources and histories. A child who says [pu] for both *spoon* and *pudding* will have produced the utterances via different rules from the underlying forms 'XpuC' and 'puCX' where X represents noise and C some unidentified consonant.

For Waterson (1971), the most attractive way of relating the child's production to his perception of the adult form rests in proposing an underlying form which is a reduced form of the adult word. She argues for this approach on two counts. In the first place, it has similarities with the notion of telegraphic speech which was an attempt to characterise the early syntactic efforts of the young child (Brown, 1973). The suggestion was made that children selectively attended to the informationally rich parts of adult utterances. In drawing this parallel, Waterson invites a continuity between explanations of syntactic and phonological development. The other evidence for this relation between perception of the adult form and production of the child's form is empirical. Waterson first analysed her child's words into five types and then found that the adult words to which they corresponded similarly fell into five categories. Applying an intuitive notion of salience to these adult forms, Waterson was able to indicate how reduced versions of these forms, which retained their most salient elements, could give rise to the child's productions, via processes similar to those outlined by Ingram.

The debate continues. Smith brandishes Occam's razor over Waterson and Ingram, denying the need for extra levels of representation when the insertion of a modest perceptual filter will account for the major divergences between the adult correct form and the child's underlying representation (Smith, forthcoming). Most of the discussion to date has been at the level of elegance and economy of formal descriptions. In the future it may have a sounder and more detailed empirical basis.

4.3 Awareness of phonological structure

When a child begins to learn to read, he is faced with an experience of language quite different from anything he has come across before. Instead of a more or less continuous flow of speech, enriched by intonation, gesture and non-linguistic context, he has to contend with written words, separated from each other, composed of letters which somehow correspond to the sounds he has been listening to and producing for the past four or five years. It can be a bewildering time for a child: just how bewildering is likely, in part, to be related to how much he understands about the nature of language, whether he can segment speech into words and syllables and whether he knows that some combinations of sounds which are physically possible to produce are, none the less, not permissible sequences in English. Gibson and Levin (1975) discuss in some detail the linguistic skills which are prerequisite to learning to read.

Preschool children have difficulty in segmenting speech into a sequence of words, and studies which attempt to encourage them to do this find that they are more inclined to base their segmentation on features of the rhythm of the sentence or on semantic considerations. Holden and MacGintie (1972) asked children to repeat a sentence and, for each word, as they said it, to point to a counter. They found that the children frequently missed function words, pointing only once for sequences like *the men* or *to go*, and that their pointing was often determined more by the rhythm of the sentence than by its lexical content. Huttenlocher (1964) asked 4-year-old children either to separate word pairs, by tapping in between each word, or to reverse them, producing 'white black' when they were given 'black white' and so on. The children had particular difficulty in both tasks with sequences such as *man runs* or *you are* which formed a coherent semantic and grammatical unit (unlike *house did* or *orange cow*). In addition, the children found it more difficult to reverse than to separate a sequence such as *man runs* which becomes ungrammatical when reversed (unlike *you are*).

A similar effect was found by Calfee, Chapman and Venezky

75

(1972) who gave a series of tests to some 5-year-old children. Among them was one where two groups of children had to learn a list of three word pairs, which were read to them five times. For both groups, the second word of each pair was the first word without its first sound, but for group A this second word was still a real word: thus, the pairs for group A were FEEL:EEL, SHOUT:OUT and PILE:ILE, while those for group B were SOAP:OAP, RIDE:IDE, CHIEF:IEF. To test their learning, the experimenter would say the first word in each pair and the children had to reply with the second. The children in group A were more often correct than those in group B on each of the five repetitions. When the group A children were then given the items in the group B list, their performance dropped, suggesting that they had been learning a semantically based rule in preference to a structural one. Bruce (1964) gave his subjects one word (such as *snail*) and asked them what word was left when a particular sound (/n/) was removed (answer: *sail*). This caused even greater difficulty and he found that it was only children with a mental age of 7 years or more who could make any progress with this task. Children with a lower mental age would reply with a letter name, or would produce another word, which was similar to the test word, for example giving *wink* when asked to take the /k/ out of *pink*. The errors of the older children were more analytic, arising from difficulties in attempting to carry out the process. Thus, they would take out the wrong sound or too many, producing *nail* when asked to take the /n/ out of *snail* or *in* when asked to take the /s/ out of *spin*.

Thus, it appears that words and phonemes have only a tenuous reality for preschool children. The children do better, however, when they have to decide whether or not a sound sequence conforms to the phonological rules of English. Messer (1967) asked children between 3;1 and 4;5 which of a pair of nonsense sequences sounded more like a word, where one member of the pair violated the phonological rules of English and the other did not. The children could do this task with a fair degree of success. In addition, when they tried to pronounce the impermissible sequences, they made them sound more like English than they had done before. Morehead (1971) explored this in his study, by repeating continuously to his subjects 'words' which violated the rules of English phonology in differing degrees and asking them to imitate them either immediately or after a delay. He found that in general his subjects either repeated the sequence correctly or changed it in some way to make it conform to the phonological rules of English. He found that his 4-year-olds were most likely to produce errors which were not real words in English but were possible ones, whereas his 7-year-olds tended to replace the sequence by an actual word in English (for example, *swum* instead of [srʌm]). From these results, it appears that by 4 years of age many children are aware of what does and what does not conform to the rules of English phonology.

5
Naturalistic studies of language acquisition

Most families have a stock of *bons mots* inadvertently produced by some luckless member in the course of his language development which survive into his adulthood in the form of nicknames or in-jokes. There is an ancient and pervasive interest in language development which constitutes a kind of popular scholarship. Such anecdotes are also the natural starting-point for consideration of the scientific studies which are or can be carried out. In this chapter we shall concentrate on naturalistic studies where the investigator records the language produced by a child in the course of his early development.

Isolated anecdotes may be interesting and amusing indices of the academic potential of the topic under discussion, but unless there is an attempt to systematise them in some way this potential remains unrealised. In practical terms, there has to be a choice between intensity and generality. Either the investigator keeps a careful record of the development of very few children which aims to be as exhaustive as possible, or he makes lightning spot-checks periodically on a large number of carefully selected children. At the outset, then, one must decide the extent to which intensity or generality is to be sacrificed. Most work has in fact favoured intensity at the expense of generality, although it is possible to strike a middle course. Wells (1974; see also Wells, 1981) used data from an extensive project as inspiration for smaller in-depth studies, and Slobin (1973) has shown how carefully selected examples from a variety of studies in several languages can be woven into an interesting account of some possible mechanisms for language acquisition.

The next decision to be made – and the most interesting one – concerns the type of data to be collected. It is a truism of the philosophy of science that when we observe behaviour, we do so with a particular question in mind. Observation can never be completely exhaustive because we cannot record absolutely everything which is happening at a particular time. Even if we constantly train a video-camera on the child we are studying, we will not necessarily have information about what he can see or how things feel to him, which might be important if we want to evaluate the accuracy of a claim like 'That's hot.'

The most enduring tradition of data collection in the subject is that of the diary study, where a particularly alert and conscientious parent keeps daily notes on a child's progress. This type of data generally emphasises changes in the child's linguistic skill along with the parent's interpretation of them, and so these studies are a rich source of ideas on the subject, although generally unhelpful if one is, for example, interested in the frequency of particular forms. However, many of the diary studies, such as Sully (1896) and Jespersen (1922), incorporate interesting surveys which compare the conclusions they draw from their data with reports already in the literature or sent to them by other parents.

The tape-recorder made it possible to keep a continuous record of all the child's utterances over a particular period, and most current studies employ a variant of this method. They differ in the extent to which they also keep account of the context in which the child's speech occurs, and in which aspect of the context they consider important. Thus Griffiths, Atkinson and Huxley (1974) kept careful note at the time of testing of which toy the child was holding, what the adults were doing and so on, although during every testing session the child spent his time playing with one of the adult investigators. On the other hand Wells (1981) categorised his speech samples principally in terms of the social context in which they occurred – whether the child was helping with the housework or being fed and so on – and only later asked the mothers to comment on the specific objects available to the child or the actions of the adults on these occasions. Clearly Griffiths *et al.* would be limited in the extent to which their data captured the full range of the child's verbal skills since, for example, they would never record the children without an adult present and so catch them practising what they had been learning (Weir, 1962), but Wells would be in a weak position to comment in detail on the development of the children's abilities to make fine linguistic discriminations, such as that between *here* and *there*.

Such studies may also differ in whether they focus attention on the speech produced by the child or the speech addressed to the child. There is a particular interest in the mother's speech as a means of investigating the nature of the linguistic environment in which the child grows up, in the expectation that this will be reflected more or less directly in the child's speech.

Thus there are three major types of study which fall under the rubric of naturalistic studies of individual children – the diary studies, which are a systematically documented series of dated anecdotes of milestones in the child's development; observational studies in which everything the child says is recorded, together with notes about the context in which it was produced, and where the child's speech is the focus of the analysis; and, finally, observational studies in which it is the speech directed to the child which is the main focus of analysis. We shall save the third kind of study for chapter 7 and here draw on work which analyses language spoken by the child.

5.1 Comprehension and production in child language

According to Chomsky (1965) it is not enough to write a grammar for the utterances a native speaker actually produces: we must also make it comprehensive enough to include all sentences he can understand and could produce if the occasion demanded it. However, at least in adult studies, it is common to assume, to within idiolectal variation, that a common competence serves both comprehension and production of speech in the individual (but see Matthews (1979) for a discussion of the problems arising from this assumption). In other words, if we can understand a sentence, it is assumed that we could and might produce it on some other occasion. Perhaps not without hesitation: it is a well-known result from studies of memory that it is easier to recognise an item with which we are familiar than to recall it (Baddeley, 1976:285) – an observation which supermarket displays exploit to advantage! It is also common to assume in adult studies that if we can produce a sentence then we can also understand it, unless we are 'producing' the sentence under relatively unusual conditions, such as reading out a speech or reciting some poetry.

It has often been assumed that child language is similar to adult language in this respect. As soon as a child is able to show evidence of creative use of language, this is attributed to the contribution of an elementary linguistic competence which is expected to serve the child's comprehension and production in the same way as an adult competence does. Gradually, rules are added to the competence: the child *acquires* his language bit by bit, picking it up rather like mud on his shoes, without disturbing the relation between linguistic competence and language performance which is found elsewhere. In child language, the relation between different parts of language performance may be more obvious than in other cases. In particular, it is commonly reported that production of language lags behind comprehension quite markedly. Mothers frequently report that their preverbal child already understands a lot of what is said to him, and experimental studies with older children often find better performance on tests of comprehension than on corresponding tests of production.

Unfortunately, the relation between comprehension and production in child language is not as simple as this (Bloom, 1974; Bloom and Lahey, 1978). Children come out with a lot of language which appears to indicate a more sophisticated level of language development than they have actually attained. For example, they sometimes go through a period of echoing the last parts of utterances addressed to them, often after a delay, so that it is difficult to tell whether an utterance has been spontaneously created by the child or is an imitation of an adult utterance. They often learn stock phrases – *in there* is quite a common one – without being able to segment the phrase and recombine its parts with other lexical items, and so produce fresh phrases such as *in the box*, *on there* and so on. And it is well known that they can repeat songs and nursery rhymes almost correctly without understanding what they are singing. Thus much of the language children produce may not be backed up by understanding.

At the same time, children may appear to understand much more language than they actually do. Clark, Hutcheson and van Buren (1974) point out that we overestimate a child's comprehension unless we check carefully that the child could not have based his response on paralinguistic cues or redundancy in the situation or in the language itself. To test whether a child understands the difference between two linguistic constructions we have to ensure that both could lead to appropriate responses in a situation and then check on whether the child can regularly match the language used with a correct choice of action. For example, they showed that Adam, the child they were studying, did not understand the difference between *up* and *down*. They went to visit a friend whose house could be approached either by going up one flight of steps or down another, and at the point where the choice had to be made, the adult said to Adam 'Let's go down today.' Adam then sometimes chose to go up the steps and sometimes to go down them, with no clear preference and no obvious understanding of the adult's comment. From this they could show that Adam's comprehension was no better than his production since at this stage he was using *down* to refer to vertical movement in either direction.

Both comprehension and production of a linguistic structure undergo development, probably at different rates. It is also easy to overestimate the extent of both in casual conversation with a child, and so it is important that we should be clear about the criteria we are going to use if we want to claim that a child can understand or produce a particular linguistic structure. What criteria should we use? Should we ask them to imitate examples of the structure (for example, the plural inflection), understand it under natural conditions, understand it under controlled, experimental conditions, produce it spontaneously (if so, how often?), generate examples of it using novel, or nonsense, lexical items (as Berko (1958) asked her subjects to do), or explain to an adult under which conditions particular forms should be produced (in other words, formulate and articulate the rule)?

Each of these abilities shows a certain control by the child over part of his language. In adults, these abilities may all come together, so that one can at least propose that there might be a single body of knowledge underlying use of the language. In children, they certainly do not, and so the image of a budding competence, growing by the gradual acquisition of linguistic rules, has to be treated with considerable suspicion.

However, we can still ask at any stage of a child's linguistic development what degree of control, or what kind of control, he has over aspects of his language. Does a certain word have any meaning for him and, if so, what meaning is it? Under what conditions might he use it? How much of the potential of this part of the language can he exploit? Can he use the relations between parts of the language, such as lexical opposites or active–passive equivalences, to increase the flexibility of his linguistic system?

The next chapter looks at how some of these questions can be approached using experimental techniques. Here we are concerned with studies which try to answer these questions using naturalistic data, and it is worth considering briefly how such data may best be used. The investigator has two major sources of information – put simply, these are the occasions on which the child uses a form appropriately and the occasions on which he uses a form inappropriately or constructs an idiosyncratic form.

A natural starting-point for many investigations is a count of the frequency with which a particular form appears in the data. This is generally preparatory to a claim such as '*wh*-questions are more frequent than *yes/no*-questions in the language of 2-year-olds' or 'Verbs of experience appear late in child language.' One must be cautious about making these claims, however. In the case of the first example, it may be that a similar distribution would be obtained from adults under similar circumstances. Drummond (1907) reports an interesting debate over Tracy's claim (Tracy, 1893) that children begin language acquisition by learning proportionately more verbs than nouns. From a dictionary count, Tracy estimated the adult ratio of nouns to verbs to be 60 : 11, while the ratio in child language studies was 60 : 20. However, the ratio in connected writing is quite different: a frequency count of the nouns and verbs both in an action-packed novel (*Robinson Crusoe*) and in a more descriptive work (*Glaciers of the Alps*; both are Drummond's examples!) produces a noun–verb ratio closer to 45 : 24. In adult speech, of course, the ratio is likely to be different again. The point is that one must be careful in choosing an appropriate comparison group for statements about relative frequencies of forms. Frequency counts are also very sensitive to changes in the context in which the children are speaking: locative expressions increase remarkably if you give children lots of detachable toys to play with. The danger with the second statement, that a particular form appears late in child language, lies in the fact that, as they get older, children become more voluble, and so, on statistical grounds, they are more likely to produce a form which in adult speech is infrequent, just because they are saying more in any half-hour period. (See Bowerman (1975) for a discussion of this point in connection with the data of Bloom, Lightbown and Hood (1975).)

Naturalistic studies often try to represent the full power of the child's language at any stage. Experimental work, of necessity, probes the child's skill only in those areas in which he is interrogated, and so misses the wider picture of what the child is capable of at any time. Naturalistic work can often be a useful check on theories proposed by experimentalists, which are liable to emphasise the errors children make in learning their language. However, naturalistic studies also may concentrate on the errors children make. An isolated error can prompt the investigator to look for the idiosyncratic basis for a lot of the generalisations children make about the language they are learning, which, in many cases, may coincide with adult usage, but for different reasons (Bowerman, 1978a; Edwards, 1978; Griffiths and Atkinson, 1978). Systematic error can reveal a productive rule in the child's system, as in the well-known example of children applying to all verbs the rule 'to form the past tense, add *-ed* to the present form', and so generating *buyed*, *comed* or *falled*. Treated carefully, children's spontaneous errors can provide evidence for a variety of claims. Bowerman (1978b), for example, collected substitution errors from her two daughters, and cites the instance of Christy (at age 3; 4) saying *put* when she meant *give*, as when the utterance 'You put the pink one to me' was used as a request for her mother to give her a pink cup. The interesting feature of this example was that Christy had been using both verbs appropriately since she was 2 years. Bowerman interpreted these substitution errors as indicating that the child was beginning to organise her semantic memory so that verbs of exchange or causation were becoming confusable for her: slips of the tongue by adults have been interpreted in a similar way (Fromkin, 1973). Clark (1974, 1980) has assembled examples of errors in her sons' speech, such as 'That's mine jam', to argue that an important process in the development of syntax is that of coupling together imitated, but unanalysed, phrases, prior to attending to the appropriate syntactic relations between the elements. In the next section, we shall find that children's errors are an important source of information for an understanding of the development of word meaning.

84

5.2 The development of word meaning

When we compare the comprehension and production of single words, we find ourselves investigating the relation between vocabulary development and conceptual development. Brown (1958) has proposed a model of the way in which both developments influence each other in his description of the rules for 'The Original Word-Game', played by a tutor (who knows the language) and a player (who is learning the language). The rules are as follows (p. 194):

(i)   The tutor names things in accordance with the semantic custom of his community

(ii)   The player forms hypotheses about the categorial nature of the things named

(iii)   He tests his hypotheses by trying to name new things correctly

(iv)   The tutor compares the player's utterances with his own anticipations of such utterances and, in this way, checks the accuracy of fit between his own categories and those of the player

(v)   He improves the fit by correction

This model is instructive in exposing the points at which misunderstanding may occur between child and adult. In the first place, the child may be wrong in assuming that the adult is naming an object at all. Jespersen (1922) tells the story of an adult who was being pestered by his son's demands for some beer and finally gave in, saying 'Let's have some peace in the house', and was asked the next day by a thirsty child for more 'peace-in-the-house'. Similarly, we may make wrong assumptions about what the child is trying to say and so 'correct' him wrongly. Jespersen again suggests an example of this. If a child points to a model horse, saying 'horse', and is given the object, he may assume that *horse* can be used to request items he wants. If he then points to a china cow, and says 'horse' in the hope of being given the cow, we might correct him by suggesting he say *cow* instead of suggesting *please*, which would be more compatible with his hypothesis. We cannot be sure how far-fetched this example may be, but it is part of the aim of theories of semantic development to find out.

The way they attempt to do this is by trying to chart the sorts of

85

hypotheses the child makes at stage (ii) in the game. Several kinds of hypotheses are possible. The child may assume that the word refers to a class of objects which all share particular features, so that its meaning can be represented as a set of semantic features (Katz and Fodor, 1963; Bierwisch, 1967, 1970). These features can be seen as being present in an all-or-none sense or in varying degrees (Rosch, 1973; Andersen, 1975), producing two models of the concepts – one where a given item either is or is not an example of the category named, and another where one item may be a better, or more central, example of the concept than another, although both would share the name in question. Alternatively, the child may apply the same name to a sequence of objects A, B, C in such a way that A and B have something in common and so do B and C, but A and C are quite dissimilar. Vygotsky (1962) calls this a chain complex. A final model might be that of the associative complex (also Vygotsky), where there is some event or item around which all instances of the concept centre, in that each of them shares some feature with it but may have nothing in common with each other. There is evidence to suggest that children may use some or all of these models on different occasions.

The evidence takes the form of the mistakes which children make in labelling objects. Such misnamings are called 'overextensions' since the child is assumed to have wrongly extended the meaning of the adult name.[1] In the simplest case, children overextend by using a single adult lexical item (such as *ball*) to name a variety of objects which all share a certain property (such as roundness). Thus Bowerman (1978a) reports that when her daughter, Eva, was about 13 months old, she used *ball* for rounded objects of a size suitable for handling and throwing, such as a rounded cork pincushion, a round red balloon, an Easter egg, a small round stone, a plastic egg-shaped toy, and a round cannister lid. We also have examples where children appear to apply their vocabulary according to hypotheses based on chain complexes or associative complexes. Clark (1973a) quotes an example where a child extended *bébé* first to a photograph of himself, then successively to all photographs, all pictures, all books with pictures and finally to all books. Bower-

---

1. Sometimes children 'underextend' the meaning of an adult word, restricting its application to a subset of the adult referents, as when they apply *furniture* only to chairs.

man's daughter's use of *kick* had as a prototypical referent the event of kicking a ball with the foot so that it was propelled forward. She then extended it on the basis of three features of that event: the waving limb (reflected in her application of *kick* to a moth fluttering on a table), the sharp contact of the foot with the ball (explaining her use of *kick* when she pushed her chest against a sink) and the sight of an object being propelled (leading to her use of *kick* before throwing an object). Each of these uses relates to some aspects of the original event, but they have very little similarity to each other.

The fact that a young child overextends a lexical item can be interpreted in at least two ways. It may mean that he believes that all the objects which he names with that item belong to a single category and that the lexical item provides the adult name for all these objects. Thus, when he refers to both a pig and a cow by the word *pig*, we can interpret this as indicating that the meaning of *pig* for him has to do with whatever a pig and a cow may have in common, and we would then expect him to use *pig* to name other animals sharing these properties – for example, we may expect him to call a sheep or a horse *pig* since they are all farm animals. Alternatively, a child may overextend a lexical item, not because he thinks it is the correct name, but because he has no better word in his vocabulary for the occasion, or because he is unable to remember the correct name. Thus, when he calls a cow *pig* it may be that this is equivalent to an utterance such as 'like a pig' or 'Is that a pig?' If this is the case, we would expect him to be able to choose a picture of a pig in preference to one of a cow if he was asked 'Where's the pig?'

Clark (1973a) exploited the first interpretation of children's overextensions, and she suggested that children's early errors could be explained by assuming that they learn the semantic features of the adult name one by one and so begin by having a concept which is too inclusive since it lacks many of the features which restrict its application. For example, if they have acquired only the feature of roundness for *ball* they will apply the word to apples and door-knobs as well as balls. She further proposed that the earliest features acquired are perceptual ones and so the child's earliest overextensions are according to such features as shape or colour. This account is known as the Semantic Feature Acquisition

Hypothesis (see also section 6.4.2). Bowerman (1978a) found several examples of perceptual overextension, in her children's speech, as when Eva said 'moon' when touching a ball of spinach she was being offered, looking at a grapefruit-half, looking up at the inside of the shade of a lit floor lamp, or at a wall-hanging with pink and purple circles.

Sometimes children apply a phrase to situations which all share a feature which is not criterial, in adult terms, for the phrase. Sully (1896) reports that Taine's child extended his word for railway engines to 'a steaming coffee-pot and everything that hissed or smoked or made a noise'. When this happens, it fails to support Clark's Semantic Feature Acquisition Hypothesis, in that the basis for the child's overextension does not correspond to a semantic feature in the adult representation. This begs the question, of course, of what the correct featural analysis for *railway engine* would be in the adult language: the point is that children very often base their language use on categories which an adult mind finds unfamiliar.

One feature which seems to be very important in the young child's experience is that of constraint of one kind or another. For example, Bowerman found her daughter saying 'too tight' to protest about situations involving physical restriction or interference as when her mother tried to wash her ears. Edwards (1978) has shown how his daughter used possessive forms, not to indicate ownership, but rather on occasions when she had been prohibited access to an object by the person in question. Thus, when her mother asked her not to touch her father's tape-recorder, she commented 'Mummy's tape' which was, in fact, incorrect. He suggests that the origins of the child's understanding of many parts of the language, including negation and possession and words such as *dirty* or *hot*, are to be found in situations where freedom of action is restricted in some way. Griffiths and Atkinson (1978) report four children who shared with one of Sully's (1896) children the tendency to extend *door* to everything that stopped up an opening or prevented an exit. The major point of interest of their example, however, was that the children used the word as a general purpose verb to request an adult to operate on something, whether this involved separation or closure, and later used it statively. Other children in their sample used *stuck* or *on* or *off* in similar ways. This example defies the boundaries common to adult linguistic categories, and so again casts doubt on a theory such as the Semantic Feature Acquisition Hypothesis which sees the child's lexicon as an incomplete version of the adult's.

Returning to the two interpretations given above for children's overextensions, we find that there is some evidence in support of the second interpretation. Huttenlocher (1974) observed that children probably overextend more in their production than in their comprehension, and Thomson and Chapman (1977) found that 2-year-old children could often point to the picture appropriate to a word which they had used on other occasions to name an object depicted in the alternative picture. There was a lot of variation between the children, however, and often they overextended both in comprehension and in production. In some cases, the child had an appropriate name in his vocabulary for the alternative picture, and so Thomson and Chapman suggest that children may overextend in production, not because they believe they are correctly naming the object or because they are deliberately misnaming it, but because sometimes they cannot remember the correct name. If this is so, then it would be useful for children to build up a stock of general-purpose lexical items, verbs like *make* and *do*, deictics like *that*, or a general locative marker like [ŋ] which can be interpreted as *in*, *on* or *and* as appropriate. Clark (1978b) explores the use children learning various languages make of these general-purpose words in the early stages of their language development.

There are other reasons for being reluctant to deduce from the way a child names objects what meaning these words have for him. It may be that, although the objects to which a child applies a word all share certain perceptual properties, the concept underlying the use of the word may not simply consist of a list of perceptually based features. Nelson (1974, 1977) took heed of the Piagetian literature on the development of the concept (see section 3.2.5) and proposed that it was important to make a distinction between the processes of concept formation and of concept identification. She suggested that the child was interested in what objects did or what he could do with them and so formed a concept which had a functional, action-based, core. However, identifying new examples of a concept was done on the basis of perceptual features and so she predicted overextensions similar to those predicted by Clark. A further distinction in this area has recently been explored by Nelson (1978). She analysed the answers children gave to the two instructions 'Tell me what X is' and 'Tell me what you know about X', where X could be words like *tiger*, *animal*, *zoo*, *striped*, or *run*. She found that the 4-year-old children gave different kinds of answers to the two types of questions, while the 3-year-olds did not make a great distinction of this kind in their answers. She interprets this as meaning that it takes time for a distinction to develop between concepts, or knowledge about objects, and word meaning.

5.3 Holophrases

In the last section we concentrated on the confusions of reference which children commonly make. Here we shall embed the single words in discourse and explore further their semantic analysis.

It is common for children to pass through an early period when most of their utterances consist of a single word. Many of them are conventional performatives, such as greetings, or vocatives such as *Mummy* or *see*. However, there appears to be little restriction on what other words can appear on their own at this stage. When a child hands an adult a toy with detachable arms and says 'off', or points to the mantlepiece and says 'clock', the adult is likely to respond as if the child has said 'Could you take this off', or 'There's a clock' or 'Where's the clock?' depending on whether the clock is in its place or not.

This holophrastic speech has a pivotal status in language development. It marks the start of what we recognise as speech, in that it is vocalised, and yet it seems a poor advance on the cries and gestures of the days before, and a long way from the richly inflected utterances children will be producing a year later. The dilemma centres round the question of the kind of linguistic knowledge we should attribute to the child at this stage: if we say he is simply naming features of his environment (even in their absence!), then we are going to have difficulty in explaining the sudden emergence of grammatical structure out of disjointed comments; if we say he has knowledge of the full *sentence* of which he is producing a single element, we soon find ourselves attributing full *sentential* knowledge to every animal which makes a noise when it is hungry; if we say that the child is using the word, suitably inflected, as part of an economical communicative act over which he has control, we may be more successful.

McNeill (1970) argues that 'The facts of language acquisition could not be as they are unless the concept of a sentence is available to children at the start of their learning', but this still leaves open the question of how differentiated the concept may be. If we assume for a moment that a full sentence underlies the child's single word, do we assume that the word expresses the whole sentence or only part of it? De Laguna (1927), Leopold (1949) and Nelson (1974) emphasise how nebulous and indefinite the child's early concepts are, and so they could argue for the first alternative that for the child at this stage word and sentence are one. On the other hand, Ingram (1972) and Antinucci and Parisi (1975) make explicit the structure underlying the utterance, representing it as a tree with several nodes empty except for the single word which is uttered. To the extent that these represent the child's linguistic knowledge, they claim that the child *expresses* only part of the sentence in his utterance. In this, the child is like the adult sitting in the doctor's waiting-room who looks at a youngster's swollen eye, enquires 'Ball game?', then himself holds up a bleeding finger saying 'Car door'.

Two features of the adult example are important. Because the speaker has mature competence, we assume that on other occasions he could produce a fully grammatical utterance conveying the same information as this shortened form, and so we are entitled to attribute to him knowledge of the full sentence plus mechanisms for producing the elliptical final utterance. Since our holophrastic children have given no evidence of fully grammatical sentences, we cannot use this justification for them. The second important point is that the adult's utterances are carefully selected so as to convey maximum information. If we assume that 'Car door' derives from *'I hurt my finger in the car door'*, we see that the speaker has chosen *not to express* elements of the sentence which can be deduced from the context.[2] If we can show that children are similarly selective in which aspects they express of the sentence which we assume to be underlying their utterance, then we might have an alternative basis for attributing to them a differentiated concept of a sentence.

2. We are in a double-bind here, since we use the context to expand his utterance into the sentence 'I hurt it in a car door' rather than 'My car door needs a new coat of paint' but this is a characteristic of communication in general.

De Laguna argued that it was important not just to consider the word the child expressed but also the gestures with which he accompanied the utterance and other aspects of the context of utterance. She proposed that the child drew attention to an object by gesture and then commented on a particular property of the object in his speech. In this account, the paradox of the 'sentence-word' is reduced by widening the anlysis to include the context of utterance as well as the utterance itself. How do these young children make use of context in their communication?

Greenfield and Smith (1976) looked at the way the holophrase developed in the speech of two boys. They showed that the functions which the one-word utterances served changed gradually over the period of investigation. To begin with, language was used just as an accompaniment to action, conveying no information of its own. Next, the boys restricted attention to a single object and action associated with it, using language to express functions such as agent, object, action or state of agent or of object, and dative. Then they took note of the relations between two objects and finally commented on an event, for example, asking for something to be repeated by saying 'again'. This shows that the account of the holophrase given by de Laguna was too rigid in that it did not allow for the different uses children make of the single word as they develop. However, it also shows that children do make use of the context of utterance to expand their expressive power. Greenfield and Smith go on to suggest that at the next stage, once the children had shown that they could use language for a variety of functions, it was possible to predict which function they would express with their one word. The children seemed to use language to express that part of their message which was least obvious in the context of the rest of their action, so maximising the informativeness of their communicative act. Greenfield and Zukow (1978) have tested this claim more directly. Greenfield's approach makes the most of one of the most striking features of children in this period – although they are not advanced linguistically they have considerable skills at communicating. They can do several things while speaking – draw attention to objects, protest about a state of affairs, query and comment. Although they seem to use language to refer to a single feature of the event, they embed their utterance in other activity which confers an extended meaning on the word and leads adults to use a full sentence to paraphrase the total meaning which they convey.

Dore (1975) proposes an analysis of the child's skill which separates out its functional and referential components. He shows that at this stage children have skills of labelling, repeating, answering, requesting, calling, greeting, protesting and practising. Each of these he calls a primitive speech act consisting of a primitive force and a rudimentary referring expression. In time, each of these components develops, the primitive force into the illocutionary force of an adult utterance, and the referring expression into a full sentence. He suggests that the force of the child's utterance is, in large measure, carried by the intonation of the utterance.

This analysis is attractive. It explains why adults use a full sentence to paraphrase the child's single word – they are in fact describing the force of the child's utterance. It has developmental continuity in that it does not attribute grammatical competence to animals simply on the basis of a few grunts of pain. It also gives due credit to the children's skill at communicating and shows this to be a central feature of their early language and one which a purely grammatical account fails to handle adequately (Campbell and Wales, 1970).

5.4   **Writing grammars for child language**[3]

If we accept Brown's (1970a) rule of thumb that psycholinguistics takes five years to catch up with developments in linguistics, we look to 1962 as the year of transition into the era of studies dominated by a Chomskyan theory of language, introduced in 1957 in *Syntactic Structures* (Chomsky, 1957). Indeed, we do find this year straddled by studies which fall into pre- and post-Chomskyan positions.

Bellugi and Brown (1964) documents a conference held in 1961 on the acquisition of language which includes reports of studies falling into several psychological paradigms. Miller and Ervin's report is of note for its caution. They had studied two children and produced a distributional analysis of all the utterances collected from the children in terms of the adult syntactic categories of which

---

3.   Brown (1973) gives an excellent account of these studies and contains greater detail on the work than we can incorporate here.

the utterances were composed. That done, they highlighted one group of utterances of particular interest. They noticed that one of the children always placed the words *on* and *off* second in the utterance, and that there were restrictions on the classes of words which could come first in these utterances. This regularity was worthy of note but no excessive claims were made for its overall importance or generality.

That paper is also well-known for the comment it drew from Chomsky who was its discussant at the conference. In this he made two main points, giving with the one hand and taking with the other. He reminded the participants of the proper goals of linguistic theory and the importance to language study of being able to characterise, by a set of rules, all and only the grammatical sentences of the language – that is, the importance of writing a grammar for the language. This was as important for the language of children as for the language of adults. However, his second point was that while judgments of grammaticality could be elicited from adults this was far more difficult in the case of children[4] and, because of the distinction between competence and performance, whatever the proper data for developmental psycholinguistics might be, it certainly could never be the bald transcript of the utterance which the child produced.

This advice was seized on selectively by McNeill (1966a), exploiting data from studies by Braine (1963a), by Brown and Fraser (1964) and by Miller and Ervin (1964). He proposed that the early two-word speech of children could be captured by a 'pivot–open grammar'. The rules of the grammar were very simple – in fact they reduced to the single rule that an utterance consisted of either an open word, or a pivot word followed by an open word. This rule is best viewed as an empirical prediction that for the early speech of a child it will be possible first to isolate two groups of words – one group, called pivots, will be few in number but will occur with great frequency in the child's speech, and the other group, called open words, will be large in number but will occur infrequently in the child's speech. When they do, they will conform to the rule above. Thus, a child whose pivot class

---

4. Just how difficult this is can be seen in the paper by Gleitman, Gleitman and Shipley (1972) and in the section on metalinguistic skill in de Villiers and de Villiers (1978).

contained the words *there* and *Mummy*, and whose open words included *biscuit*, *chair*, *down* and *birdie*, would produce utterances like 'there birdie', 'Mummy biscuit' or 'down' but not 'chair down' or 'there'.

Other formulations of the grammar (McNeill, 1970; Brown, 1973) allowed two open words to occur together, without a pivot, and also divided the pivot class into two subclasses. The pivots in one subclass were always expected to appear first in an utterance and those in the other always appeared second. Thus, if in the above example *there* was an initial pivot and *Mummy* a final pivot, the grammar would now predict the occurrence of 'there birdie', 'biscuit Mummy', 'down', and 'chair down' but not 'there' or 'Mummy biscuit'. In this way, the grammar could still predict a restriction on the set of permissible utterances – some utterances would occur, others would not.

On the face of it, child language study was moving in the same direction as adult psycholinguistics with both producing syntactically based grammars as the best description of their data. This made the developmental story easy to relate and gave support to the claims that linguistic ability was innate, since right at the start of language acquisition children were producing language in a severely constrained manner which had no obvious model in the supposedly convoluted language of the adult user.

The enthusiasm with which this tale was told obscured two major flaws in it. The first flaw was that as more evidence was collected it became clear that the very strong empirical claims which constituted the pivot–open grammar were not being supported. Bloom (1970) and Bowerman (1973a) each found the model inadequate to account for their data. The second, more serious, flaw had to do with the rationale of the grammar-writing activity itself. Chomsky's caution that the child's spontaneous utterances were not the appropriate input to the linguist's description had been ignored. Therefore, even if the pivot–open grammar had correctly summarised the utterances which the child produced, it would not have been a grammar of the same kind as was being sought for the adult's language. A grammar (Chomsky, 1965) characterises the native speaker's linguistic competence and as such embodies his knowledge of his language. This epistemological claim was not being tested by such purely distributional studies.

Bloom (1970) recognised that this approach underrepresented the expressive power of child language and as such did not adequately describe the child's linguistic competence. In a famous example, she pointed out that the utterance 'Mommy sock' had appeared on two separate occasions in her corpus and meant something different each time. On one occasion Kathryn had used it to refer to her mother's sock and on another occasion she had used it when her mother was putting her sock on her. Clearly these two surface forms should be accorded different deep structure representations in the grammar, just as they would in the adult case. She therefore advocated that careful attention be paid to the context of the children's utterances so that their semantic content could be ascertained. The grammar she produced for her corpus was still based solely on the surface forms produced by the children, supplemented by these adult-attributed meanings, and was of generative syntactic form with a small transformational component.

In producing a 'rich interpretation' (McNeill, 1970) of her children's utterances, whereby the adult investigator describes what he thinks the child was 'really' trying to say for each utterance, Bloom joined up with another tradition of grammar writing which had been continuing throughout the 1960s, although it had been largely elbowed out by the pivot–open controversy. The major contribution came from Brown and his colleagues although the work of Gruber (1967) and Schlesinger (1971, 1974) is also worthy of note. All were working with the aim of characterising their total corpus of utterances in a small set of rules, and so to that extent were more ambitious than Miller and Ervin had been, for example, or than many people have been since, and aimed to do so by postulating some richer structure of which the child's utterance was a reduction.

Brown and Fraser's (1964) paper at the 1961 conference had paved the way for much of Brown's later work. In it, they observed that it was possible to take many of the utterances in their sample and, keeping the order of the words constant, fill out the utterances to produce an utterance which was fully grammatical in adult terms and appropriate to the context of utterance. In general, the items which had to be added to give the adult utterance were function words, while most of the child's utterances contained the substantives which formed the skeleton of the sentence. Turning the method on its head, Brown suggested that the children's utterances resembled the language adults use when sending telegrams, where the cost is minimised by omitting function words which are usually redundant, but retaining substantives, which conveys the message efficiently. He hypothesised that the children's utterances resulted from their selective imitation of the highly informative substantives of adult speech and called this 'telegraphic speech'.

This model made the strong prediction that function words would hardly ever occur in two-word speech. Since many children had words like *off*, *this*, *by*, and *other* as part of their 'presumptive pivots', and so frequently incorporated them in two-word utterances, the prediction could not explain the same data. Clearly, there was an element of truth in both telegraphic and pivot–open grammar accounts of two-word speech, but since evidence for the one acted as counter-evidence for the other, neither could be an adequate explanation on its own of a particular set of data. To combine both accounts would lead to the position where any combination of word classes could be expected, and so there was no value in producing such a description. If we are to make any interesting claims about the child's language at any point we have to be able to exclude certain word combinations as being utterances which do not, or are not likely to, occur in the child's speech. This separation of grammatical from ungrammatical sentences is the normal aim of linguistic description. How was it to be done here?

Several suggestions can be made. It may be that a child's early two-words combinations are more amenable to a pivot–open analysis than his later ones, which may be better described in terms of telegraphic speech. It is not clear, however, how the child might develop from the one kind of organisation to the other. Alternatively, telegraphic speech could be seen as a way of analysing only combinations of open words and so be treated as a subpart of a pivot–open grammar. On the other hand, Bloom, Lightbown and Hood (1975) draw attention to individual differences in language development. Two of the children they studied, Peter and Eric, adopted what they called a 'pronominal' strategy during the two-word period, whereby a small number of morphemes, such as *it*, *my*, *there*, had constant functions and were added to other words to signal certain semantic relations, such as affected-object, possession or location. However, Gia and Kathryn adopted a 'categorisation' strategy, apparently collecting words into groups, which each performed a particular function. Bloom *et al.* suggested that the speech of children following a pronominal strategy might look relatively 'pivotal', while that of children following a categorisation strategy might look more 'telegraphic', and that variation between children of this kind might explain why the two analyses looked feasible for two-word speech.

Earlier, Bloom (1970) had tried to reconcile pivot–open grammar and telegraphic speech by proposing a grammar which contained a transformational component and a phrase-structure component which expanded the sentence symbol either into Nom (Neg) {NP/VP} or as Pivot + Noun. Pivot constructions cannot be handled adequately by the normal transformational grammar account, but as Schaerlaekens (1973b) points out, this pivot rule is also inadequate. It cannot simultaneously handle the fact that although *more* is restricted to appearing with a following noun, Bloom also has examples like *this ride* or *that's cold* in her data which do not fit the P + N expansion.

Perhaps more rules could be added to the grammar. However, it is argued, particularly by Bowerman (1973a,b), Brown (1973) and Schaerlaekens (1973b), that Bloom's grammar already contains far too much structure for which there is no evidence in the children's speech, so echoing the discussion we have already encountered over the appropriate account of holophrastic speech. Brown notes that if the representation of a short, two-word string consists of the derivation of a full sentence plus some reduction transformations, we are ascribing a more complex description to utterances which appear earlier in the child's linguistic development than to those which appear later. This would violate the general principle which he proposes that there should be a match between developmental priority and linguistic simplicity. Bowerman (1973a) argues forcibly that there is no justification for attributing to these children any knowledge of the grammatical relations subject and direct object, and that the data can be more adequately accounted for by representing their knowledge in terms of semantic relations.

She observed that the Finnish children she was studying were more likely to combine subject and verb in their utterances, omitting the object, than they were to combine verb and object. A transformational account would predict greater cohesion between verb and object than between subject and verb, so she interpreted this evidence as indicating that an analysis based on these grammatical categories was inappropriate for her data. In addition, she found that her children initially used verbs which took only agentive subjects (such as *hit*) and later started to use verbs like *fall* which took patients as subjects. She proposed that an analysis based on Fillmore's version of case grammar (Fillmore, 1968) might be more appropriate for her data.

5.5 Semantic relations in two-word utterances

Bowerman was not entirely successful in accounting for her data using a case grammar, as she acknowledged. However, Brown decided that an approach to these data based on semantic relations was the most fruitful one that had been suggested, and so he tried to see whether he could capture restrictions on the child's utterances by exploring the semantic relations they expressed. He did not restrict himself to the relations proposed by Fillmore. Out of the relations he himself proposed, he identified eight which occurred frequently in the two-word utterances of a dozen samples taken from children who were learning to speak either English, Finnish, Mexican Spanish, Samoan or Swedish (Brown 1973:173). These were agent and action, action and object, agent and object, action and location, entity and location, possessor and possession, entity and attributive, demonstrative and entity. In addition, he proposed that during this period there were three basic categories of reference available to the child: nomination (*this necklace*), recurrence (*more cookie*) and non-existence (*sun gone*).

These eight semantic relations do not account for all the two-word utterances in Brown's sample. Some, such as agent–object, appear only marginally in the sample and others, such as *sweep broom* or *Mommy lady*, which Brown describes as instrumental and classificatory, do occur, although infrequently. Brown claimed that his eight relations accounted for around 70 per cent of the utterances in his sample. On the other hand, Arlman-Rupp, van Niekerk de Haan and van de Sandt-Koenderman (1976) report that these relations describe a far smaller proportion of the utterances in their sample.

What of the claim that these utterances express semantic relations at all? They certainly name items which are linked in a particular way by what is happening. By claiming that the child is expressing a small set of semantic relations in his speech, Brown claims that the child is doing more than naming items between which there is a relation (the 'collocational hypothesis' of Matthews (1975)): he is in fact expressing the relation itself in his language. Can we justify this claim?

Consider the relation 'entity and location'. As a semantic relation this expresses the position of an object and it does so in a fully grammatical sentence by casting the 'location' in the locative case and marking it with an appropriate preposition. Thus, once a spatial configuration is mapped into a language, one element of it is characterised as the location of some other element. The language does not simply reflect the situation: it imposes a perspective on it. Often, it is obvious that only one characterisation is possible. If a person is sitting in a chair, it is unlikely that we would describe the position of the chair as being related to the person. However, there are occasions when language has a choice over which element to mark as the location. Thus we can describe the position of the sugar as being on the shelf above the butter, or the butter as on the shelf below the sugar. In this example, language imposes two semantic interpretations on the same spatial relation. Thus it is possible to draw a distinction between the semantic relation of entity and location and the contextual relation of spatial contiguity.

How do we know whether the children are expressing the semantic relation or simply collocating words which refer to items which are spatially related? So long as they fail to use prepositions it is hard to see how we could decide. If we could trust their ordering of the words and found that in relatively unambiguous cases the location was placed second, we might accept that when a child, for the example above, said 'Sugar butter', he was telling us the location of the sugar and so expressing a semantic relation. Without this reliability, however, we have no way of deciding whether or not he is imposing a semantic interpretation on the configuration (Macrae, 1979).

Unfortunately, we cannot rely on the word order in these utterances. Brown emphasises that the relations are not grammatical ones. It is possible to find both the orders entity–attribute, for example, and attribute–entity (as in *dog big* and *big dog*). Presumably word order stabilises at some point, but until it does there seems to be very little reason to claim that children are expressing semantic relations in their two-word utterances rather than observing that they successively refer to aspects of the situation in which they find themselves and which are contextually related in ways which reflect the child's interest.

Brown observes that many of the semantic relations he has identified in early two-word speech are closely related to the achievement of the sensorimotor period of cognitive development from which these children are emerging (section 3.2.5). He interprets this as evidence in support of his analysis of their speech: if his analysis shows a child talking about the kinds of relations which a sensorimotor child is expected to have mastered, then it is more likely to be valid than one which shows the child talking about relations of reversibility, say, which children do not understand until much later (see section 3.3). However, the same observation could equally support the view that the children are successively referring to features of their environment which they find interesting, without necessarily expressing a semantic relation in their speech. The restrictions which Brown observes would then be simply a reflection of the children's cognitive development, rather than an achievement in language development.

The source of the analysis produced by Brown and his colleagues lies in the method of rich interpretation, whereby the investigator uses as much information as he can from what he knows about the child, from the context of the child's utterance and from its intonational pattern to produce an interpretation of what the child intended to express by his utterance. This method has been widely used in child language, particularly at the two-word stage but also with younger children. We have seen that Greenfield and Smith (1976) described the emergence of semantic functions in the one-word speech of two children, using the method of rich interpretation, and Bruner (1975) uses a similar method to point to parallels between grammatical structure and the structure of action in the play of preverbal infants. The method is usually justified by the observation that this is what adults normally do while talking to children – it is the source of the phenomenon of the holophrase, discussed in section 5.3. But precisely this example should encourage us to make a distinction between what the child is trying to express and how adults interpret what he manages to communicate

(Howe, 1976). Olney and Scholnick (1978) found, by dubbing children's speech onto new contexts, that adults' interpretations of their speech were based on the visual context of its occurence rather than on features of the linguistic signal itself.

Perhaps the best reason for proposing that children are learning to express semantic relations during the two-word period is that, very shortly afterwards, they begin to produce prepositions and inflections which are the hallmark of grammatical speech. However, the details of how the child learns to express these relations are probably obscured by the tendency of most of the studies reviewed here, to treat the two-word period as a homogeneous stage, rather than an important period of development.

5.6 **Over the threshold**

The title of this section comes from Halliday's (1975) description of his son Nigel's entry into adult language. It comes at the end of a book which aimed to show the way that one child gradually discovered the various functions which language could serve and the various meanings it could express. Armed with these insights, Nigel sets out to learn the linguistic code being used around him. Two main points are obvious from the examples of his efforts which Halliday offers: he still has a lot to learn, and his output is considerable. Thus we face the major frustration of the study of child language – just when the child begins to make big advances he becomes so voluble and his language so varied that we have to turn to other means of collecting and organising our data. So long as he was producing occasional utterances two or three words long, we could hope to collect samples which appeared to be typical of his output and therefore attempt to characterise in some way the whole language at that stage.

However, once the child starts to produce inflections, it becomes obvious that he is doing so very rapidly, and in several areas of language at once, so any sample of his speech is going to be so selective as to be a misleading index of his total linguistic development. At this point, the studies themselves become selective. People choose to concentrate on the development, say, of deictic expressions or question forms, and most turn to experiments instead of naturalistic studies.

It also becomes desirable to have some indication of how far a particular child's language has developed. Early language often does give the impression, as indeed we have given in these sections, of beginning with the production of words one at a time, then moving into a relatively stable period where words are concatenated two at a time, and then taking off into multi-word utterances. However, development is probably far smoother than that, with these periods shading into each other. It might be useful to know, for example, how far a child had advanced through the two-word period.

Brown proposed that a useful index of language development would be the child's mean length of utterance (MLU). He suggested that one should collect a sample of 100 utterances from the child under observation and for each utterance calculate the number of morphemes which it contains. The mean of these utterance lengths, calculated in morphemes, is taken as the child's MLU. This measure increases relatively smoothly over time for children (Brown, 1973:57), and it is widely used to compare the interpretations of data from different authors. Using it, Brown also proposes five stages of development. Stage I lasts to MLU 1.75, and is the stage of two-word speech that we have been investigating, and Stages II–V correspond to MLU values of 2.25, 2.75, 3.50 and 4.00.

There have, however, been criticisms of the MLU, as defined by Brown. To start with, it is often difficult to decide what constitutes an utterance in child speech. Griffiths (1974a) criticises Brown for using the mean instead of the median as his measure of central tendency. Some peculiarities arise in deciding which morphemes should be counted separately: past tense forms of irregular verbs count as one morpheme, those of regular verbs as two, *Mummy* counts as one morpheme because its diminutive suffix is not thought to be productive in the child's system. Arlman-Rupp *et al.* (1976) observe that for children between 2;0 and 2;6 there is a high correlation between calculations of MLU based on morphemes, on words and on syllables, at least in Dutch. The advantage of a morpheme-based MLU was expected to be that it would allow comparison of development between languages of different types. This has been done by Varma (1979) for a Hindi-speaking child and she finds that, although there are similarities between her child and the English-speaking Stage I children described by Brown, her child increased his MLU, not by concatenating words, as the English-speaking children did, but by learning several grammatical markers, such as tense markers and functors to mark the possessive.

Brown described Stage II as the stage of the development of grammatical morphemes and the modulation of meaning. Over this period, he traced the development of fourteen grammatical morphemes in the speech of the three children he was studying. These were the present progressive, the prepositions *in* and *on* (two morphemes), plural inflections, past inflections on irregular verbs, possessive inflections, uncontractible copula (the forms *is*, *am* and *are*), the articles, past inflections on regular verbs, regular third person forms, irregular third person forms (*does*, *has*), uncontractible auxiliary forms, the contractible copula and, finally, the contractible auxiliary. He traced the order of development of these morphemes, proposing as a criterion of acquisition that the morpheme should be present in the child's speech in at least 90 per cent of the contexts in which it is obligatory in three successive two-hour samples. Using this criterion, Brown found that the order of acquisition of the morphemes correlated well between children and that the order outlined above was representative of them. He also found that the rate of acquisition varied considerably between the children.

Why should there be consistency across children in the order of acquisition of these morphemes? One possible reason might be that this order reflects the frequency of these morphemes in the parents' speech so that children learn first the elements they hear most often. Brown checked this and found it not to be the case. Another candidate is semantic or grammatical complexity. It may be that children will first acquire those morphemes which an adult grammar would treat as being simpler either semantically or structurally. Unfortunately very few of the morphemes Brown considered are comparable in terms of adult complexity as derived from the analysis in Jacobs and Rosenbaum (1968) which he used as his model of adult grammar. In those few cases where comparison is possible, order of acquisition does reflect increasing complexity but since grammatical and semantic complexity happen to coincide in these cases, the most parsimonious conclusion is that the acquisition order reflects cognitive development.

One way of sidestepping these difficulties in determining complexity is first to choose forms which can be graded in complexity and then to predict beforehand what the order of acquisition of the particular forms will be. Brown and Hanlon (1970) did just that. Basing their analysis on a rather idiosyncratic grammatical model, they noted that the derivation of a truncated negative question involved *the same* transformations as that for a negative question plus an extra one. On that basis it was possible to claim that a truncated negative question was linguistically more complex than a negative question. Using the same argument, they claimed that a negative question was more complex than a question, which was more complex than a simple active affirmative declarative. Using this they tested the Derivational Theory of Complexity, which stated that if the derivation of a sentence was cumulatively more complex than that of another, then that sentence would appear later in the child's speech than the less complex one. Notice that they are using appearance as the variable, not full acquisition, requiring six examples of the utterance type per sample as a measure of appearance. They predicted nineteen orders of appearance of which only two were disconfirmed for any one child. Brown (1970a) later observed that he had found several more counter examples since the paper had been published.

More important than the fate of the data for this particular test of the hypothesis is the hypothesis itself. It articulates the assumption behind much of the work in language acquisition which looks to linguistic theory for the determinants of acquisition, and we shall meet it again in the background to the experimental studies. It is impressive when two measures of complexity, such as the child's difficulty in learning a form and the linguist's difficulty in describing it, do match up in this way. However, knowing that they coincide does not explain why they should do so, and it is important to look at such results critically, to see whether there is another way of describing the increasing complexity which would explain the difficulties of both child and linguist. In this particular example, the same measure of complexity could have been derived by counting the number of times the operations of addition, deletion and permutation had been carried out on elements of the surface string. Thus even if the data had supported the hypothesis, they would not have confirmed that the children had necessarily been acquiring the transformations in the linguistic analysis.

5.6.1   *The development of negation*

A more fruitful way of approaching an explanation for a developmental sequence is to look at the sorts of mistakes made by the children as they are mastering the construction. This was the plan of Klima and Bellugi (1966). Again using Brown's data, they plotted the course of development of negatives and question forms. For each form, they chose three samples of increasingly advanced examples. They then produced transformational accounts of the regularities at each of the stages. At successive stages, the accounts became more complex. For example, at the first stage, negatives are formed by *no* or *not* being placed either before or after a corresponding sentential nucleus, stage two sees the appearance of negative sentences containing auxiliaries (*I can't catch you*), and by stage three two transformations are required to account economically for the utterances produced. This account is subject to the criticisms made earlier of Bloom's grammar, for example, and Huxley (1966) accuses them of obscuring distinctions in their early data and so producing a description for it which is too simple.

Bloom (1970) also paid special attention to the development of negation in her sample. In line with the rest of her thesis, she pointed out that a single form frequently has more than one function, and that a single function may be expressed by different children by the use of different forms. She identified three main functions for negation in her sample: denial, rejection and non-existence. McNeill (1970) reports that he found a similar analysis useful in his study of the development of negation in Japanese.

Form and function come together in Wode's (1977) survey of studies of development of negation in several languages, including German and Swedish. He proposes three main stages in the development of negation. In the first stage, the child uses a negative morpheme on its own – *no*. The particular morpheme chosen for this, Wode suggests, will be the one used in isolation by adults. The second stage has two parts to it. In this stage the child combines a negative element with another word, producing utterances at least two words long. To begin with, he uses negation anaphorically: in Bloom's terms, he uses negation to deny a suggestion made by someone else. For example, Wode's daughter Inga retorted 'nein, Milch' ('no, milk') when her father tried to offer her some other kind of fluid. Later, and generally still using the same negative morpheme as in the earlier examples, the child uses negation non-anaphorically, to negate the information contained in the rest of the utterance. Thus, at this stage, Inga commented 'nein schaffe ich' ('I can't manage it') after several attempts to shoot with a bow and arrow. Wode comments that non-anaphoric negation is not common in these children and he observes that Bloom decided that all negation at this stage is anaphoric. On the other hand, Park (1979) found that all the multi-word utterances containing *nein* in the early recordings of the German girl he was studying were non-anaphoric, and that anaphoric uses did not appear until his later recordings, six weeks later. The third and final stage considered by Wode is characterised by the appearance of negative elements inside the child's utterance and also by the appearance of other negative morphemes, such as *not* or *nicht*. For example, Wode describes Kathryn's comment 'Kathryn not quite through' from Bloom's data as a third-stage utterance. Similarly the comment from his son, Lars, 'Henning braucht nicht in die Uni' ('Henning doesn't have to go to the university') is taken as an example of intrasentential negation from this period.

5.6.2   *The development of questions*

Children's errors in the production of question forms have also been analysed. McNeill (1970) identified three stages of development, taking as evidence data from Klima and Bellugi (1966). In the first stage, children form questions by the use of rising intonation and a few *wh*-words. In the second stage, similar to the pattern with negation, a *wh*-word is used to introduce an utterance which, in other respects, does not differ from a statement (for example, *Where my mittens?*, *Why you smiling?*). In the third stage, auxiliaries appear but, in *wh*-questions, subject and verb are not inverted, as they are in adult questions. Thus the child produces questions like *What he can ride in?* or *Why kitty can't stand up?* instead of the corresponding adult forms *What can he ride in?* and *Why can't kitty stand up?* At the same time, however, the children can produce correctly inverted *yes/no*-questions (*Can he ride in it?*).

Other peculiarities have been observed in children's question forms. Hurford's (1975) daughter, Eve, asked questions like 'What's that is?' or 'What did you did?', between the ages of 1;10 and 2;6.

Hurford analyses these utterances transformationally and proposes that his daughter was operating in terms of an 'Aux copying rule' instead of the adult 'Aux inversion rule'. Instead of moving the auxiliary from one part of the sentence to another, Eve appeared to copy the auxiliary in a different place in the sentence, leaving both forms intact. Hurford describes his data in terms of the child internalising an imperfect version of an adult transformational rule, and a lively debate has arisen over this interpretation (Kuczaj, 1976; Fay, 1978; Maratsos and Kuczaj, 1978).

Beside studies of children's errors in the production of question forms we can place an analysis of the frequency with which particular kinds of questions appear in children's speech. Tyack and Ingram (1977) asked the parents of twenty-two 2- and 3-year-old children to collect a corpus of about 200 questions produced naturally by their children. They found that 60 per cent of the questions produced were of the *yes/no* form. *What* and *where* questions were very frequent at all ages. *Why* and *how* questions increased in frequency as the age of the child increased. *Who* and *when* questions accounted for only about 2 per cent of the data in all the samples. Tyack and Ingram propose that the variation in the frequency of the questions can be explained as a reflection of the child's cognitive development.

Finally, having looked at the production of question forms, we should ask how children's understanding of question types develops. Tyack and Ingram studied the development of the comprehension of question forms by asking children from 3;0 to 5;5 to look at a picture and then answer a *wh*-question about it.[5] They found that children were better able to answer the questions as they got older. Their difficulties with the question forms showed interesting interactions between the particular *wh*-word in the question and semantic properties of the verb or between animacy and grammatical form (*who*-subject questions, like *Who is helping the girl?*, were easier than *who*-object questions, like *Who is the girl helping?*, but *what*-object questions were easier than *what*-subject questions). They proposed that the children seemed to have the following two strategies for answering *wh*-questions:

5. Steffensen (1978) has analysed the strategies used by two children for answering *yes/no*-questions.

(i)   If you have acquired the particular question word, give
           an appropriate subject
(ii)   If you have not acquired the question word, respond on
           the basis of the semantic features of the verb (for
           example, focusing on cause when the verb is *help* or on
           location when the verb is *ride*)

And, of course, part of understanding how to answer the
questions is understanding when not to answer them! The
appropriate response to *Can you shut the door?* is not *Yes* but is the
action of complying with the request and shutting the door. Shatz
(1978) has looked at the responses of three 2-year-olds to requests
of this sort made to them by their mothers while they both played
with a large toy. She found that, if the children responded at all to
the mothers' requests, they did so appropriately, and that they were
as likely to respond to requests given in question form as those
given in an imperative form. Similar results were obtained from
two younger children at ages 1;7 and 1;8. Garvey (1975) has traced
the development of the ability to use and understand indirect and
inferred requests in older children. She observed pairs of nursery
children (3;6–5;7) playing together and analysed their use of various
request forms. She found that both her younger and older groups
produced similar numbers of direct requests (for example, *Open the
door*), although only half of them were successful in producing the
desired effect. Younger children, however, were less likely to
produce indirect requests (for example, *See if you can open the
door*) than the older children. According to her analysis, indirect
requests were more successful than direct requests, being complied
with 75 per cent of the time.

6

Experimental studies of linguistic development

An experimental study of child development can have one of two principal aims. It can try to change the course of a child's development, as is the case with training programmes for children whose development is retarded for some reason. Alternatively, it can try to probe, in detail, the natural course of development, without intending to interfere with this development in any way. Most of the studies reported in this chapter are of the second kind. As such, they are really just a special kind of observational study and generally follow a characteristic pattern. Groups of children at one or several ages are interviewed one at a time by an adult investigator, commonly called the experimenter. The interview generally lasts about fifteen minutes and is structured insofar as the experimenter has a list of questions or instructions which he gives to each child in the group. He probably also watches out for particular actions or replies on the part of the child which he records and which form the main part of his reported analysis of the study, although of course other behaviour that has not been anticipated may be noticed, or recaptured from a video-tape of the interview, and may prove useful in interpreting the child's other actions. Generally, the children are at least 3 years old, because at a younger age many children are uneasy in such a situation. Also, most of the studies look at children's comprehension of language rather than their production: in a situation such as the one described, it is much easier to arrange instructions and materials with a view to discovering whether a child understands an adult when he uses a particular linguistic construction than to try and elicit that construction from the child himself.

Experimental studies of language development became popular in the 1960s. Compared with longitudinal studies, they had the advantages that a large number of children could be tested, the experimenter could control and hold uniform the material given to the children and he could specify fairly clearly what responses he was interested in. Thus the method saved time, both in collecting the data and in its analysis. The aim of such studies was to discover which features of language were difficult for children and which were mastered early. Predictions were made about which parts of the language the child should find difficult, and these predictions guided the choice of materials and design of the experiments carried out. The earliest predictions were based on a developmental form of the Derivational Theory of Complexity (section 5.6). Given two sentences, S_1 and S_2, such that S_1 can be shown to be linguistically more complex than S_2, it can be predicted that S_1 will be psychologically more complex for the child than S_2. In particular, the child will find S_1 more difficult to understand than S_2, and so will make more errors on test items which require him to understand S_1 than those which require him to understand S_2. Thus, for example, it was proposed, using arguments from transformational grammar, that passive sentences would be more difficult for the child than active ones, and the child would be correct on tests involving active sentences at a younger age than he would be correct on the same tests involving the passive transform of that sentence (Fraser, Bellugi and Brown, 1963; section 6.1 below). It was proposed that exceptions to a rule would be more difficult than sentences which obeyed the rule, and so children would understand the sentence *John told Bill to leave* before the sentence *John promised Bill to leave* because the latter is an exception to the Minimum Distance Principle, whereby the subject of a verb is taken to be the noun closest to it, while the former obeys the principle (Carol Chomsky, 1969; section 6.3 below). It was proposed that lexical items would be ordered in their acquisition relative to the number of semantic features necessary to their analysis and so, when considering polar opposites, such as *long* and *short*, the positive term (*long*) would be acquired before the negative term (*short*) since the negative term was accorded an analysis which was more complex by one feature (Clark, 1973a; section 6.4.1 below).

It was also proposed that the errors which children made during language development could be predicted on the same basis, namely, that the more complex item would be assimilated to the less complex one at a certain stage of development. Language development was seen as being simply a process of acquisition: the child gradually added extra transformations, or rule exceptions, or semantic features to his grammar, and at any stage his understanding of the language could be derived from inspection of his grammar. Therefore, if in the adult grammar *short* was analysed as having the same semantic features as *long* plus one extra, then a child who had not yet acquired that extra feature would interpret *short* as if it meant the same as *long*.

Not all hypotheses at this stage allowed linguistic complexity on its own to predict psychological complexity. Bever (1970) proposed that the difficulty of a construction, both for an adult and for a child learning his language, would owe as much to the type of perceptual problem it presented as to its linguistic analysis. He proposed several perceptual strategies by which one could uncover the grammatical analysis of a surface string, and used these to predict the child's difficulties. For example, one of the strategies proposed that the first noun of the sentence should be taken as referring to the actor. From this one can predict that, in general, passive sentences will be misinterpreted as meaning the same as an active sentence, with the roles of actor and object transposed relative to the original passive sentence. In this case, Bever makes the same prediction as the Derivational Theory of Complexity but his reasons for doing so are different in an important way.

To begin with, the results of experiments were encouraging for an account of language development which looked only to linguistic criteria for an explanation of the child's difficulties. Complex constructions or lexical items did cause more problems for the children. Also many of the predicted confusions were found. It soon became clear, however, that experimental results could not be predicted purely on the basis of the language being tested. Interactions were found between the linguistic factor and other aspects of the experimental design, such as the objects used in the test, the kind of response required, discourse features and the child's experience of the materials of the task. Many of these results were unexpected – for example, why should children base their judgment of the truth of the statement 'All the cars are in the garages' on whether or not the row of garages was full, irrespective of the number of cars relative to the number of garages (Donaldson and Lloyd, 1974)? Across sets of experiments it became clear that the children's performance was extremely task-sensitive and their errors were better described in terms of features of the experimental design than as confusion with other lexical items or as impoverished linguistic constructions. Clark (1973b) proposed that the children were following non-linguistic strategies[1] in their attempts to understand the experimenter's demands, rather than simply consulting an immature grammar. Clark suggested that the children were attending to the language but did not understand it sufficiently to decide on one response rather than another and so they then appealed to their non-linguistic strategies. Donaldson (1978) has suggested that a more thoroughly interactive account of the children's responses might be necessary. It is by no means obvious that nursery children can give separate attention to the language of the experiment, in isolation from other clues which they may pick up in their attempt to give meaning to the whole situation. Thus, it may not be possible to conclude much about children's linguistic development from these studies until a great deal more is known about how children approach semi-formal settings of this kind.

So far, these comments advise caution in the interpretation of experimental results. Their implications for theories of language development are not clear. It may be, as Karmiloff-Smith (1979) suggests, that these strategies are generated *ad hoc* by the children in an attempt to understand the experimenter, and have no consequences outside the laboratory. It would be remarkable that children should agree so well on these strategies if they were generated purely for the purposes of the experimental session – an event outside most children's experience – but as the dynamics of an experiment are at present so poorly understood, there may eventually be ways of explaining this agreement. It would be more optimistic to propose, with Clark (1977), that these strategies capture the way in which children approach language outside the laboratory as well. She proposes that children start out with certain expectations about the way the world operates and the sort of behaviour they are likely to encounter in certain contexts. For example, nursery children, when asked to point to one of two piles

1. Cromer (1978) summarises many of the strategies which have now been proposed.

of objects, have a strong tendency to point to the larger pile (Trehub and Abramovitch, 1978). Clark proposes that they assimilate the language they hear to these assumptions or tendencies, assuming that the language will be compatible with their non-linguistic expectations. As a result, certain parts of language will cause them fewer problems than others. From the example given above, we expect that children will quickly pick up the lexical items *more*, *big*, and *large*, while the terms *less* and *small* will puzzle them. Sorting out the differences between the opposite pairs will then lead to a restructuring of their expectations, or language strategies, and so development proceeds, with language, perception and aspects of social understanding closely bound together.

These are only outlines of what a theory of language development might have to look like. They raise questions about the relation between the child's performance in the experimental laboratory and his language use outside. They raise again the question of the relation between comprehension and production and the possibility that children also have strategies for production which are poorly understood. They direct attention to the peculiarities of the child's own experience of objects and people as well as his exposure to a linguistic input. These issues are at present still only challenges to research. In the following sections it should become clear why they have to be faced.

6.1 Active and passive sentences

The passive is frequently quoted as an example of linguistic complexity, relative to active sentences. Adults are reported to take longer to react to a passive than to an active sentence (Olson, 1972; Olson and Filby, 1972). Full passives are infrequent in casual conversation and are even less frequent in speech to children. Thus all the signs point to the prediction that young children will find passives harder to understand than actives.

One of the earliest experimental studies to trace the development of the passive was by Slobin (1966). His subjects were 6-, 8-, 10- and 12-year-olds and adults. The task was sentence–picture verification; that is, subjects were presented with a picture and a sentence and they had to decide as quickly as possible whether the sentence was a true description of the picture. He found that his subjects made more errors and took longer to make their decision when the sentence was in the passive voice than when it was in the active voice, but right at the outset there was a qualification to the result. The difference held only in reversible sentences; that is, sentences such as *The boy followed the girl* where the semantic constraints between the verb and its arguments are weak enough to allow *The girl followed the boy* to be a perfectly acceptable sentence. For non-reversible sentences, the difference between actives and passives disappeared; that is, for sentences such as *The boy drank the milk,* where the semantic constraints are such that the alternative sentence *The milk drank the boy* is not acceptable. The point is that one can extract the meaning of a non-reversible sentence without attending to the syntax at all: a simple sentence containing the words *boy, milk* and *drank* plus some function words can have only the one interpretation whereby the boy is the agent and milk the patient. However, *boy, girl* and *follow* are not so constrained and so one must understand the relation between grammatical category and case role to decide on the correct interpretation: in this case, one must understand the difference between active and passive sentences. Thus Slobin's conclusion is that passives are harder than actives, for all age groups, only in reversible contexts. It should, however, be noted that Forster and Olbrei (1973) found difficulty in replicating this reversibility effect with adult subjects when they used a non-pictorial testing method and when they controlled for the verbs in their items, so that for each verb there would be a reversible and a non-reversible item. They suggest that Slobin's results may in part be due to the greater difficulty of depicting the activities described in his reversible sentences than those in his non-reversible items.

His work was extended in two ways by Strohner and Nelson (1974). Their children were younger, aged between 2 and 5 years, and the sentences which they contrasted varied in the probability that the events they described would happen. Thus, they had sentences such as *The car followed the lorry*, which they described as equiprobable since the event described by *The lorry followed the car* is just as likely. They also had pairs of sentences, such as *The dog chased the butterfly* and *The butterfly chased the dog*, where the former example was described as a probable sentence and the latter as an improbable sentence. They used a different task from Slobin. It was an enactment task where the children were provided with dolls or puppets and asked to act out the event described by the sentence. They found that the 2- and 3-year-olds predominantly used a 'probable event strategy'. They were correct on all the probable sentences, whether active or passive, and incorrect on 90 per cent of the improbable ones. 4-year-olds also found the probable sentences easier than the improbable ones, but the result was not so marked as for the younger children. Strohner and Nelson suggest that the older children, with their slightly wider experience, may realise that many improbable events are still possible. It is also likely that the 4-year-olds are beginning to be able to analyse the sentences syntactically and so have less cause to rely on a probable event strategy. This interpretation is also supported by the results on the equiprobable sentences. The youngest children followed a 'word order strategy' whereby the first nominal was ascribed the role of actor and the second the role of object of the action. This led them to the correct interpretation for most of the active equiprobable sentences, and the wrong interpretation for most of the active equiprobable sentences, and the wrong interpretation for most of the passive ones. The 4-year-olds again did better on the active equiprobable sentences but managed to be correct 67 per cent of the time on the passives. By the time they were 5 years, the children had difficulty only with the improbable passive sentences.

The same word order preference was found by Segalowitz and Galang (1978) in their study of the development of sentences in Tagalog, a Malayo-Polynesian language, which have either agent focus or patient focus and correspond functionally to active and passive sentences in English (but see Kess, 1979). They found that in a sentence–picture identification task, the children produced higher scores on the sentences with patient focus (corresponding to the passive) than they did on those with agent focus. These results could be explained, in part, by assuming that the children were following a word order rule, whereby the first noun was taken as agent, since in the sentences tested the subject, or the focused noun, was placed last in the sentence.

It is noteworthy that similar results have been obtained in these studies although they used different tasks for assessing comprehension. Other studies have compared a variety of methods for assessing competence and some have introduced variations to the

task itself which affect the children's ability to handle the construction. The most famous study of this kind was by Fraser, Bellugi and
Brown (1963). They investigated several morphological and syntactic constructions, including the passive, and compared 3-year-old
children's performance on three tasks – the imitation task, the
comprehension task and the production task. They found that the
children did best in the imitation task, less well in the comprehension task and least well in the production task. They also found that
performance on the active construction was better than that on the
passive. For tasks on the passive, they compared two sentences
such as *The train is bumped by the car* and *The car is bumped by the
train*. In the imitation task, the experimenter spoke the two
sentences. He then spoke one of them again and the subject had to
repeat it. He then spoke the other and the subject repeated that one.
In the comprehension task, the experimenter showed the child two
pictures which could, respectively, be described by the two sentences. He described the pictures in this way. He then spoke one of
the sentences and the subject had to point to its corresponding
picture. In the production task, the experimenter described the two
pictures and then pointed to one of them, which the subject had to
name. As tests of the control of language in imitation, comprehension and production, these studies have been criticised. Certainly,
it is unusual for the experimenter to demonstrate initially the
information he wishes to test in this way. To generalise from these
results that imitation precedes comprehension, which precedes
production in development is also unwise, given the specific details
of the experimental method employed (Clark, Hutcheson and Van
Buren, 1974). However, the empirical result has been replicated
(Lovell and Dixon, 1967; Turner and Rommetveit, 1967; see also
Baldie, 1976), and it demonstrates at least that it is important to
take into account the method used by the investigator when
assessing his claims about the development of linguistic control.

There have been other studies of the passive which compare the
children's performance on a variety of tasks. Beilin (1975) compared performance by 4- to 7-year-olds on recall tests, recognition
tests and tests of synonymy, and found that it was not until 7 years
that children were able to handle passives competently in these
tasks. Olson and Nickerson (1977) also tested 5-year-old children's
ability to use the synonymy of a passive and its active transform.

They asked their children questions of the form *John is hit by Mary. Does Mary hit John?*, and varied the extent to which the event described could be given a vivid pictorial representation. They found that the hardest condition was the John and Mary item quoted, and then, in order of decreasing difficulty, one where the characters mentioned were those from the Peanuts series, then these items embedded in a story and, finally, a condition where a picture of the event was shown to the child at the same time. Horgan (1978), in a survey of the spontaneous speech of children from 2 to 14 years old, found that children younger then 4 years used the wrong word order when producing reversible passives, as would be expected from Strohner and Nelson's results. She also found that agentive non-reversible passives (*The milk was drunk by the boy*) did not appear until 9 years, and that between 11 and 13 years the children distinguished between instrumental passives, which they marked with *with* (*The door was opened with a key*) and agentive passives, which they marked with *by* (*The door was opened by a man*).

The difference in difficulty between the comprehension and production tasks of Fraser *et al.* (1963) may reside in the relative complexity of the response required in the two cases. There are more opportunities for error when producing a complex sentence than when pointing to a picture. Other studies have controlled for the difficulty of the process of choosing a response on the basis of the information given.

Huttenlocher, Eisenberg and Strauss (1968) used an enactment task which tested comprehension of sentences such as *The red truck is pushing (is being pushed by) the green truck*. The children had to arrange one truck in front of the other to demonstrate which truck was pushing and which being pushed. The children were 9- and 10-year-olds, and it is interesting to note in connection with the relatively advanced age of their subjects that another study, by Sinclair and Ferreiro (1970), has reported that passives involving the verb *push* are relatively difficult. They had tested comprehension, production and repetition of passives and had found that difficulty was also a function of the verb used in the sentence: *break, spill, wash, push* and *follow* were found to increase in difficulty in that order. Huttenlocher *et al.* added a further consideration: they fixed the position of one of the trucks and handed the other one (the mobile truck) to the child. They found that when they measured reaction times the children did better on actives than on passives, but also better when the mobile truck was the actor in the sentence than when it was the object of the action. In other words, if they were holding the red truck they found an increase in difficulty over the following four sentences:

(1)   The red truck is pushing the green truck
(2)   The green truck is pushing the red truck
(3)   The green truck is being pushed by the red truck
(4)   The red truck is being pushed by the green truck

A similar result was obtained by Dewart (1975) with 4-, 5- and 6-year-olds. She measured the errors made by the children when acting out passive sentences with normal and deviant word orders containing verbs such as *kick* when the child was holding one of the two dolls at the start of the instruction. She also found that children who were given a training session during which they were always handed the actor of the action in the sentence improved on a post-test in which their comprehension of passives was tested without any contextual cues as to the role of the nominals. Children who were always handed the object of the action in the training session failed to improve their pretest scores.

These results are interesting when they are considered in conjunction with studies which have looked at focus effects on passive comprehension. The passive construction is useful in two principal situations: where the object of the action is the focus of attention and where the agent of the action is unknown or where it is tactful not to name him. Unsurprisingly, perhaps, passives are less difficult when they are used in such appropriate contexts.

Turner and Rommetveit (1968) manipulated focus effects in a recall test. Testing 4- to 9-year-old children, they first showed the child a picture (called the storage picture) which corresponded either to the agent, or to the object of the action, or to the whole event described by the test sentence. Next, they told him the test sentence, then followed it with a 'retrieval' picture from the same set as the storage pictures. The child was then asked to recall the sentence. They found that the retrieval pictures had a stronger effect than the storage pictures on performance. They also found that passive sentences were recalled better than active ones when the object of the action was depicted in the retrieval picture.

Notice the difference between this study and the studies which involved enactment tasks with one item mobile. The focusing experiment found that performance was best in conditions where the item attended to was the subject of the sentence tested: in other words, performance was best when the passive was being used to topicalise the item of interest. In this experiment, however, the response demanded was recall of the sentence. When the response is an action, as in the experiments by Huttenlocher *et al.* and by Dewart, it is important, not that the held item be the subject of the sentence, but that it should be the agent of the action, leading to an interaction between item of attention and semantic role, rather than grammatical category.

Passives are also useful in their truncated form (for example, *We were taken to the zoo*) when for some reason the agent is not mentioned in the sentence. Slobin (1968) told primary-school children stories, using either full or truncated passives. He then asked them to recall them verbatim. He found overall that 61 per cent of the truncated passives were retained as they stood in retelling, but that 62 per cent of the full passives were converted into their corresponding active form. Harris (1976) has also demonstrated that children as young as 3 years do better on a picture identification task when truncated passives are employed, rather than full passives.

In conclusion, the question of whether a young child will understand or be able to use correctly an utterance cast in the passive voice does not have a simple answer. His ability will depend on aspects of the event described by the utterance, what he is expected to do with the information extracted from the utterance, and aspects of the wider conversational setting. If we change the question and ask at what point children begin to notice the syntactic differences between actives and passives we could suggest tentatively, on the basis of the results of Strohner and Nelson and of Dewart, that the process starts around age 4, but we know from Beilin's work that an understanding of the relation between the two constructions, which we might want to take as important for ascribing control of the construction to the child, does not begin to appear before age 7.

6.2 'John is easy to see'

Passives are not the only kind of sentence which can create confusion over the identification of actor and patient. Certain complement constructions also cause difficulty, and in this case the difficulty is not satisfactorily resolved until the children are much older. Some aspects of this development in primary-school children were investigated in a book by Carol Chomsky (1969) which has led to many other studies.

Chomsky set out to investigate the assumption, held by many who argued for the remarkable speed of language development, that syntactic development was virtually complete by the time the child started primary school. Her subjects were forty children aged between 5 and 10 years. She explored in particular their understanding of sentences of the same form as *John is easy to see* and complement constructions involving the verbs *ask*, *promise* and *tell* (see section 6.3). She found that these structures were still causing problems till at least age 9, and that one 10-year-old had difficulty with sentences of the form *John asked Bill what to do*. As we should expect from our consideration of the passive, however, such statements are subject to many modifications and various investigators have questioned the generality of her results. We shall therefore look in detail at some of her tests.

The materials for the test of *John is easy to see* consisted of a doll which had a blindfold over her eyes. The child was asked 'Is this doll easy to see or hard to see?' After the child had replied, he was asked 'Would you make her easy/hard to see?' depending on whether the child had answered 'hard' or 'easy' to the first question. The child was then asked various questions, particularly if he had answered 'hard', to try to determine the reason for his decision. Fourteen children answered incorrectly: most of the 5-year-olds were in this group, but it also included children as old as 8. All of these children removed the blindfold when asked to make the doll easy to see, and the subsequent discussion centred on the properties of a blindfold.

In this test, the most unusual feature and so, one might expect, the most salient feature for the child, was the blindfold. It drew attention to the fact that the doll could not see and centred interest on the doll as perceiver and not as object of perception. As a result, the child would have to be very secure in his understanding of the language and convinced of its importance to ignore these cues and give the correct answer that the doll was easy to see. It is therefore a very stringent test and one would expect that other versions of the test could reveal an earlier understanding of the language.

Morsbach and Steel (1976) showed how insecure the younger children were in their control of this construction. Testing 5- and 6-year-olds, they administered Chomsky's test before or after a test of their own, which biased interpretation in the opposite direction. The test which they devised consisted in placing the doll, without its blindfold, behind a semi-transparent screen which was placed in front of the child. They replicated Chomsky's results with the group which were given her test before the screen test, but found that performance on the second test a child was given was influenced by which test the child had been given first.

Chomsky saw her results as evidence about the kind of rule children were using to assign a subject to *see*. She proposed that, since the surface subject was the deep structure object in these sentences, they would cause difficulty because children would be more likely to take the surface subject as also being the deep structure subject. She therefore interpreted her results as indicating that the young children were following a rule which identified surface and deep structure subjects. Morsbach and Steel's results propose an alternative explanation for the young children's difficulties by suggesting that they were misled into error by aspects of the perceptual array. A similar criticism of Chomsky's method was made by Kessel (1970), who proposed a more neutral test. He showed the child two Peanuts dolls and told him that they were playing hide and seek. He then said that Lucy was easy to find, for example, and then asked the child who was hiding and who was seeking. He found very few errors among his 6- to 12-year-old children. It seems clear, then, that some of Chomsky's children may have made the wrong decision because they were responding to non-linguistic features of the situation, rather than because they were following a linguistic rule about subject identification.

However, it is important to note that there was some evidence in both Morsbach and Steel's and Kessel's results that some children were following this syntactic rule. Kessel found that ten of his group were predominantly correct on *eager* sentences, such as *John is eager to see*, in which surface and deep structure subjects are the same, but wrong on *easy* sentences, suggesting that they were following a rule which identified surface and deep structure subjects. Morsbach and Steel found three children who managed to resist their contextual manipulations to the extent of being incorrect in both conditions even though they were given the screen condition first. These children could also be said to be following the linguistic rule in a very determined manner.

Cromer (1970) extended the discussion to other adjectives which share the characteristics of *eager* in identifying the surface subject with deep structure subject (*happy*, *anxious*, *willing*, *glad* – S-adjectives), those like *easy* which identify surface subject with deep structure object (*tasty*, *hard*, *fun* – O-adjectives) and those which are ambiguous in that they allow both interpretations (*bad*, *horrible*, *nice*, *nasty* – A-adjectives). His task was an enactment task. The children were given glove puppets of a wolf and a duck and had to show which was doing the biting in a sentence such as *The wolf was tasty to bite*. He found a large group of 'Primitive Rule Users', all having a mental age less than 5;9, who followed Chomsky's proposed rule throughout the task. All the children who performed adequately on the task ('Passers') had a mental age greater than 6;8; and at all mental ages there were children whose performance was intermediate and unstable, even from one day to the next. In the absence of cues of a non-linguistic kind, it appears that young children do tend to follow Chomsky's primitive rule, so scoring highly on S-adjectives and making errors with O-adjectives.

A third explanation of the reason for the difficulties of Chomsky's youngest children has been suggested by Cambon and Sinclair (1974). They emphasised aspects of the meaning of the verb *see* which may be developing in the children of this age. They included Chomsky's blindfold condition in a more extensive design which involved half-covering the doll with a cloth, covering her mouth or chest with a bandage, and placing her face-downwards on the table. Considering performance on all these conditions, they divided their children into those who made the doll the subject of *see*, those who made her the object and those who gave a mixture of responses. They agreed that the construction was not generally understood until age 8, but found a surprising number of 5-year-olds who gave the correct answers. They were a larger group than Chomsky's correct 5-year-olds and also a larger group than the correct 6- and

7-year-olds. They explain the discrepancy between their results and Chomsky's by pointing out that there seems to be an ambiguity in what is meant by *being easily seen*: it can mean 'being visible' or 'being recognisable because the face is visible'. They suggest this may have been part of the reason why Chomsky's young children objected to the blindfold, and that she may have been too quick to interpret reasons like 'because she's got a scarf over her eyes' as meaning that it was important that the doll should see rather than that her eyes should be seen. They also appeal to the egocentrism of the younger children in explaining their high performance level relative to the 6- and 7-year-olds. They suggest that the younger children readily jump to the conclusion that they should be the active perceivers and only later realise that the doll can also be regarded as a potential perceiver, so resulting in the depressed performance of the older children.

Again we see the pitfalls in designing a valid test of linguistic understanding. Children of this age do not think primarily in terms of logical possibilities and are eager to respond to anything which might be a cue to the expected answer. Other linguistic factors may also intrude, such as the semantics of *see* in these examples. However, as with actives and passives, a residual effect does remain which is the confusion between the constructions contrasted and a marked preference for one of the possible interpretations.

6.3 Word order in other constructions

The studies in the last two sections emphasise the important contribution contextual cues can make to the interpretation children give to two particular syntactic constructions. Through the forest of these modifications, however, two early perceptual mapping rules (Bever, 1970) can be detected. In *The doll is easy to see* type of item, in which there is only one verb and one noun mentioned, young children follow a primitive rule (Cromer, 1970) which assigns to the noun the grammatical role of subject of the verb, rather than object. In the interpretation of passives, in which a verb intervenes between two distinct nouns, a common tendency is to take the first noun as deep subject of the verb. Some other studies have looked at more complex constructions with a view to uncovering similar mapping rules of surface features on to semantic roles. Two candidate rules which emerge are ones which coincide in the rule for the interpretation of passives: separated out for consideration in more extended constructions they are the rule that the first noun should be subject of the verb, or actor, and that the noun nearest to the verb should be its subject.

This latter rule has been called the Minimum Distance Principle (MDP), and most complement constructions in English can be decoded by appealing to this principle. Some verbs, however, fail to conform to the principle. Consider sentences (5)–(7):

(5)   John asked Bill to leave
(6)   John told Bill to leave
(7)   John promised Bill to leave

The MDP asserts that the subject of *leave* should in all cases be *Bill*, the noun closest to *leave*. We see that *ask* and *tell* conform to the MDP and that *promise* does not.

Carol Chomsky (1969) took this as the starting-point of her study of syntactic development of children between 5 and 10 years, predicting that children would initially assimilate *promise* to the more inclusive MDP to which it is an exception. She also observed that *ask* is semantically more complex than *tell* since it has both a 'command' interpretation, in which it parallels *tell*, as in (5) and (6) above, and also a 'request information' interpretation in which it contrasts with *tell*, as in (8) and (9) below:

(8)   John asked Bill the time
(9)   John told Bill the time.

She found that children found (8) and (9) highly confusable, predominantly choosing to interpret (8) as if it were synonymous with (9). There may have been an effect here of the children's state of knowledge about information being exchanged, since Chomsky tested the structures by asking one child to ask or tell another classmate things to do with their common experience, such as their teacher's name. Kessel (1970) indeed found that children could discriminate *ask* and *tell* by age 8, rather than 10 as found by Chomsky, in a picture selection task where they had to decide, for example, which picture depicted the situation where *The boy tells/asks the girl what shoes to wear*. More interesting for our present purposes was Chomsky's finding that her prediction about the difficulty with *promise* was confirmed. She tested this by giving the children two dolls, Donald Duck and Bozo, which had to perform the actions requested or promised in the test sentence. Thus when the children were told 'Donald promises Bozo to do a somersault. Make him do it', the children were expected to make Donald perform the somersault. If the verb was *ask*, however, Bozo would be the actor required by the verb. Chomsky found that the younger children overextended the MDP and chose Bozo as the actor whatever verb was used in the matrix sentence.

Unfortunately, the MDP does not always work even for *ask* and *tell*, as was pointed out by Maratsos (1974a). If the matrix sentence is made into the passive as in (10), it is not the case that the noun nearest to *leave* is its subject.

(10)   Bill was told/asked by John to leave

Maratsos suggested that Chomsky's young children may have been following a Semantic Role Principle (SRP) rather than an MDP. This principle states that the goal of the verb of instruction should be the actor of the complement action. In other words, in both (6) and (10), the instruction is directed towards Bill, so Bill is the goal of the verb of instruction. The SRP states that Bill should also be the actor, as indeed he should be in both sentences. Thus the SRP survives the syntactic manipulation of passivisation and will assign the correct subject to *leave* in (10), unlike the MDP. If Chomsky's subjects were overextending the MDP, and were therefore applying it to their decoding of sentences such as (7) as well as to (5) and (6), then they should be led into error on (10). However, if they were following the SRP, they should not make errors on (10) but should still make errors on (7). He tested in an enactment task some 4- and 5-year-olds who could correctly interpret simple passive sentences and found that they had no difficulty with the passive forms of (5) and (6), as indicated in (10), but overwhelmingly misinterpreted sentences of form (7) which included *promise* as the matrix verb, so replicating Chomsky's result with younger children. It is apparent, then, that children do not slavishly follow the MDP in all situations and can assign correct interpretations to quite complex sentences which do not follow the principle. Unfortunately, Maratsos' study leaves us uncertain about what governs the children's decisions in the *promise* items, since he did not include a passive form of this sentence, and there is no reason *a priori* (other than reasons of economy) why the same explanation should serve both in cases where the child has mastered a construction and where he is still learning one.

An important assumption behind many experimental studies in language development is that, since the young child must be encountering novel constructions frequently, he must have strategies for interpreting these constructions. It is further assumed that these strategies will be uncovered if he is asked to interpret sentences involving nonsense words or deviant constructions. Now, not all strategies will be uncovered by this method: ones which rely on semantic or pragmatic cues will be of no avail in the face of these manipulations. However, to the extent that children agree on interpretations of deviant syntax, one can claim that a strategy for syntactic interpretation has been uncovered. If in addition such a strategy helps to explain results such as the *promise* example, one can be reasonably confident that it is part of the child's natural repertoire of learning skills.

This method was explored by Sinclair and Bronckart (1972). Children between 2;10 and 7;0 were asked to act out with dolls 'instructions' which contained either two nouns and a verb or two verbs and a noun, and in which the order of the words in the instruction was varied systematically, so producing instructions which were not well-formed. They also varied the transitivity of the verbs and the reversibility of the resulting instruction. Most interesting was the case where two nouns and a transitive verb were involved and the situation was reversible. An English example of this item would be *boy girl hit*. Four strategies emerged. The youngest children gave the verb an intransitive interpretation, ignoring one of the nouns, for example making the boy hit out, but not at the girl. 4-year-olds tended to choose the noun nearest to the verb as agent, in accordance with the MDP, so making the girl do the hitting. 5-year-olds, on the other hand, chose the noun nearest the verb as patient, so making the boy hit the girl. Interestingly, this strategy was also evident in a study by McNeill, Yukawa and McNeill (1971) in which Japanese-speaking children had to assign nouns in deviant instructions to the grammatical category of either the direct object or the indirect object. The two strongest strategies for choosing the direct object that emerged were to choose the noun nearest to the verb or to choose the noun first in the instruction.

Sinclair and Bronckart's oldest children finally favoured the strategy of taking the first noun as agent and second as patient, a strategy one might have expected to come in earlier on the basis of many of the studies of the passive and the perceptual mapping rules proposed by Bever (1970).

Unfortunately, there is not much evidence from studies of naturally occurring constructions to support these strategies. Garman (1974) explored Tamil-speaking children's understanding of complex sentence types related to restrictive and non-restrictive relative clauses in English. He did conclude that, in assigning subjects to verbs, there was a developmental change from choosing the noun in front of the verb to choosing the first noun in the sentence. This is compatible with Sinclair and Bronckart's data. Brown (1971) looked at the comprehension of relative clauses by nursery-school children using a picture selection technique. Among other conditions, he compared their understanding of centre embedded clauses with either subject focus or object focus, as in (11) and (12):

(11)   The boy who is talking to the girl is wearing a hat
(12)   The boy who the girl is talking to is wearing a hat

In the light of our discussion of these strategies, we could expect that younger children would do better than older children in assigning a subject to *talk* in (12), but such a development is not reported, although overall the children found (12) much more difficult than (11). Finally, Segalowitz and Galang (1978) found that the sentences which their Tagalog-speaking children found easiest were ones where the agent was both closest to the verb and was the first noun in the sentence, which happened to be the sentences in Tagalog equivalent to the English passive.

6.4 Relational terms

Several studies have looked at the development of specific relational terms, often choosing pairs of opposites which are inherently relational, in that correct application of each term requires a comparison between at least two objects or events. Word order considerations are still with us, as many of the opposites contrast with each other in terms of which of the compared objects should be referred to first. For example, with respect to height, correct use of *taller* requires that the taller man should be ordered first in the comparison, while correct use of *shorter* requires that the taller man should be ordered second. Thus (13) and (14) refer to the same comparison:

(13)   Bob is taller than Pete
(14)   Pete is shorter than Bob

Therefore this area of language solidly straddles the syntax/semantics boundary and has proved an extremely fruitful one for study.

6.4.1   *Dimensional adjectives*

Children's understanding of relational terms is of special interest for developmental psychologists, because they are frequently used in tests of cognitive development. In these tests the major concern is not whether the children understand the language used, but whether they understand the properties of the objects and situations which are the topic of conversation. The possibility that there is a linguistic barrier to understanding as well as a conceptual one operating in these tests was one which Donaldson and Wales (1970) set out to explore by carrying out a series of experiments on nursery children's understanding of terms such as *more/less*, *same/different* and dimensional adjectives.

The specific study of dimensional adjectives they reported consisted of a comprehension test and a production test designed to compare the comparative and superlative forms of the opposite pairs *big/small*, *long/short*, *thick/thin*, *high/low*, *tall/short* and *fat/thin*. Wales and Campbell (1970) also reported some longitudinal comparisons of the development of these same terms. In the comprehension test, the children were shown four objects and asked to show the experimenter the biggest one, for example, or one which was bigger than the one the experimenter identified. In general, the children were more accurate with the positive adjective than with the negative one and this effect was more obvious with the superlative items than with the comparative ones. In the light of later studies, one of the most interesting results from the production test was the fact that, although there was a general improvement in the appropriate use of the terms, there was an indication that in the six months between the initial and later testing of the same children, some of them had specialised their use of *big* in the sense that they no longer used it as a general, multi-dimensional adjective, but restricted its use to comparison along a single dimension.

Later studies have confirmed the polarity effect, whereby the positive term is associated with a higher level of accuracy than its negative counterpart (Eilers, Oller and Ellington, 1974; Brewer and Stone, 1975), although Eilers *et al.*, whose subjects were only $2\frac{1}{2}$–$3\frac{1}{2}$ years old and had been requested to *give* the experimenter the specified object, had to correct for a tendency by their subjects to choose the smaller object before the polarity effect was apparent. Klatsky, Clark and Macken (1973) investigated the basis for the polarity effect. They argued that the superiority of the positive term could be either the result of the children's encountering it more frequently in adult speech or the result of a difference in conceptual complexity between the positive and negative ends of dimensions. To decide between these explanations they took a group of 4-year-olds and taught them nonsense words for the positive and negative ends of the dimensions of size, height, length and thickness. They found that the children had greater difficulty in learning the nonsense words for the negative pole than the one for the positive pole, which is consistent with the results from the language development studies, although a post-test indicated that the children had not tumbled to the fact that their nonsense words were equivalent in meaning to perfectly ordinary English words which they understood quite well. They concluded that there was a conceptual basis to the children's difficulty with negative dimensional adjectives and not just a problem of less frequent exposure to them in adult speech.

An asymmetry in difficulty has also been found between different pairs of dimensional adjectives. *Big* and *small* are handled more accurately than the other terms by 3-year-old children (Eilers *et al.* 1974). This early facility with the most general dimensional adjectives is consistent with Clark's (1972) finding that if 4-year-olds are asked for the opposite of a dimensional adjective, they are likely to substitute either *big* or *small* for a more specific adjective of the appropriate polarity.

An alternative explanation of Clark's result may be found in the results of attempts to specify more precisely the development of the meaning of *big* itself. Maratsos (1973) claimed that 3-year-olds had a better understanding of *big* than 4-year-olds. The young children appeared to have a truly multi-dimensional understanding of the adjective,[2] while the 4-year-olds tended to base their answer to the question 'Which is the big one?' on a consideration of height alone. Their judgments were also more susceptible to experimental cues than those of the 3-year-olds (Maratsos, 1974b). This difficulty appears to be a linguistic one unconnected with the ability to coordinate information on several dimensions, since they could correctly decide which object would be heavier. 4-year-olds have better understanding than 3-year-olds of the more specific dimensional adjectives, so it appears that once the children start attending to dimensions one at a time and learning specific adjectives for them, they become confused over the meaning of the more general term. This is consistent with the longitudinal observations by Wales and Campbell (1970) and may provide an alternative explanation for the tendency of Clark's 4-year-olds to substitute *big* or *small* for the more specific item. The children may have been confusing *big* with the more specific term rather than using the more general term to mask their lack of knowledge of the more specific one.

6.4.2 *'More' and 'less'*

One of the common words children use very early is *more*. For many, it has a pivot-like function (see section 5.4), frequently heralding a request for extra food (*more biscuit*) or for the repetition of some pleasing activity (*more swing*). Even *more gone* has been reported. From these examples, it is clear that the meaning of the word has still a long development ahead of it. By contrast, *less* appears late in children's speech and may even have a restricted use in the speech addressed to children. It has been suggested that children's early encounters with this term may be in utterances such as *Give him less* where some quantity is being offered and the comparison is unspecified. Such usage is of little

---

2. However, Bausano and Jeffrey (1975) claim that 3-year-olds have a unidimensional understanding of *big*. Their children had to choose the biggest of three stimuli, which varied from one trial to another. It seemed that their children chose either the tallest item or the widest item, depending on whether height or width was more salient for a particular trial, but did not combine the dimensions in making their choice.

help for the static comparison of quantity which has been the focus of much of the research into the understanding of these tems.

Donaldson and Balfour (1968) devised eight types of settings in which their children (aged 3;5 to 4;1) could be asked for judgments involving *more* and *less* or asked to carry out instructions involving the same terms. All made reference to two cardboard apple trees, each of which had six hooks on which a number of cardboard apples could be hung. The children were asked to make static comparisons of the two trees, to imagine and carry out transformations of the numbers of apples on the trees and, in a follow-up study six months later, to transform the number on a single tree in accordance with a specific instruction. The overall result was that the children did not discriminate between items which involved *more* and those which involved *less*, and in general their responses were those appropriate for the *more* items. Only one child was consistently correct on *less* items.

This result was seized upon by H. H. Clark (1970), who related the experimental results to the linguistic structure of the terms. A distinction can sometimes be made between the members of a pair of opposites, whereby one term is described as being marked, while the other is unmarked. The marked term can only be used contrastively, but the unmarked term also has a neutral use, in addition to its contrastive meaning (Lyons, 1968). He observed that *more* was the unmarked, and *less* the marked, member of the pair and that a semantic analysis based on semantic features (Bierwisch, 1970) would therefore accord to *more* a less complex analysis than to *less*. He already had evidence from adults (Clark, 1969) that it was more difficult to reason about information expressed in utterances involving marked adjectives. Subscribing to the psycholinguistic theory that psychological complexity directly reflects linguistic complexity, he proposed that in language development children would acquire unmarked terms before corresponding marked terms, and that when the marked terms first made their appearance their meaning would be assimilated to that of the unmarked term. This proposal was further developed by E. V. Clark (1973a) into the Semantic Feature Acquisition Hypothesis and then modified into the Partial Semantics Hypothesis (Clark, 1973b). The results of Donaldson and Balfour's experiment lend support to Clark's structural theory, if they are interpreted as indicating that nursery children understand *more* and interpret *less* to mean *more*.

This interpretation of the results has been explored by subsequent studies. They have focused on the two questions; (a) do nursery children always interpret *less* to mean *more*, and (b) do nursery children have a sound understanding of *more*?

Children certainly have difficulty with the comprehension of *less*, but they do not necessarily give it a consistently wrong interpretation. Palermo (1973) did, indeed, replicate the Donaldson and Balfour study and found that even some 7-year-olds were still performing well below chance on *less* items. Palermo (1974) compared the ability of 3- and 4-year-olds to judge 'Which has less?' when applied to apple trees, beakers of water and linear arrays, and found that on all these tasks there were some 4-year-olds and even more 3-year-olds who made systematic errors on the question. These children stuck to their erroneous interpretation of *less* even in the face of a strong inducement (in the form of candies) to bias their choice in the correct direction. Townsend (1974) extended the investigation to questions in which an explicit standard was mentioned (e.g. 'Who has more apples than Carl?'). He found that 3- to 5-year-olds did well on *more* instructions but performed only a chance on *less* items. Pike and Olson (1977) also found worse performance by 5- and 7-year-olds on *less* items than on *more* items, but not systematic confusion. Carey (1978) included a condition in which the comparative adjective was replaced by a nonsense word and found that the response patterns for *less* items and nonsense items were similar. Since it is not likely that one would wish to argue that the children had a semantic reading available for the nonsense word, this experiment points out the danger of concluding from these results anything about the meaning of *less* for the children other than the fact that it appears to cause them considerable difficulty.

One source of the difficulty was explored by Pike and Olson (1977). They divided their 5- and 7-year-olds into two groups on the basis of their ability to rearrange piles of marbles in response to instructions to make it so that one pile had more or less marbles than the other, under conditions where the child was allowed to change the quantities in either pile and where he was allowed to change the quantities in only one of the piles. Children in the pass operations group were correct on all the instructions in this task: the other children formed the fail operations group. These groups were found to differ in the patterns of reaction times they produced to items on a similar task where they had to decide which of two beakers had more or less marbles, after one marble had been added to or subtracted from one of the beakers which had previously held an equal number. Pike and Olson were able to interpret these different patterns in the following way. The children in the fail operations group always interpreted the arrangement in terms of which beaker had *more* than the other. When they then had to judge a statement which used the word *less* they had to reinterpret the arrangement in terms of which beaker had less and then compare this with the statement. However, the children in the pass operations group showed from their reaction time profile that they could interpret the arrangement equally well in terms of which beaker had more or in terms of which beaker had less. When the less advanced children were trained to focus on the lesser amount, their reaction time profiles then matched those of the more advanced children.

Thus, comprehension tests for *more* and *less*, which require matching a description to an arrangement, have to face the problem that nursery children quite simply seem to *see* the arrangement in terms of which part has greater quantity. This makes performance on *less* items doubly difficult whereas it may make *more* items spuriously easy. Trehub and Abramovitch (1978) also showed that when nursery children were asked to point to one of two piles of objects they had a strong tendency to point to the pile with the greater number of objects, even when the instruction contained no reference to *more* or *less*. A similar effect was shown by Estes (1976), who found that children made more errors in learning a discrimination where the positive stimulus has fewer objects than the negative stimulus, than they did when learning the opposite discrimination.

Children sometimes have surprising difficulty in judging which arrangement has more items in it. 4-year-old children, in particular, frequently use length as a criterion of quantity (Siegel, 1977), to the exclusion of considerations of density, so that they will judge that a row of three counters spread out is bigger than a row where five counters are placed close together. There is some indication (Bever, Mehler and Epstein, 1968) that younger children are less susceptible to this illusion, and Weiner (1974) has reported that 3-year-old children can perform above chance both on *more* and on *less* judgments of quantity, applied to rows of objects. In a study by Donaldson and McGarrigle (1974), there were some nursery children who attended not to length of the arrays of objects about which they were required to make a judgment, but instead chose as their criterion the fullness of the containers in which they were placed. Gordon (1978) found that some nursery children erroneously judged a three-dimensional array as having more than a two-dimensional array. Although his results may be explained in other ways, they are consistent with the conclusion that nursery children's judgments of relative numerosity are unreliable and are based on a variety of criteria, better suited to judgments of relative mass. In the light of these considerations, it is clear that proper application of *more* is still developing in the nursery child.

6.4.3   *'Same' and 'different'*

Other studies have asked children to select an object which is the same as or different from one indicated by the experimenter. These studies are not tracing the development of descriptions of quantity, but are frequently discussed along with the studies of the previous section, largely because the initial result was similar to the systematic confusion found for *more* and *less*. Donaldson and Wales (1970) found that their children were as likely to choose a maximally similar object to the standard whether the instruction asked for one that was 'the same in some way' or one that was 'different in some way'. Webb, Oliveri and O'Keeffe (1974) supported the interpretation that, to begin with, children treat *different* as meaning *same*, on the basis of the explanations offered by the children for their choices in a similar task. They proposed that, while *different* separated off from *same* semantically, it went through a period where there had to be a certain dimension of similarity between the objects for them to be judged different.

As in the case of *more* and *less*, subsequent discussion has centred on whether the two terms are indistinguishable for the young child, and also on what the positive term (*same*) means for the children. Wales, Garman and Griffiths (1976) analysed the pattern of selections their children had made over a series of repetitions of the test questions, and found different patterns for the two terms. Glucksberg, Hay and Danks (1976) challenged the assimilation of *different* to *same* in another way, by creating a context in which adults as well as children, when asked for an object that was different from the one held by the experimenter, chose a maximally similar object. Karmiloff-Smith (1977) explored nursery children's interpretation of *the same X* when they were asked to act out a sentence such as 'The girl pushes an X and the boy pushes the same X', where their opportunity to choose a different object of the same kind as the original X varied between items. She found that her 3-year-olds were more likely to choose an object of the same kind for the action than to choose the original object itself, but, by the age of 5, they reliably chose the original object.

In the case of *same* and *different*, it soon becomes particularly clear how difficult it is to separate information about semantic development from considerations of the development of cognitive skills, such as estimations of quantity; from social skills, such as assessing the reasons behind the experimenter's questions; and from other features of language use, such as the use of determiners and anaphoric reference.

In the light of these results, it now makes less sense to ask whether there might be a purely linguistic barrier in tests of cognitive ability. There is no simple answer to the question 'Do children of a certain age understand *more* and *less*?' The way children interpret a question containing these words will depend on the various features we have so far uncovered. It is, therefore, not possible to explain their difficulties with tests of conservation, for example, by proposing that their language is not adequately developed. What can be proposed, however, is that it is just as unlikely that the way they perform in conservation will be simply a function of their level of cognitive development (Elliot and Donaldson, forthcoming). Several studies have shown that children who do not show the ability to conserve when given Piaget's standard test, can produce conserving responses when features of the testing situation are altered slightly. For example, Rose and Blank (1974) found that performance improved if discourse features were changed so that a particular question was not repeated. McGarrigle and Donaldson (1974/5) varied the extent to which the transformation (which is irrelevant to the question being asked) would be seen as deliberate or accidental, and they found that performance was better when the transformation was made accidental. Light, Buckingham and Robbins (1979) have also found this effect with a different scenario, where the transformation is made incidental to a more absorbing game. Sinha and Walkderdine (1978) found that children did better in a test of conservation of inequality of liquid when both the setting of the test and the language used was changed. Instead of pointing out to the children that one beaker had more liquid in it than another, they told them that the beakers contained the drinks for two toys – the horse liked a lot to drink and the dog liked a little to drink, and the rest of the test was conducted using these expressions rather than the quantifiers *more* and *less*. Piaget himself (Piaget, Inhelder and Szeminska, 1960) demonstrated that children's difficulties with conservation of length could be lessened by weakening the visual illusion involved. Thus the judgments children make in conservation tasks are the product of a whole range of factors which compete for their attention.

As a test of the relation between cognitive and linguistic development, Sinclair (1967) took a group of conservers and a group of non-conservers and asked them to describe pairs of objects, such as two pencils of different lengths. She found that most of the non-conservers used absolute adjectives in their descriptions ('This pencil's long and this one's short'), while over 70 per cent of the conservers compared the lengths. Similarly, if the objects varied on two dimensions, such as length and width, the conservers tended to coordinate the dimensions in their descriptions ('This, pencil's longer but thinner than that one'), while the non-conservers treated each dimension separately. This difference in language use between the groups shows that an important factor in conservation may be the ability to attend to features of the visual array in a particular way. Sinclair then demonstrated that training the non-conserving children to describe the objects comparatively, and by coordinating the dimensions, did not help them to conserve when they were tested later. This may indicate that a certain amount of cognitive insight is required in addition to knowing which features of the array to attend to, or it may mean that the children had not had time to assimilate the lessons of the training session before the post-test (Karmiloff-Smith, 1979). It is evident that cognitive, linguistic and interactional factors are too closely entwined in these tests to make it useful to try and see language as dependent on cognition or the reverse.

6.4.4   *Locative prepositions*
A final set of studies on relational terms centres on the development of the understanding and use of some locative prepositions. Clark (1973b) set out to find an order of acquisition for the prepositions *in*, *on* and *under*, hypothesising on the basis of the Semantic Feature Acquisition Hypothesis (Clark, 1973a) that children should find *in* most difficult, since it required reference to a three-dimensional object, and *under* more difficult than *on*, since *on* was the positive term of the pair and *under* the negative. She tested children from 18 months to 5 years of age. She had a collection of small objects, such as toy mice, and a set of reference objects. Each reference object allowed one of the small objects to be placed either in it and on it (a tunnel), or on it and under it (a table), or in it and under it (a truck). She would than ask the child, 'Put the mouse in the tunnel', 'Put the mouse on the table', and so on for each of the possible relations for each reference object. She found that her predictions were not upheld. In fact, the young children (below 3 years) were nearly always correct on *in* items, next most successful on *on* items, and hardly ever correct with *under*. Clark found that her data were described best if she assumed that the children first picked up from the instruction that they had to arrange the two objects spatially in some way and if she assumed that they then followed the ordered rules:

(i)   If the reference object is a container, put the small object in it

(ii)   If the reference object is a surface, put the small object on it

She referred to these rules as non-linguistic strategies with which the child supplemented his partial semantic entry for the prepositions (assumed to be something like [+Locative] for all these prepositions).

Wilcox and Palermo (1974/5) were quick to point out that the physical properties of the reference objects were not the only features which were important. Children also were sensitive to the extent to which the resultant relation between the objects was congruent or not. By selecting their small objects carefully they showed that, if the child was asked to put a piece of track in a truck, he was likely incorrectly to place the track under the truck despite the difficulty of doing so.[3] As a result, he was correct on the *under* item and incorrect on the *in* item, although the reference object was a container. Thus, the children's expectations of which arrangement is more natural is an important factor in the way they handle the task, particularly with the 2-year-olds. This is compatible with the proposal made by Strohner and Nelson (1974) that, in understanding passive sentences, 2- and 3-year-olds follow a 'probable event strategy'.

The children's expectations can be manipulated over quite a short interval. Grieve, Hoogenraad and Murray (1977) gave their child subjects instructions such as 'Put the baby in the bath.' The difference this time was that the 'baby' and the 'bath' were just two boxes which child and experimenter had agreed to name in this way at the start of the item. The 2- and 3-year-old subjects arranged the boxes in different ways depending on the way in which they had been named as well as on the preposition in the instruction.

These studies reveal that children invest a lot of meaning in the materials used in experiments, and are constantly searching for ways to build sense into the game they are playing with the adult. However, most of the studies report that by 3 years of age the children can overcome many of the expectations they might have of what they are being asked to do, and are able to follow simple instructions involving these three prepositions. Other locative prepositions are still being learned. Macrae (1976) explored the range of prepositions 4-year-old children would use to describe objects vertically aligned and found that, while *on top of*, *under* and *underneath* were frequently used, *over* and *below* were very infrequent and *above* was never used. There were virtually no confusions of polarity by the children at this stage. Some of them produced interesting composite constructions, such as *up beside* and *down beside*, during this experiment.

Macrae noticed that there were some constructions which the

3. They found that their youngest children (18–24 months) did tend to make the response which was easiest to carry out, resulting in their performing better than the older group on incongruent items, for which the correct response often happened to be also the easier one.

children seemed to avoid using. When asked for the position of a television in a picture containing a vase of flowers on top of a television set, the children would avoid saying 'The television is under the flowers', but would either hesitate and produce the more natural description, 'The television is . . . the . . . the flowers are on top of the television', or would say things such as 'The television is over in the corner.' In this situation there is a conflict between the discourse demands to make the television the topic of the utterance and the natural perceptual analysis, which takes the flowers as figure and the television as ground. When either adults or children describe such an arrangement, without these discourse constraints, they generally take the ground of the perceptual analysis to be the reference object of the prepositional phrase (Macrae, 1978). Later studies showed that when 4-year-old children were asked to point to the picture where 'the chair is under the cushion' they would in fact point to the picture of a cushion under a chair, despite the fact that this arrangement is the less congruent one. Macrae concluded from these results that, although nursery children appear to have a good grasp of some of the locative prepositions and rarely use the incorrect word order with them, they do not in fact have a syntactic rule associated with their use. In other words, instead of deriving from the order of mention of the two objects related which is to be taken as reference object, they assign the status of reference object to one of the items on either discourse or perceptual grounds, and then use the preposition as a clue to the relative positioning of the objects. Consequently, the children are using pragmatic rules for comprehension and production which are qualitatively different from those which adults are supposed to use but which, outside psycholinguistic experiments, coincide in their application with the adult syntactic rules.

6.5 Deixis and reference

In view of the way in which studies of semantic and syntactic development keep returning to the need to take account of the context of utterance of the instructions, it makes sense to spend time considering how children come to master those features of language which themselves depend on the situation of utterance for their interpretation – the deictic features of the language. These include pronouns, demonstrative adverbs and adjectives and the verbs *go*, *come*, *bring* and *take* (Lyons, 1977). They depend on the situation of utterance in the sense that the person referred to by a pronoun, the object indicated by *this* or *that*, the location described by *here* or *there*, and the direction of the movements referred to by the verbs, cannot be identified without taking into account the identity of the speaker, sometimes that of the addressee, and the place and time of the utterance. A single individual will be referred to as *I* when he is speaker, as *you* when someone else is speaker. Thus, on the one hand, deictic terms are extremely useful ones for a child in his attempts at reference and description when he has a limited vocabulary. On the other hand, when used appropriately, they share the difficulty of shifting reference and require the coordination of several pieces of information about the situation of utterance.

All but the singular pronouns also have the difficulty of shifting boundaries (Clark, 1978a). The distinction between *here* and *there* revolves round whether the location is in the vicinity of the speaker, a vague concept which allows *here* to refer to 'at the table', 'in the flat', 'in Bedfordshire', 'down south', depending on which contrasts most appropriately with the addressee's presumed location. This also interacts with the topic of conversation: during a discussion of the weather, the location is likely to be taken as Bedfordshire, but if the topic changes to central heating then 'here' will be the flat. The conditions of application soon become complex in the adult language (Fillmore, 1973) and vary between languages. There is plenty of room for confusion by the child. However, given that his early language is so embedded in context anyway, we might expect him to give his full attention to the problem.

'Deixis' is the Greek for 'pointing', and before looking at the way mastery of these deictic terms develops, we shall look briefly at some studies on the development of the deictic function of language. This function could be described as the act of successfully focusing an addressee's attention on the item the speaker wishes to topicalise. Ultimately, this becomes the act of successful reference in general. For the prelinguistic infant the act of securing joint attention on an object is frequently accomplished by pointing, and so it is perhaps not surprising that Lyons (1975) was able to trace out a hypothetical course of development which had 'Deixis as a source of reference' (to quote the title of his paper). Since then, various authors have sought to establish a continuity between these acts.

By the age of 12 months, infants appear to use pointing communicatively (Bates, 1976) to ensure that they and their interlocutor are attending to the same object (Bruner, 1975). However, pointing is successful only when the addressee is capable of sharing the same visual field as the infant, and so an early achievement (Lock, 1980) is the discriminative combination of speech and gesture to ensure attention, where the child learns first to call his mother into the room, or away from her more absorbing activity, by calling her name or crying and only then pointing to the object of interest. This important phenomenon is seldom picked up by teams of investigators who concentrate all their attention on the child and his activities while they are visiting him, but it may be quite frequent in a normal family environment.

This attention-drawing function of language can be served by a variety of linguistic devices which do not necessarily develop into the deictic forms of the language. Many children do, however, have a deictic word in their early vocabulary which is invariably accompanied by pointing, and this frequently has a phonetic form related to the adult demonstrative (see Clark (1978a) for a summary of diary studies which report this). The correspondence between form and function is seldom simple, however. Griffiths (1974b) has traced the development of the demonstrative *that* in the case of a single child, who first drew attention by using *see* (cf. Edwards, 1978), and whose early use of *that* had two functions, distinguished by intonation – one to draw attention to an object and simultaneously request its name, and the other both to draw attention to an object and to refer to it, as an elementary deictic pronoun. The child also developed the ability early to distinguish by use of stress between the given and the new parts of utterances containing the pronoun, producing '*That baby* in answer to 'Which is baby?', and *That 'Mummy's* in answer to 'What's this?'

Difficulties arise, however, when the child has to learn to pick out a required referent or set of referents from a wider set of objects without using gesture. The distinction between *this* and *that* can sometimes be used for this function. Clark and Sengul (1978) have traced the development of this distinction and the related one between *here* and *there* by giving a comprehension test to children between the ages of 2 and 5 years. Two identical animals were placed on a table in front of the child, both within his reach but one close to him and the other farther away. An experimenter sat either beside the child or across from him so that closeness to the experimenter either coincided with closeness to the child or was directly in opposition to it. The experimenter would ask the child to make one of the animals perform some action, specifying which animal by using one of the terms of interest, *this*, *that*, *here* or *there*. The locative distinction was mastered before the adjectival one (see also Wales, 1979), and the children appeared to follow one of two paths in their development of the distinction. Some used child-centred strategies while others used speaker-centred strategies. The youngest children made no contrast between the opposite terms, always choosing either the animal close to (or, less frequently, far from) the child or the animal close to (or, less frequently, far from) the speaker, depending on the strategy they were following. At a later stage, a partial contrast was developed, whereby they discriminated between the locatives correctly either while the speaker was beside them (child-centred) or while the speaker was opposite them (speaker-centred), and failed to discriminate them in the other condition. Finally, the full contrast was developed.

Similar strategies were produced by some of the 4-year-old children to whom Webb and Abrahamson (1976) gave a comprehension test of *this* and *that*. They also found that several of the children in their 7-year-old group demonstrated an egocentric understanding of the terms, interpreting *this* as always referring to the object closest to themselves, irrespective of the speaker's location and *that* as referring to an object far from their own position. The role of egocentrism in the acquisition of deictic terms is a curiously elusive one, both conceptually and empirically. Certainly, to use the terms in their contrastive sense, a speaker has to take account of locations relative to his own position, and so it is natural to expect that a child who is egocentric in Piaget's sense (section 3.1) might misinterpret the deictic terms addressed to him in terms of his own perspective, rather than that of the speaker. The paradox is that, in order to acquire the deictic contrast in the first place, the child must notice the regularity between the use of a lexical item and the location or identity of the referent *relative to the speaker*. In other words, he has to recognise the correct, speaker-centred use of the terms before he can produce the incorrect egocentric pattern, as some of Webb and Abrahamson's and Wales' 7-year-old subjects did.

Other attempts to find egocentric patterns in comprehension tests of deictic terms have been unsuccessful. De Villiers and de Villiers (1974) found good discrimination of *here* and *there,* and of *this* and *that* by 3-year-old children. The child had to find a candy hidden under one of two cups placed on either side of a wall, which was between the child and the experimenter, who was also speaker. The wall served to differentiate clearly the two locations of relevance and may have helped the children. The children were only given a single trial for each lexical item, unlike in the other studies (Tanz (1980:94) explores the consequences of this difference). Charney (1979) proposed that younger children may show an egocentric tendency and so tested understanding of *here* and *there* by children between 2;6 and 3;6. She did not find any evidence for an egocentric stage among her children, but did find several children who discriminated correctly and others who had difficulty only when their perspective was in direct opposition to that of the speaker.

Finally, Tanz (1980) tested comprehension of *this*, *that*, *here* and *there* by preschool children in a design where there was no opportunity for the children to use egocentric interpretations of the items. The child was equidistant from two plates, beside each of which was a doll. The dolls took turns to be speaker and to refer to one of the plates. Tanz found a tendency for the children to choose the plate beside the speaker, irrespective of the lexical item. She also found that the ability to differentiate the deictic pairs increased with age, and she found some 3-year-olds who could discriminate some of the pairs.

These demonstrative adjectives and adverbs are useful for specifying identity when only two items or sets of items are competing for attention, but various other linguistic devices have to be used when a larger contrast class is involved. Karmiloff-Smith (1979) has carried out a series of studies on the use of the articles, some quantifiers and possessive adjectives by French-speaking children. She found that the descriptor function of these determiners appeared before their determinor function: that is, the children were able to use these terms first to add information about a referent to which the addressee was already attending, before they were able to use them to direct the addressee's attention to a particular referent or group of referents. The definite and indefinite articles appeared to have distinct functions from the start and quite separate courses of development. The deictic function was the first function of the definite article in that it was used to direct attention to the object to which the child was attending. The plural definite article then appeared, to indicate plurality within the deictic function, and only later to indicate totality, without the support of *all*. Meanwhile the indefinite article had been used in its nominative function, and later the distinction of definiteness appeared, with the definite article(s) being used to identify a unique referent or set of referents and the indefinite to specify one of a class of similar referents. However, this distinction was initially made only where the competing objects were actually present (the exophoric function) and it was not until the children were 9 years old that they used the definite article to refer to something previously mentioned in the discourse (its anaphoric function).

These results are compatible with Warden's (1976) conclusion that children are still confused about the introductory function of the indefinite article until 9 years of age. Moreover, Karmiloff-Smith failed to replicate Maratsos' (1976) results that some 4-year-old children could use the anaphoric contrast between the articles in their understanding of a story to enable them to distinguish between conflicting referents.

Another related contrast which does not appear to be mastered until 9 years is that between the deictic verbs of motion. Clark and Garnica (1974) designed a comprehension test in which the children had to use the deictic contrast between the verbs *go* and *come*, or between *bring* and *take*, to identify either the speaker or the addressee of an utterance. Their youngest children tended to identify both speaker and addressee with the animal which was located at the goal of the movement described by the utterance. Thus, when asked 'Which animal can say to the lion "Go into the garden"?', where they had a choice between an animal located inside the garden and two outside, the youngest children chose the animal inside the garden. This strategy was replaced by one in which the children were able to give the correct identification to the speaker but not to the addressee. It was not until the children were 8 or 9 years old that a reasonable success rate was achieved for this task. The children found *go* and *come* easier than *bring* and *take*, but a similar pattern was found for the development of both pairs of verbs. Macrae (1976) also found that children were unable to discriminate appropriately between *go* and *come* until 8 years, in a series of comprehension tests in which they had to use the deictic information in the verbs to decide between two actions they were asked to make some dolls perform. Two dolls, Alice and Peter, were standing on the table, with their pet tortoise, Terry, equidistant from them both. Beside each of Alice and Peter stood two identical chairs. The children were told: 'Alice says to Terry "Come to the chair". Make him do it.' The most popular action by the children in this test was to move Terry towards the speaker, irrespective of whether the verb used was *come* or *go*.

This might be taken as an indication that the children, by their attention to the speaker, were beginning to accord a special importance to those features of the situation which are central to the deictic contrast (cf. Tanz's (1980) study on demonstratives and locatives mentioned above). Similarly, Clark (1978a) has argued that the fact that so many of the children in the Clark and Garnica study chose the animal at the goal of the movement is significant for an understanding of the development of the meaning of the verbs. However, it appears to be the case that both of these results reflect characteristics of the experimental design, rather than stages in the semantic development of the verbs. Macrae found that the same tendency to move a doll towards the speaker appeared when non-deictic verbs were used and, as a result of this and other studies, she came to the conclusion that the children were drawn to the speaker, not because of his deictic role but rather because he had been mentioned in the instruction. Tanz (1980) failed to find a tendency to choose the goal in her study, with preschool children, in which the goal did not figure as prominently in the instruction as it had in the Clark and Garnica design. Macrae has recently shown (unpublished data) that when there is only one goal and one non-goal, and when the instruction, as in Tanz's experiment, is of the form 'May I come up the steps?', then the children are just as likely to choose the non-goal on every trial as to choose the goal on every trial.

Richards' (1976) data on children's use of deictic verbs in contrived situations show that, in some conditions, her 4-year-old subjects were using *come* and *go* correctly and that, in general, her subjects performed better than Clark and Garnica's data would lead one to expect. It is possible that the children first observe the distinction in their own speech before seeing it as significant in the speech of others. What is not clear from Richards' data, however, is the extent to which the verbs themselves carried the deictic information. These verbs occur frequently in collocations such as *going to bed*, or *coming home*, which can be seen as activities which hold far greater significance for the child than would be apparent in a cold linguistic analysis of the phrases. The children may be able to use these expressions appropriately without being aware of the deictic contrast carried by the verbs they use. Clark (1978a) reports that children, when asked what the verbs mean, appear to offload the deictic component on to a supporting phrase: for example, '*Come* is *come here* and *go* is *go away*.'

This interpretation is interesting in the light of Karmiloff-Smith's main thesis (1979), which is that in mastering the system of determiners, the child moves from using a set of juxtaposed unifunctional markers to using a fully relational system of pluri-functional markers. For example, the word *mes* in French has two descriptor functions of describing the referents as plural and as belonging to the speaker, but it also may have the determinor function of indicating the totality of the set of the objects belonging to the speaker and may be sufficient to contrast them with the objects belonging to someone else. Karmiloff-Smith suggests that children set out with the hypothesis that each word has a single function and, once they realise, around the age of 5 in her studies, that they are using the same word to mark several functions, they start restricting the function of the markers. However, they add other indications of the rejected functions and so overdetermine in their production. *Mes* principally indicates plurality rather than possession by the speaker, at this stage, and so the children produce phrases such as 'les voitures rouges, c'est les miennes', or 'mes camions bleus à moi', which in the latter phrase overdetermines the referent. Similarly, *les* indicates plurality rather than totality and so is frequently used within the phrase 'tous les X' in the early stages. Later, the children coordinate form and function and use the markers plurifunctionally.

This has consequences for comprehension tests of these terms. Several authors, relying on comprehension data, have produced componential analyses of the development of deictic systems. Clark (1978a) analysed the deictic markers of English in terms of the number of elements which had to be considered. The *I/you* contrast involves attention to speaker. In addition, *here/there* requires specification of place, *this/that* includes an object, *go/come* adds movement of the object and *bring/take* includes a component of causation. This analysis successfully allows a match to be made between the lateness of acquisition of the terms and the number of components underlying the distinction. Componential analysis of a similar kind has been done for the system of German pronouns (Deutsch and Pechmann, 1978) and another match has been found with the order of acquisition, and Baron and Kaiser (1975) have found that their data on the confusions made between pronouns by children on a comprehension test can be explained by assuming that the children have not attended to all the features of contrast between the pronouns.

It does not follow from these studies, then, that the children who fail to observe distinctions in tests of comprehension will produce ambiguous messages in their production, because they may have other ways of marking these distinctions in their speech. Ford and Olson (1975) have shown that young children tend to overspecify in their description, and economy of message is a late development. The lesson to be learned, yet again, is that comprehension and production should *both* be examined in studies of the development of any distinction.

7
The communicative context of language acquisition

Much of the work on language acquisition studies the way in which the language produced by the child grows in complexity and the various paths it follows in trying to approximate to the target language. The focus of that work is on the growth of a formal system, as demonstrated by the child's attempts at learning. It studies the products of the learning process and tries to propose mechanisms whereby the observed sequence of these products could be obtained.

Other methods are open to us, however, for discovering the various mechanisms underlying the acquisition process, and the one on which we shall concentrate in this chapter is that of observing the way language is used by the child and by other people with him in direct communication. The mechanisms proposed by this approach and the explanations offered are naturally of a different order from those discussed in the section on experimental studies, where the emphasis was on changes in the formal structure of the language. At the end of the day, however, both explanations should complement each other and so produce a more comprehensive picture of language development. Indeed, since the child's major source of knowledge about a particular language is the conversations directed at him by older people, it is important to study this communicative context to appreciate accurately the problem facing the child. Only much later will other sources of language be available to him which lack such contextual support, such as the written word.

7.1 Mothers' speech to children

How do we speak to children? A moment's reflection shows that we speak differently to children from the way in which we address fellow adults. We don't complain to them about the difficulties of obtaining a mortgage, or if we do, we don't expect them to understand and reply intelligently. We don't expect that they will follow long explanations without frequent checks that they are understanding the steps in the argument. We do comment on what they are doing, frequently showing exaggerated pleasure or disgust in their accomplishments. We may use a special vocabulary which we would use with adults only in special situations of great affection. In other words, a child's experience of language styles is different from our own, and so it is worth asking precisely what these differences are and whether they may contain a clue to the child's success in learning language.

The differences lie principally in the nature of the speech which is specifically addressed to the child, often called 'motherese', to be distinguished on the one hand from 'baby-talk', which is one component of motherese, and on the other from 'environmental language', which refers to all speech which a child may hear or overhear, only some of which will be addressed to him, and which includes voices on the television and conversations between adults within hearing distance. Other authors use these terms differently. Snow and Ferguson (1977) extend 'baby-talk' to refer to what I have called motherese. It is not clear what effects environmental language may have on language development. Shipley, Smith and Gleitman (1969) report that children at the start of language acquisition attend only selectively to the speech they hear even when it is directed to them. On the other hand, many parents find to their distress that children quickly pick up phrases which were definitely not meant for their ears!

Motherese seems to have two principal components. In some cases it has features which are missing in the adult model or would be deviant within it, features commonly referred to as baby-talk. In addition it displays characteristic modifications of the adult model, particularly at the levels of paralinguistic features, syntactic features and discourse features.

Baby-talk is most noticeable in its special vocabulary: words like *tummy* for *stomach*, *choo-choo* for *train* and *doggie* for *dog*. Many of these nursery forms display characteristics which also appear in the nursery forms of other languages. For example, *tummy* involves the reduction of the initial consonant cluster (*st*) of *stomach*, *choo-choo* involves syllable reduplication and *doggie* involves the use of an affective ending which can be added to other adult forms. Ferguson (1977) summarises many studies of baby-talk in languages other than English. It is interesting to speculate on the origins of this vocabulary. Jespersen (1922) suggests that they represent attempts by adults to accommodate to features of child phonology, and Jakobson (1960), in his survey of nursery forms for *mother* and *father* in over 500 languages, observes that they conform to the easiest phonological units which the child can manage, all lacking consonant clusters, but predominantly containing stops and nasals. However, the extent to which baby-talk mirrors child phonology is limited. Ferguson (1977) notes that English baby-talk has no examples of the omission of a nasal before a voiceless consonant, although Smith (1973) has reported such a reduction in the speech of his 2-year-old son (e.g. [bʌp] for *bump*). The other principal feature of baby-talk is its deviant use of pronouns. Adults frequently use phrases such as 'Now Mummy's going to give baby his dinner' in addressing a very young child, dispensing with all pronouns except the third person, which would be unacceptable in adult–adult speech.

Several studies have compared the speech used by adults when addressing young children with that used when addressing other adults or older children. Snow and Ferguson (1977) includes reports of such studies, and Slobin (1975) and Bard (1980) give detailed summaries of this area. The following modifications appear to be characteristic of motherese:

(a)	Paralinguistic features	(i)	High pitch
		(ii)	Exaggerated intonation
(b)	Syntactic features	(i)	Shorter mean length of utterance (MLU)
		(ii)	Fewer verb forms and modifiers
		(iii)	Fewer subordinate clauses/ embeddings per utterance
		(iv)	Shorter mean preverb length
		(v)	More verbless utterances
		(vi)	More content words, fewer function words

(c)	Discourse features	(i)	More interrogatives and imperatives
		(ii)	Speech more fluent and intelligible
		(iii)	More repetitions, whether complete, partial or semantic

Differences arise in the extent of the modifications produced by adults, depending on the age of the child addressed. Snow (1972) asked some mothers to play with 2-year-old and 10-year-old children in three conditions: telling a story to the child about a picture, sorting some toys and explaining some physical phenomenon. She found various modifications in the speech addressed to 2-year-olds relative to that addressed to 10-year-olds. Garnica (1977) found differences in the incidence of rising terminal pitch in speech addressed to 2-year-olds, but not in that addressed to 5-year-olds, relative to adult-directed speech. Motherese is even sensitive to the age of a preverbal addressee. Sylvester-Bradley and Trevarthen (1978) and Snow (1977) have explored changes in the characteristics of mothers' speech to infants between 8 and 20 weeks and 3 and 18 months respectively, changes which they attribute to changes in the interaction between mother and infant over this period.

It seems that children are subject to modified speech of some kind, no matter who is speaking to them. Snow (1972) asked both the mothers in her study and a comparable group of women who were not mothers to speak as if they were addressing 2- or 10-year-old children and found that both groups produced similar speech. Gleason (1973) studied the modifications made by children between 4 and 8 in their speech to babies and found that, although there were differences between children of different ages, all children attempted to change their speech style, a finding supported by Shatz and Gelman (1973) and Sachs and Devin (1976). These results are important, in that they show that motherese is not the prerogative of mothers, and, in many cultures, the responsibility for looking after young children falls on older siblings rather than on mothers. Harkness (1977) reports a comparison of the speech to young children by mothers and older children in a small agricultural community in Kenya. She found that mothers tended to use more questions than did the children and the children used more statements than did the mothers. This suggests that, in that community, mothers and children provided differently modified language environments for the young child.

The view of the linguistic input which emerges from these studies is in sharp contrast to that of speech as complex and ungrammatical, which was one of the factors supposed to contribute to the difficulty of the task facing a child learning language. Given the assumption that the raw material for acquisition was chaotic, it was held to be remarkable that children could produce comparatively tidy linguistic skills in a short space of time. This lent plausibility to the idea that children were endowed with special abilities for cracking the language code. If, instead, adults speak to children in short, grammatical utterances, which give the appearance of ideal language lessons, much of the mystery about the process is reduced, and one should consider more seriously theories of development which give greater weight to environmental factors than has been the case recently.

Of course, it does not follow that the modified linguistic input to which the child is exposed significantly simplifies the language-learning task. Children may still have a special ability for language learning which could operate on a wide variety of linguistic styles. Adults may modify their speech for reasons which have little to do with the child's linguistic needs: indeed the child himself may be eliciting these modifications from adults. The effect of the modified adult input on the child's facility and success at learning language and the child's contribution to the whole process are still subject to empirical test. The following studies show how this can be done.

Schaerlaekens (1973a) studied the effect of environmental factors on language development by looking at a situation where different children were learning their language from the same people and receiving arguably the same input. She took samples of the first 200 instances of two-word utterances from each of two sets of Dutch triplets. Each set was of mixed sex and in each family the children were treated alike and not separated from each other by sickness or other factors. Schaerlaekens constructed a grammar for the speech of each child, and on comparing them found considerable differences which were not related to family differences. The children differed in both the rate and the nature of their development, in that some children would have control over structures which others did not attempt but lack ones which their siblings had mastered. When the children were older (4 years) she scored them on an analogy test to see whether the linguistically more advanced children would have a higher IQ than the others but found no correlation: the most advanced speaker scored lowest on the analogy test. From these results we see that attention focuses sharply back on the child's contribution. Either each child made something quite different out of the same raw data or, alternatively, the data were not, in fact, the same in each case (cf. Staats, 1975). It may be that each child elicits a subtly different type of interaction, and so linguistic input, from his mother and other adults. This then might produce the differences observed in the children's grammars but, in this case, note how sensitive the mechanism must be.

Cross's (1978) approach was different. She selected pairs of children who were matched for MLU but who differed in age by about 7 months. The younger child of each pair was assigned to the 'accelerated' group of children. She then compared samples of the speech used by mothers talking to their children in the two groups to see whether the mothers of children whose development was accelerated made different modifications to their speech from those made by the other mothers. The mothers' speech was scored on sixty different measures, including many syntactic criteria (e.g. complexity and sentence types used), discourse features and records of the content of the speech, such as whether it referred to events in the here-and-now or not. Cross found that the mothers of accelerated children spoke more clearly – they produced fewer unanalysable or unintelligible utterances – than mothers of normal children, and they also produced more utterances which were semantically related to the children's contributions and fewer semantically new utterances. These mothers therefore were careful to tailor their utterances to the semantic intentions of their child and to allow the child to take the lead in the interaction.

No other differences were evident between the mothers, except for a difference in preverb complexity, which Cross attributes to the age differences between the groups. It is important to notice that, although the children were distinguished from each other on grounds which were principally syntactic (MLU and comprehension of syntactic constructions), there was virtually no evidence that their linguistic input differed in its syntactic complexity. Notice also that the groups were chosen in such a way as to ensure that the level of complexity of the child's language was held constant across a pair so that differences in the mother's speech could not be attributed to the mothers of the more accelerated group receiving a more advanced feedback from their children. It is evident that the relationship between features of a mother's speech and her child's linguistic development is far from simple or obvious. Again, it may be that credit for the acceleration may rest with the child, in his being able to communicate his semantic intentions clearly.

In her study, Cross controlled for the effect of the child's linguistic sophistication but retained age as a difference between her groups, which may have accounted for some of her results. Other studies have tried to control this as well. Newport, Gleitman and Gleitman (1977) analysed the speech of fifteen mothers to their daughters, who ranged in age from 12 to 27 months and in MLU from 1.00 to 3.46. They returned to the mother–child pairs six months later and so could estimate a child's 'language growth' on various dimensions by comparing her scores in the two recording sessions. They analysed their data, using statistical techniques which removed any effects which could be attributed to the child's age or MLU, leaving only the effect of mother's speech on the child's linguistic development. They found no effect of intelligibility of the mother's utterances, unlike Cross, and, in agreement with Cross, also found no effect on the child's language development of the mother's length or complexity of utterance. They did find that the number of *yes/no*-questions produced by the mothers correlated with an increase in the number of auxiliaries in the child's verb phrase. Since *yes/no*-questions generally have an auxiliary in initial position (*Did you enjoy your pudding?*), Newport *et al.* interpret this as an indication that children have a processing bias to attend to the beginnings of utterances. They also found a weaker relation between the frequency of deictic utterances (*Those are apples*) in the mothers' speech and the increase in the number of noun phrase inflections in the child's speech. Bard (1980) points out that this indicates the children must have been paying special attention to the ends of utterances as well, and she invites suggestions as to why the children's attention to parts of utterances should be selective in this way.

Support for Newport *et al.*'s result that mothers' use of *yes/no*-questions is related to the development of verbal auxiliaries in the child's speech is provided by Furrow, Nelson and Benedict (1979). They complained that Newport *et al.* had assumed that the effect of motherese on language development would be the same at all stages of development and therefore adopted a different experimental design. They found seven children all aged 1;6 and all with the same MLU of 1.00. They recorded them with their mothers at this stage, and then again nine months later. They were particularly interested in the correlations between aspects of the mothers' speech at the 1;6 recording and aspects of the children's speech at 2;3. Some significant correlations were found between syntactic features in the mothers' speech and that of the children nine months later. In addition to the effect on the development of auxiliaries, they found negative correlations around −0.70 between the frequency in the mothers' speech of pronouns, verbs, copulas and words in general (i.e. length of utterance) and the child's MLU and the number of verbs and of noun phrases per child utterance. Thus there is now some indication that the syntactic properties of mothers' speech may have an effect on their child's linguistic development.

The importance of the mother's sensitivity to her child's semantic intentions found in Cross's study is consistent with the results of a famous study on the effect of linguistic input, that of Cazden (1965). She ran a short study of twelve children, divided into three groups. The children in the control group were not given any special treatment, but each day for twelve weeks the other children spent a special forty minutes with the investigator. With the expansion group, she took each utterance by the child and expanded it into the full adult form of which it seemed to be a reduction, retaining the child's words in the order in which they were uttered. With the modelling group, she commented on utterances made by the child, continuing the theme suggested by the child but without necessarily incorporating any of his lexical items into her utterance. She then compared the child's level of language development at the end of the intervention period with that at the start and found that the modelling group had made rather more advance over the period than the other two groups.[1] Her results are sensitive to the particular tests of language development used and also to the type of expansions used in the expansion group. By varying these factors, other investigators have found expansion also to be effective (Farwell, 1973). As they stand, however, Cazden's results are compatible with other studies reviewed here in demonstrating the effectiveness for the development of structural properties of language of a linguistic environment which is in tune with the child's immediate semantic interests.

This conclusion, imprecise though it may appear, is what would be expected if one subscribes to the Semantic Primacy model of language acquisition proposed by Macnamara (1972), which has heavily influenced theoretical work since it was published. He proposed that children come to the acquisition task with certain concepts already worked out. Children start with semantic intentions, and the acquisition process consists in finding an acceptable linguistic expression for these meanings, rather than the child having to build a concept to fit the use of the linguistic expressions he hears. Even if this is only part of the process it is likely to be particularly important in the early stages, and so it is clearly advantageous if the mother is sensitive to her child's language proposals.

Nelson (1973) argued for the importance of the mother's sensitivity in this sense on the basis of her study of eighteen mothers and children at the start of language learning. She was primarily concerned with the composition and rate of acquisition of the children's first fifty words. On the basis of these data she divided her children into a referential group, for whom the majority of their first words fell into the general nominal category, and an expressive group. She also classified them according to whether there was a cognitive match or mismatch between their early concepts and English word meanings, basing this on the extent to which they overextended common vocabulary. Mothers were then characterised as either accepting or rejecting their children's language

---

1. The children in Cazden's study were speakers of Black English, while the investigators spoke Standard American English. Bard (1980) suggests that the improvements noted may have had more to do with how children learn a new dialect than linguistic development as such.

proposals, using as indices, for example, how persistent they were in trying to decode their children's more garbled efforts.

Each of these dimensions contributed to the rate and smoothness of the development. Children who had shown a cognitive match tended to start speaking early and develop smoothly, while those with a cognitive mismatch were characterised by a late start or sometimes a false start followed by a period of silence while they tried to find the key to the puzzle. Referential children appeared to have a faster rate of development than expressive ones; but remember that as the measure of development was vocabulary size this result is not very surprising: there is probably more opportunity for children to learn the names of objects quickly if that interests them than to learn terms referring to social functions. Nelson suggested that the acceptance/rejection dimension might be the one with the most important long-term effects. It affected both the rate and smoothness of development, and she proposed that a rejecting milieu might turn children into passive learners at a later stage.

It appears, then, that the most important factor influencing children's linguistic development shown in these studies is the extent to which mothers are sensitive to their children's linguistic attempts and try to extend the conversation, using these attempts as a starting-point. As a discourse feature this also throws the spotlight on the child himself – it takes two to make a conversation. Much of the smoothness of the interaction depends on the child's own contribution and this may create difficulties for a sensitive and well-motivated mother. Lieven (1978) reports that characteristics of her speech changed markedly when she was addressing the different children in her study, and the changes were in the direction of the characteristics of the speech of the respective mothers. Children at this stage are developing characteristic styles of interaction as well as language, and the style of interaction may well limit or increase the amount of useful linguistic input they can elicit from their adult partners.

Now although there appears to be very little graded effect of the other characteristics of motherese, such as syntactic modifications and baby-talk, this does not mean that they are not important for successful development. Since all studies report modifications to some degree in the speech of children's caretakers it may be that a certain minimal modification is necessary for successful language acquisition to take place. It is difficult to decide whether this is the case, but some light can be thrown on the subject by considering why adults modify their speech at all in this way.

If asked why they modify their speech to children, adults often say it is to help teach children how to speak – for pedagogic reasons. However, as Brown (1977) points out, if you ask adults to show you how they would try to teach a child to speak, they go about the task in a particularly awkward way, concentrating on basic vocabulary training. It may therefore be that parents rationalise their use of motherese by claiming that they are doing it for pedagogic reasons but that this is not really their primary motivation. Few of the modifications can be said to be made consciously and rationally by adults: what they are doing is demonstrating a particular speech style which is deemed to be appropriate for use when addressing young children. As has been indicated, there may be aspects of the speech style which have evolved from their usefulness in providing an optimal input for a child learning his language but these aspects, apart from sensitivity to the child's language proposals, prove to be very resistant to discovery.

A sociolinguistic approach to motherese, treating it as a single package with the properties indicated, and considering it as one of various speech registers which a native speaker has at his disposal, is a fruitful one, carefully examined by Ferguson (1975, 1977). It widens the discussion away from *ad hoc* speculation on the origins of particular aspects of motherese, inviting comparison with other registers and careful attention to the conditions under which it will be used. For example, one might suppose that motherese represents an attempt by an adult to simplify his language for the benefit of an uncomprehending infant. Certainly many of the features of motherese (in particular the syntactic features) do appear to be simplifications of the adult model in an obvious sense. Exaggerated intonation can also be seen as an attempt to clarify speech and so make comprehension simpler, and even the deviant use of pronouns can be seen as a simpler system in that it excludes first and second person uses. Using this approach, however, one soon starts to create *ad hoc* criteria of simplicity to cover the data. Ferguson (1975) used a different approach. He observed that we simplify our speech in other contexts as well – for example, when we speak to foreigners. He proposed that 'foreigner talk' of the *me Tarzan – you*

Jane variety represents another register, characterised by the need to simplify speech, which native speakers control and which is also widely used as a literary device (Ferguson refers to C. S. Lewis; see also Corder's analysis of the speech of a character in *Watership Down* (Corder, 1975)). He elicited foreigner-talk versions of standard English sentences from a class of students and isolated some characteristic modifications which they made. There were some similarities with motherese – exaggerated intonation, shorter MLU, special vocabulary including forms such as *savvy?* and *bang-bang* for *gun*, etc. However, it was also common to omit forms of the copula, substitute *me* for *I,* him for *he* and replace all negatives by *no*, features not found in motherese. Thus, although both registers undoubtedly involve simplifications of the standard adult language, we cannot explain their characteristics solely by saying that adults simplify their speech when talking to children and foreigners since the simplification is tuned differently in the two cases.

Perhaps adults imitate the children they are addressing. Again, a case can be made for this suggestion, strengthened by the observations that in early development mothers typically follow their baby's lead in play with them. But again it runs into difficulty. For a start, motherese is used in addressing babies far too young to produce any speech. It is also used (or something akin to it) between adult lovers and sometimes in speech to animals. It is not adequate to explain the speech style by saying the adult is spontaneously imitating the child in front of him. It may be that many of the features of the style have their origins in imitation of children's attempts and the role of child phonology in baby-talk forms has been discussed. Jespersen (1922) discusses the impossibility of sorting out the causal relations in this issue once forms such as *tummy* and *gee-gee* become institutionalised in the baby-talk vocabulary.

Of course, the search for a unitary explanation of a phenomenon like this, though the aim of the tidy-minded scientist, is seldom successful, and many authors have decided to break up the motherese package into more homogeneous parts for which explanation may be more readily forthcoming. Brown (1977) first outrages his reader's sensitivities by representing the human infant 'without significant remainder' as a conjunction of the features 'inspiring affection, tenderness and intimacy' and 'lacking verbal production, verbal comprehension and cognitive competence' in order to analyse motherese into two principal components – a communicative component (COMM) and an affective component (AFF). He proposes that COMM is present in motherese because children are linguistically and cognitively undeveloped, and the COMM component is evidenced in devices whose aim is to clarify the adult speech for ease of communication and comprehension by the child. AFF represents an expressive dimension along which adults can give vent to their feelings of tenderness for the infant. If this analysis is correct, then features of COMM should be shared by foreigner talk, while features of AFF would extend to speech to infants, lovers and pets. Much of this comparative work remains to be done.

Garnica (1977) also sees motherese as serving two functions – an analytic function and a social function. In her analysis of prosodic and paralinguistic features of speech to 2- and 5-year-old children, she proposed that some characteristics helped the children to analyse the linguistic content of the speech. For example, rising intonation at the end of a sentence signalled the completion of a linguistic unit, and use of primary stress and longer duration on verbs and colour terms helped to draw attention to the main informative units in the sentence. (This was in a puzzle task where mother and child had to assemble a barrel composed of colour-coded pieces of wood.) Other features served the social function of regulating the conversation between adult and child and gaining and maintaining the child's attention. For example, she suggests, along with other authors, that the higher pitch of motherese indicates to the child that this is speech addressed to him and not to some other adult (whispering may serve a similar function), and the rising sentence-final intonation can also be seen as a signal to the child that it is now his turn in the conversational sequence. She supports her proposal by observing that many of the features of the social function are less marked in speech to the more attentive and socially sophisticated 5-year-olds, while some of the clarifying features of the analytic function persist.

Snow has also explored the suggestion that many motherese features are a byproduct of the type of interactions one has with young children, and she noted (1972) that the presence of the child is important in eliciting motherese. In that study, she had a 'present' condition, where adults talked to 2- and 10-year-old children, and also an 'absent' condition, where she asked them to talk into a tape-recorder, imagining that they were talking to 2- or 10-year-old children. She found that there were considerable differences between the 2-year-old and 10-year-old conditions when the child was present but that the differences were less in the absent conditions. Snow (1977) then reported a study of the way in which motherese characteristics change as the age of the child increases from 3 to 18 months. Initially, there was a high incidence of questions which declined by around 7 months, to pick up again temporarily around 18 months. There was also a change in the topics of conversation, from initially being centred on the child and his internal state to becoming more focused on external topics. Utterance length and sentence type were otherwise fairly constant across the age span. Since most of the changes occurred before the child had any productive control of speech himself, this demonstrates that the adult's speech is not simply tuned to the child's linguistic level (a conclusion shared by Newport *et al.* (1977) and also evident in Cross (1978)) but may change with age. Snow suggests that her mothers are trying to hold a conversation with their children, and their valiant attempts to pass the turn on to the child result in the high incidence of greetings and question forms which are found in motherese.

This method of studying in detail ways in which motherese changes as the child addressed becomes older or more linguistically proficient has much to recommend it as a way of identifying the function of parts of the speech style. For example, Seitz and Stewart (1975) found a negative correlation between the percentage of child utterances expanded by the mother and both the child's MLU and the frequency of child utterances elicited by questions from the mother. From this they conclude that as children become more efficient at speaking for themselves, mothers expand proportionately fewer utterances, suggesting that expansions occur when adults step in to help a child who is having difficulty in expressing himself, just as they feel tempted to speak for other adults who have speech impediments of various kinds.

The story of the study of mothers' speech to children is a curious one. Initially embraced in an attempt to strengthen the environmentalist position that the clue to the child's success in learning language would be found in a careful analysis of the speech addressed to him, it quickly came up against partial success and disconcerting failure. The success was the demonstration that linguistic input to children was different from that experienced by adult linguists, vindicating the assertion that careful empirical attention would have to be paid to the details of a child's early linguistic environment. Disappointment lay in the elusiveness of any clear demonstration that this modified environment could contribute to the child's linguistic success. Indeed the evidence persists in turning the spotlight back on the child and his ability to make use of the material offered or to elicit appropriate speech from his interlocutor. Where then did motherese come from? Rather than postulate an innate 'baby-talk device' available to all adults, a search was initiated for the sources of the speech style. Surviving much initial *ad hoc* explanation, this line of research is now producing interesting studies of the way in which features of the child's developing linguistic system and the mother's style of address arise out of the dynamics of the social interaction between them. At the end of the day we are discovering much which is useful about the linguistic and social context of language learning even though an explanation of the development of syntax still appears as far off as ever.

7.2   **Language and social class**[2]

The linguistic environment of the young child has come under scrutiny from another direction in recent years. In an attempt to understand why the measured scholastic achievements of middle class children in Britain should be superior to those of working class children, Bernstein raised the possibility that an explanation may be related to differences in patterns of language use between different social classes. Notice that the emphasis is quite different from that in the preceding sections. There the search was primarily for the source of children's control over basic structures in their language – primarily ones of syntactic complex-

2.   Dittmar (1976:4) characterises the lower class as 'social groups in the low income bracket who have little social influence' and the middle class as 'groups who are assured powerful and influential positions because of their material and intellectual privileges'.

ity. Now the spotlight is turned to highlight differences between children, not to look for common sources, and also to concentrate on their control of speech styles appropriate to particular social contexts, rather than of basic syntactic structures. Much of the work in this area has been done with older children.

Various studies have shown how the incidence of specific phonetic values in speech varies with social class and the degree of formality of the eliciting situation. Labov (1970) noted how the incidence of features such as postvocalic *r*, unstressed *-ing* and substitution of a stop for a fricative varied as the socio-economic index of the speaker differed, and also varied with whether the speaker was speaking spontaneously about an emotional issue or was reading a word list. Labov's subjects were from New York City and similar studies have been done by Trudgill in Norwich and Macaulay in Glasgow (Trudgill, 1974; Macaulay, 1977). While these linguistic indices of social class membership can be important where they affect attitudes of employers and interview boards (Macaulay, 1977) they are not the kinds of social class differences Bernstein considers most important.[3]

Bernstein distinguishes between a restricted and an elaborated speech variant. An elaborated speech variant is a style of speech which assumes very little background or contextual knowledge on the part of the listener; a restricted speech variant is one which is understandable only by someone with considerable background or contextual knowledge which supplements the speech itself. Certain social contexts are more appropriately served by an elaborated speech variant – for example, giving telephone instructions on how to drive to your house to someone who has never visited the area before – and others give rise to a restricted speech variant – Bernstein gives the example of a couple discussing a film they have just seen. Use of an unsuitable speech variant leads to contravention of Grice's conversational maxims (Grice, 1975). Overuse of a restricted variant is likely to diminish the informativeness of the speech in certain contexts, while overuse of an elaborated variant results in a turgid speech style, lacking conciseness. Bernstein then turns attention away from types of speech variant, which describe a

3. Bernstein's theory has been developing at least since 1958. The account given here is based largely on his paper 'Social class, language and socialisation' (in Bernstein, 1971).

specific speech event, to what he calls speech codes, which characterise the pattern of language use of an individual. He says someone operates with an elaborated code if they can easily produce elaborated speech variants when necessary and says someone operates with a restricted code if they have difficulty in producing elaborated speech variants. He proposes that restricted codes are more characteristic of working class speech and elaborated codes are characteristic of middle class speech.

The evidence in support of this characterisation is hotly disputed (see Edwards (1976a) for a review and discussion). Differences in language use between social class groups have been reported, despite debates about the appropriate way of specifying membership of social classes. Bernstein's original study (1962) was followed up by Lawton (1968) on a slightly larger sample. They both analysed the speech used by groups of adolescent boys (aged 16 (Bernstein) and 12 and 15 (Lawton)) in conversation on various topics, and Lawton also analysed written work by the children. Bernstein noted that the middle class boys hesitated more often than working class boys which indicates, according to Goldman-Eisler's theory of speech planning (Goldman-Eisler, 1958), that they were less likely to produce clichés in their speech (but see Coulthard, 1969). He also noted that working class boys used more pronouns than the middle class sample, suggesting a more contextually bound, and thus restricted, speech variant. Lawton found the differences between his samples were also present in writing. Among other measures, such as analysis of content, he concluded that the middle class boys showed a greater tendency than the working class boys to switch styles when the topic under discussion changed from a descriptive to an abstract topic. This ease of code switching (as it is confusingly called) among middle class children has also been reported among 5-year-olds by Henderson (1970a). On the other hand, Edwards (1976b) failed to find differences on these measures in his study of 11-year-olds. The age of the children may be important here. Macaulay (1977) found social class differences more marked between 15-year-olds than among 10-year-olds, and Lawton similarly found greater variation in his older sample.

The main debate surrounding these studies centres on the task-dependent nature of the results. In a formal interview or in a discussion about capital punishment, middle class adolescents use a speech style similar to the elaborated variant Bernstein described, while working class children do not display the relevant characteristics so clearly. In other contexts, however, the differences are less marked. Higgins (1976) concludes, from a literature survey, that social class differences in communication accuracy are most likely to be found if the communication task is sensitive to possible social class differences in vocabulary or perceptual skills or if it does not reflect normal conversation. He decided that there was little support for the hypothesised social class differences in verbal communicative style. The most celebrated challenge to Bernstein's proposals came from Labov in a paper (1972) in which he extrapolated Bernstein's theory to apply it to the characteristics of Black American English. He reacted strongly to the 'deficit theory' implied by the codes, whereby working class speech is represented as being inferior or deficient relative to middle class speech. After some careful fieldwork aimed at establishing a good relationship with his informants, he demonstrated that Black American English can be as forceful and logically clear as standard English, and also that an elaborated speech variant can lead to so much verbiage that the meaning becomes totally obscure. This demonstrates the difficulty of pinpointing easily scored linguistic measures of logical clarity and so communicative effectiveness.

The debate behind this debate, then, had to do with the implications for educational policy stemming from the conclusion that middle class children cope better verbally in formal situations, such as a classroom provides, than their working class peers. If working class children are simply being inhibited in the classroom from displaying an elaborated speech variant of which they are capable in other contexts, one can argue that attention should be paid to breaking down this inhibition in various ways. This assumes that an elaborated variant is one that should be fostered in the schools: Labov's observations may make us doubt this. Dittmar (1976) places this discussion in the context of the wider political debate and also explores the ideological commitment of the major figures in the debate.

Bernstein continues his argument by claiming that an elaborated code is essential to facility in expressing what he calls 'universalistic meanings' which are valued and have to be valued by the educational system. Universalistic meanings are essential to theory construction while 'particularistic meanings' are more closely tied to specific examples or individual experience. An elaborated code gives easy access to universalistic meanings while a restricted code limits access to these meanings.

Bernstein would also resist the criticism that the basis for his proposals about speech codes is an artefact of the contexts in which he selected his speech samples because he suggests a source for these different codes in the family structure into which the child is born. (Incidentally, this raises the question of how valid it is to extrapolate his theory to another culture such as that of Black America.) He suggests that there are two basic family types – positional and personal. In an extremely positional family, the roles of the members are clearly defined and strictly observed. This leads to many shared assumptions among family members about what behaviour is appropriate in particular contexts and little discussion about general principles governing such behaviour. This is the atmosphere in which a restricted code flourishes. A personal family type is characterised by a tendency to treat each member of the family as an individual, not expecting them to act in role all the time and meeting each conflict with general explanations of why a particular action is hurtful or wrong. This orients the child away from his immediate situation and encourages the development of an elaborated code. For the theory to fit together, we should find that positional families are characteristic of the working class and personal families are characteristic of the middle class.

A few studies have sought to decide whether this is so. Cook (1971) investigated the control procedures that mothers reported using to correct their children's behaviour. He found no difference between his social class samples on the reported tendency to use positional appeals, such as 'Little boys don't do that.' He found that working class mothers said they used imperative techniques, such as 'Don't do that', more than middle class mothers and middle class mothers said they used personal appeals, such as 'I'll be hurt if you do that', more than working class mothers. Turner (1973) found that when 5- and 7-year-old children were asked to tell a story about a set of pictures, where children kick a ball through a window and are then scolded, the middle class children were more likely to use positional appeals than working class children. Some studies have interviewed mothers about the ways they viewed language. Henderson (1970b) asked mothers to report how often they thought they talked to other people for each reason on a given list. She found that middle class mothers reported that they talked for cognitive reasons, such as 'to exchange ideas', more frequently than working class mothers did, and working class mothers considered that they talked for interpersonal reasons, such as 'to show my feelings to others', more frequently than middle class mothers. This study provides about the only point of contact between this area of research and the studies reported in the last section. Henderson's difference is reminiscent of Nelson's distinction between referential and expressive use of language (Nelson, 1973). Also, Cook's distinction between imperative techniques in behaviour control and personal appeals may be related to Nelson's distinction between directive and non-directive mother–child interaction types. However, this link is a rather tenuous one and the evidence on either side is not particularly strong.

Bernstein's theory is impressive in its scope, but it has not yet been properly put to the test and so still requires more detailed articulation. The principal reason for this is that it straddles so many of the social sciences. We must turn to the sociologists to ask whether and why Bernstein's family types should be sensitive to social class variation. Sociolinguists may be able to help us relate family structure to patterns of language use. The psycholinguist should be able to discuss the relation between language and thought proposed between code and type of meaning. The question of which kinds of meanings should be valued by the educational system is partly political as well as of theoretical interest to a cognitive psychologist. Very little evidence has been brought forward to aid the discussion – understandably so when one starts to consider the number and complexity of the controls which have to be considered – age, sex, IQ, school type, parents' IQ and level of education, to name a few. Over and above this dearth of studies the observation which started the whole investigation rises with disconcerting certainty – the scholastic underachievement of working class children.

7.3 Contextual variation in child speech

Much debate surrounds the question of when children become sensitive to contextual constraints in their speech. As was evident from the studies discussed in chapter 5, early child language is heavily dependent for its interpretation on the context in which it occurs. In order to make better sense of the child's contribution and ease the flow of conversation between them, adults supplement the child's meagre utterances with a large dose of inferences based on his other activity and objects in his environment. Conversely, it is also often difficult to ascertain how much of the linguistic signal itself the child actually understands, since much of the language is made redundant by gestures or by habitual expectations. In chapter 6 we saw how difficult it is to control for such interpretation of accompanying non-linguistic information, even under experimental conditions, which suggests that for most children language is so embedded in its context of occurrence that it must be difficult for them to reflect on it or be aware of the constraints which efficient communication demands of speech.

This position is compatible with that taken by Piaget on the nature of pre-operational thought. He suggested that the preschool child's thought was egocentric. That is, the child always saw things from his own point of view and was not capable of decentring and seeing that things would be different from someone else's point of view. In a demonstration of the difficulty young children have in imagining what a three-dimensional display will look like from a different vantage point (Piaget and Inhelder, 1956) this was held to be literally the case, and the child's egocentrism was, by extension, thought to explain his difficulty with other cognitive tasks, such as conservation. If the bulk of a child's early language experience takes place in situations where the context and relevant background are shared by his interlocutor, then it is likely that he will have difficulty in communicating when he has access to relevant information denied his listener and when, therefore, he has to tailor his own speech to take account of his listener's needs. In other words, his language will be so context-dependent that he will find difficulty in making it sensitive to context in a controlled way.

Two principal areas have been investigated relevant to this issue. The first looks at how children learn to adjust their speech when talking to younger children lacking their linguistic skills. The second traces the development of the ability to take account of a listener's information needs in one's speech.

Shatz and Gelman (1973) asked some 4-year-old children to

explain the workings of a toy to a 2-year-old and to an adult. They also collected samples of their spontaneous speech to 2-year-olds, adults and peers. They found that the 4-year-olds produced more short utterances, more attention-drawing utterances and fewer long utterances in their speech to the 2-year-olds than in their speech to adults. They also found more coordinate and subordinate constructions and more predicate complementisers in the speech to the adult than in the speech to the 2-year-old. They found no differences between speech to peer and speech to adult, and found no difference in the tendency to modify speech between those who had younger siblings and those who had not. Thus we have a result similar to the evidence presented for motherese in adults and so a similar discussion about the source of the modifications.

The first possibility is that many of the modifications, such as an increase in attention-drawing utterances, are an effect of trying to hold a conversation with a distractable 2-year-old. This was explored by Sachs and Devin (1976), who collected spontaneous speech samples from four 4-year-olds to their mother, a peer, a 2-year-old baby and a baby doll, and also asked the children to try to speak like a baby. They found modifications in each of these situations, although not always the same ones, which were in line with those reported in studies of motherese. They also found that children modified their speech whether or not they had a younger sibling. This means that if the children were learning rules for the production of motherese, they were able to do it with a fairly limited exposure to examples of the phenomenon.

There is some evidence that motherese is a register which has to be learned. Gleason (1973) compared the modifications in speech to younger children by some children aged between 4 and 8. She found that some of the 5- and 6-year-olds made modifications which are not characteristic of the adult forms of motherese. For example, they produced *That's not bug*, omitting the article but retaining the copula, while the adult would be more likely to retain the article and omit the copula, producing *That not a bug*.

There is also evidence that children are very efficient at learning various speech registers, so the lack of difference between children with and without siblings need not be too damaging for the proposal that a large part of 4-year-olds' ability in this area is imitative in origin. Weeks (1971) reported ways in which 2- to

5-year-old children appropriately used such speech registers as whispering (in situations of intimacy or secrecy), clarification (when their earlier utterance had not been communicatively success-ful) and fuzzy speech (when they were hurrying on to a more important part of the utterance).

It seems from these studies that 4-year-old children do alter their speech when talking to children with less control of language than they have themselves. However, it is likely that these alterations are partly attempts at imitating an adult speech style and partly just the type of speech elicited by a younger conversational partner. There is no clear evidence that the children are modifying their speech because they realise the linguistic limitations of their listener.

Several studies have explored how the young child copes with a situation where he has to cooperate in a task with another child who has access to different information. The original studies were designed by Krauss and Glucksberg (e.g. 1969) who sat two children opposite each other at a table and placed a screen between them so that they could not see each other. Each child was given a stick and a collection of building blocks with distinguishing pictures on them, which could be threaded onto the stick. One child was chosen as the speaker. He picked the blocks one at a time out of a dispenser, describing each as he did so, so that the listener could choose the appropriate block and place it on his stick. The aim of the task was for both children to end up with the blocks arranged on their sticks in the same order. The question was whether the child could give sufficiently informative descriptions to his listener to enable him to choose the appropriate block each time.

An initial study in which the blocks had animal pictures on them proved too easy, resulting in too few errors to trace any develop-ment but showing that the task was one which the children could accept. The animals were then replaced by nonsense figures and this time there was a developmental effect. On the first trial, all age groups, from 4- to 10-year-olds, did very poorly, perhaps because the speaker was not sufficiently familiar with the blocks to know which ones were potentially confusable. On subsequent trials, the older children improved considerably, unlike the younger ones who con-tinued to make as many errors. This could have been because the younger listeners were inattentive or uncooperative, so the child-ren's descriptions were given to adult subjects who found the older children's descriptions far more informative, even on the first trial.

This could be taken as support for the idea that the younger children were not able to take the listener's problem into account sufficiently to make their speech informative, but other explanations are possible. The older children may have had a better memory for the alternative figures and so produced descriptions which took greater account of the contrasts among the pictures. It may also have been the case that the older children were simply more garrulous and had a larger vocabulary than the younger children, and so gratuitously produced more informative descriptions than the younger children without necessarily being more sensitive to their listener's needs.

Later studies have used simpler displays and have looked at this question of how economical the children's descriptions are. Ford and Olson (1975) hid a star under one of two blocks which were, for example, either circular or triangular in shape and black or white in colour. If a white circle was paired with a black circle, children as young as 4 years described it as the white one, but if it was paired with a white triangle, they described it as the round one. This shows that they are sensitive to perceptual contrasts and that their descriptions reflect this sensitivity. Harris, Macrae and Bassett (1978) compared young children's spontaneous descriptions of pictures of animals which contrasted in ways similar to those of Ford and Olson with their descriptions of them in a communicative task similar to that of Krauss and Glucksberg. On all items, the pictures differed in terms of colour, and on some trials they differed in the identity of the animal also. In the description task, all children mentioned the identity of the animal indicated, although on many trials this did not distinguish between the pictures, and only one mentioned colour. In the communication task, all the 7-year-olds gave informative descriptions, usually minimally so, and all 4-year-olds gave adequately informative descriptions on the first trial, although they tended to perseverate on later trials with the dimension which had been appropriate earlier in the task. This shows that even 4-year-old children can show a sensitivity to their listener's needs and tailor their speech accordingly, provided that the task is simple enough in vocabulary range and other cognitive demands.

The development of understanding of the process of communication has been approached from a different angle by Robinson and Robinson (1976). They provided two sets of cards with simple pictures on them contrasting on various dimensions. One set was given to the child and the other to the experimenter. The speaker had to choose a card and describe it to the listener who then had to hand over the same card from his set. The experimenter manufactured communicative failure on various trials and then asked the child who was to blame. The younger children (5-year-olds) mostly blamed the listener for the breakdown in communication, and it was not until much later that they suggested that the speaker might be to blame. Robinson and Robinson interpret this as meaning that children begin to realise the mechanics of successful communication through their experience as listener rather than through being misunderstood themselves.

These studies suggest, then, that young children are better able to handle clear communication than was previously thought. It is not clear how to characterise the nature of their understanding of the process. Certainly it is deficient in some ways. Part of being a good communicator is knowing what it is to be a bad communicator, and the Robinsons suggest that this awareness takes time to develop. And as everyone knows from his own experience of bad directions or obscure lectures, it is an awareness which may never be complete.

7.4   Learning more than one language

For millions of children, the environment in which they learn to speak is quite different from anything we have described so far, because they are growing up in a bilingual, or a multi-lingual, community. It is a serious shortcoming of current theories of language acquisition that they are generally formulated with the monolingual (normally English-speaking) child in mind. What is it like being brought up bilingual?

Part of the difficulty in answering this question is immediately apparent. Being bilingual in the International School in Geneva and being bilingual in the streets of Bombay are radically different experiences. There are many different kinds of bilingualism, and only some of the most important for child language study are outlined here. Some children learn both languages in the home (simultaneous bilingualism) and others learn a second language only when they go to school (successive bilingualism). Some simultaneous bilinguals hear only one language from each person around them, with, perhaps, their father speaking only German and their mother only English, while others are surrounded by people who frequently switch languages. Some successive bilinguals learn a second language without their first language losing its importance for them (additive bilingualism), while others have no choice but to learn the second language since that is the dominant language in the community (subtractive bilingualism). We shall look briefly at some studies of simultaneous bilinguals for whom each person speaks only one language. In these cases, the children's bilingualism has been carefully monitored, because virtually all the cases studied are linguists' children and so the picture may well be quite different for children with different backgrounds.

From the studies on simultaneous bilingualism a fairly clear picture emerges of the stages by which the children develop their two languages. In the first stage, the children are simply learning a single language system, which has in it contributions from both the languages the child is to learn. Imedadze (1978) calls this the period of mixed speech, and in general it lasts till the child is around 2 years old. At this stage, there is little or no syntax in monolingual development in any case. The bilingual children often juxtapose in a single utterance words from both languages (Imedadze, 1978; Volterra and Taeschner, 1978), or combine stems from one language with affixes from the other (Burling, 1959). There are few examples at this stage of the child knowing the names in both languages for an object (Volterra and Taeschner, 1978). If both languages are similar, as in the English and German which Leopold's daughter, Hildegard, was learning (Leopold, 1949), it may be difficult to tell which language is being spoken because of similarities in the phonemic structure at this stage, since the distinguishing features of the two languages are late acquisitions under monolingual conditions.

The children then begin to discriminate between the two language systems, first at the lexical level (Volterra and Taeschner, 1978) and then syntactically as well. They seldom combine lexical items for both languages in a single utterance and they begin to show an ability to translate from one language to the other. Burling played a game with his son (at age 2;10) who was learning English and Garo, which consisted of asking 'What does *hand* mean?' and then supplying the translation in the other language. His son spontaneously pointed to his nose one day and observed 'In English, it's *nose*; in Garo, it's *giŋ-tiŋ*.' At this stage, the children frequently construct 'conversion patterns' when they are at a loss for a word in one language, imposing, for example, an English pronunciation and inflectional system on a German word which does not have a cognate in English. Hildegard commented 'They are stimming', with initial [st] instead of [ʃt], as an attempt at 'They are tuning up' from the German verb *stimmen* 'to tune instruments' (Leopold, 1954). Volterra and Taeschner found that the two sisters they observed, with an Italian-speaking father and a German-speaking mother, were managing to keep both lexicon and syntax in their two languages separate by the age of 4 years, although they still kept a single language for any particular person.

An important feature of bilingualism in this period is its fragility – taken away from the bilingual environment a child soon loses the language from which he has been removed. After speaking Garo for two years, from ages 1;4 to 3;4, Burling's son forgot it all within six months of leaving India. Leopold also reports in detail the effects on Hildegard's languages of relatively short holidays in Germany or America. Gradually, the bilingualism can stabilise. Leopold considered that in Hildegard's seventh year her bilingualism became more complete in that the separate language patterns were kept distinct, with minimal interference, although her English remained stronger than her German.

From these studies, a robust picture emerges of the bilingual child, benefiting cognitively, socially and culturally (Lambert, 1977) from his experience. Future research into more varied kinds of bilingualism may require us to modify this conclusion, but at present it is a cheering image on which to end.

REFERENCES

Aitchison, J. 1976. *The Articulate Mammal*. London: Hutchinson.

Andersen, E. S. 1975. Cups and glasses: learning that boundaries are vague. *Journal of Child Language* 2, 79–103.

Antinucci, F. and Parisi, D. 1975. Early semantic development in child language. In E. H. Lenneberg and E. Lenneberg (eds.) *Foundations of Language Development*, vol. 1. New York: Academic Press.

Arlman-Rupp, A. J. L., van Niekerk de Haan, D. and van de Sandt-Koenderman, M. 1976. Brown's early stages: some evidence from Dutch. *Journal of Child Language* 3, 267–74.

Baddeley, A. D. 1976. *The Psychology of Memory*. New York: Harper and Row.

Baldie, B. 1976. The acquisition of the passive voice. *Journal of Child Language* 3, 331–48.

Bar-Adon, A. and Leopold, W. F. (eds.) 1971. *Child Language: a book of readings*. Englewood Cliffs, NJ: Prentice-Hall.

Bard, E. G. 1980. Motherese and otherese: a cold look at a warm register. Unpublished manuscript. University of Edinburgh.

Baron, J. and Kaiser, A. 1975. Semantic components in children's errors with pronouns. *Journal of Psycholinguistic Research* 4, 303–17.

Barton, D. 1978. The discrimination of minimally different pairs of real words by children aged 2;3 to 2;11. In N. Waterson and C. Snow (eds.) *The Development of Communication*. Chichester: John Wiley.

Bates, E. 1976. *Language and Context: the acquisition of pragmatics*. New York: Academic Press.

Bausano, M. K. and Jeffrey, W. E. 1975. Dimensional salience and judgments of bigness by three-year-old children. *Child Development* 46, 988–91.

Beilin, H. 1975. *Studies in the Cognitive Basis of Language Acquisition*. New York: Academic Press.

Bellugi, U. and Brown, R. 1964. *The Acquisition of Language*. Chicago and London: University of Chicago Press.

Ben-Zeev, S. 1977. The influence of bilingualism on cognitive strategy and cognitive development. *Child Development* 48, 1009–18.

Berko, J. 1958. The child's learning of English morphology. *Word* 14, 150–77.

Bernstein, B. 1962. Linguistic codes, hesitation phenomena and intelligence. *Language and Speech* 5, 31–46.

 1971. *Classes, Codes and Control*. London: Routledge and Kegan Paul.

Bever, T. G. 1970. The cognitive basis for linguistic structures. In J. R. Hayes (ed.) *Cognition and the Development of Language*. New York: Wiley.

Bever, T. G., Mehler, J. and Epstein, J. 1968. What children do in spite of what they know. *Science* 162, 921–4.

Bierwisch, M. 1967. Some semantic universals of German adjectivals. *Foundations of Language* 3, 1–36.

1970. Semantics. In J. Lyons (ed.) *New Horizons in Linguistics*. Harmondsworth: Penguin.

Bloom, L. 1970. *Language Development: form and function in emerging grammars*. Cambridge, Mass.: MIT Press.

1974. Talking, understanding and thinking. In R. L. Schiefelbusch and L. L. Lloyd (eds.) *Language Perspectives: acquisition, retardation and intervention*. London and Basingstoke: Macmillan.

Bloom, L. and Lahey, M. 1978. *Language Development and Language Disorders*. New York: John Wiley.

Bloom, L., Lightbown, P. and Hood, L. 1975. *Structure and Variation in Child Language*. Monographs of the Society for Research in Child Development, serial no. 160, vol. 40.

Bloomfield, L. 1926. A set of postulates for the science of language. *Language* 2, 153–64.

Bower, T. G. R. 1977. *A Primer of Infant Development*. San Francisco: W. H. Freeman.

Bowerman, M. 1973a. *Early Syntactic Development: a cross-linguistic study with special reference to Finnish*. Cambridge University Press.

1973b. Structural relationships in children's utterances: syntactic or semantic? In T. E. Moore (ed.) *Cognitive Development and the Acquisition of Language*. New York: Academic Press.

1975. Commentary. In L. Bloom, P. Lightbown and L. Hood (eds.) *Structure and Variation in Child Language*. Monographs of the Society for Research in Child Development, serial no. 160, vol. 40.

1976. Semantic factors in the acquisition of rules for word use and sentence construction. In D. M. Morehead and A. E. Morehead (eds.) *Normal and Deficient Child Language*. Baltimore: University Park Press.

1978a. The acquisition of word meaning: an investigation into some current conflicts. In N. Waterson and C. Snow (eds.) *The Development of Communication*. Chichester: John Wiley.

1978b. Systematising semantic knowledge: changes over time in the child's organisation of word meaning. *Child Development* 49, 977–87.

Braine, M. 1963a. The ontogeny of English phrase structure: the first phase. *Language* 39, 1–13.

1963b. On learning the grammatical order of words. *Psychological Review* 70, 323–48.

Brewer, W. F. and Stone, J. B. 1975. Acquisition of spatial antonym pairs. *Journal of Experimental Child Psychology* 19, 299–307.

Bricker, W. A. and Bricker, D. D. 1974. An early language training strategy. In R. L. Schiefelbusch and L. L. Lloyd (eds.) *Language Perspectives: acquisition, retardation and intervention*. London and Basingstoke: Macmillan.

Bronckart, J. P. and Sinclair, H. 1973. Time, tense and aspect. *Cognition* 2, 107–30.

Brown, H. D. 1971. Children's comprehension of relativised English sentences. *Child Development* 42, 1923–36.

Brown R. W. 1958. *Words and Things*. Glencoe, Ill.: Free Press.

1970a. *Psycholinguistics*. New York: Free Press.

1970b. The first sentences of child and chimpanzee. In R. W. Brown (ed.) *Psycholinguistics*. New York: Free Press.

1973. *A First Language: the early stages*. London: George Allen and Unwin.

1977. Introduction. In C. E. Snow and C. A. Ferguson (eds.) *Talking to Children*. Cambridge University Press.

Brown, R. and Fraser, C. 1964. The acquisition of syntax. In U. Bellugi and R. Brown (eds.) *The Acquisition of Language*. Chicago and London: University of Chicago Press.

177

References

Brown, R. and Hanlon, C. 1970. Derivational complexity and order of acquisition in child speech. In J. R. Hayes (ed.) *Cognition and the Development of Language*. New York: John Wiley.

Bruce, D. J. 1964. Analysis of word sounds by young children. *British Journal of Educational Psychology* 34, 158–69.

Bruner, J. S. 1975. The ontogenesis of speech acts. *Journal of Child Language* 2, 1–19.

1978. Learning how to do things with words. In J. S. Bruner and A. Garton (eds.) *Human Growth and Development: Wolfson College Lectures, 1976*. Oxford University Press.

Burling, R. 1959. Language development of a Garo and English-speaking child. *Word* 15, 45–68.

Calfee, R. C., Chapman, R. S. and Venezky, R. L. 1972. How a child needs to think to learn to read. In L. W. Gregg (ed.) *Cognition in Learning and Memory*. New York: John Wiley.

Cambon, J. and Sinclair, H. 1974. Relations between syntax and semantics: are they 'easy to see'? *British Journal of Psychology* 65, 133–40.

Campbell, R. N. 1979. Cognitive development and child language. In P. Fletcher and M. Garman (eds.) *Language Acquisition*. Cambridge University Press.

1980. On Fodor on cognitive development. In B. de Gelder and P. van Geet (eds.) *Knowledge and Representation*. London: Routledge and Kegan Paul.

Campbell, R. N. and Wales, R. J. 1970. The study of language acquisition. In J. Lyons (ed.) *New Horizons in Linguistics*. Harmondsworth: Penguin.

Carey, S. 1978. *Less* may never mean 'more'. In R. N. Campbell and P. T. Smith (eds.) *Recent Advances in the Psychology of Language: language development and mother–child interaction*. New York and London: Plenum Press.

Cazden, C. 1965. Environmental assistance to the child's acquisition of grammar. Doctoral dissertation, Harvard University.

Celce-Murcia, M. 1978. The simultaneous acquisition of English and French in a two-year-old child. In E. M. Hatch (ed.) *Second Language Acquisition: a book of readings*. Rowley: Newbury House.

Charney, R. 1979. The comprehension of *here* and *there*. *Journal of Child Language* 6, 69–80.

Chomsky, C. 1969. *The Acquisition of Syntax in Children from 5 to 10*. Cambridge, Mass.: MIT Press.

Chomsky, N. 1957. *Syntactic Structures*. The Hague: Mouton.

1959. Review of *Verbal Behavior* by B. F. Skinner. *Language* 35, 26–58.

1965. *Aspects of the Theory of Syntax*. Cambridge, Mass.: MIT Press.

Clark, E. V. 1972. On the child's acquisition of antonyms in two semantic fields. *Journal of Verbal Learning and Verbal Behavior* 11, 750–8.

1973a. What's in a word? On the child's acquisiton of semantics in his first language. In T. E. Moore (ed.) *Cognitive Development and the Acquisition of Language*. New York: Academic Press.

1973b. Non-linguistic strategies and the acquisition of word meanings. *Cognition* 2, 161–82.

1977. Strategies and the mapping problem in first language acquisition. In J. Macnamara (ed.) *Language Learning and Thought*. New York: Academic Press.

1978a. From gesture to word: on the natural history of deixis in language acquisition. In J. S. Bruner and A. Garton (eds.) *Human Growth and Development: Wolfson College Lectures, 1976*. Oxford University Press.

1978b. Strategies for communicating. *Child Development* 49, 953–9.

Clark, E. V. and Garnica, O. K. 1974. Is he coming or going? On the acquisition of deictic verbs. *Journal of Verbal Learning and Verbal Behavior* 13, 559–72.

Clark, E. V. and Sengul, C. J. 1978. Strategies in the acquisition of deixis. *Journal of Child Language* 5, 457–75.

Clark, H. H. 1969. Linguistic processes in deductive reasoning. *Psychological Review* 76, 387–404.

1970. The primitive nature of children's relational concepts. In J. R. Hayes (ed.) *Cognition and the Development of Language*. New York: John Wiley.

Clark, R. 1974. Performing without competence. *Journal of Child Language* 1, 1–10.

1980. Errors in talking to learn. *First Language* 1, 7–32.

Clark, R., Hutcheson, S. and van Buren, P. 1974. Comprehension and production in language acquisition. *Journal of Linguistics* 10, 39–54.

Cole, M., Gay, J., Glick, J. A. and Sharp, D. W. 1971. *The Cultural Context of Learning and Thinking*. London: Methuen.

Cook, J. 1971. An inquiry into patterns of communication and control between mothers and their children in different social classes. Doctoral dissertation, University of London.

Corder, S. P. 1975. The language of Kehaar. *Work in Progress* 8, 41–52. Edinburgh University Department of Linguistics.

Corrigan, R. 1978. Language development as related to stage 6 object permanence development. *Journal of Child Language* 5, 173–89.

Coulthard, M. 1969. A discussion of restricted and elaborated codes. *Educational Review* 22, 38–50.

Cromer, R. F. 1970. 'Children are nice to understand': surface structure clues for the recovery of a deep structure. *British Journal of Psychology* 61, 397–408.

1974a. The development of language and cognition: the cognition hypothesis. In B. Foss (ed.) *New Perspectives in Child Development*. Harmondsworth: Penguin.

1974b. Language in the mentally retarded: processes and diagnostic distinctions. In R. L. Schiefelbusch and L. L. Lloyd (eds.) *Language Perspectives: acquisition, retardation and intervention*. London and Basingstoke: Macmillan.

1978. Developmental strategies for language. In V. Hamilton and M. Vernon (eds.) *The Development of Cognitive Processes*. New York: Academic Press.

Cross, T. G. 1978. Mothers' speech and its association with rate of linguistic development in young children. In N. Waterson and C. Snow (eds.) *The Development of Communication*. Chichester: John Wiley.

Crothers, E. and Suppes, P. 1967. *Experiments in Second-Language Learning*. New York and London: Academic Press.

Crystal, D. Fletcher, P. and Garman, M. 1976. *The Grammatical Analysis of Language Disability*. London: Edward Arnold.

Curtiss, S. 1977. *Genie; a psycholinguistic study of a modern-day 'wild child'*. New York: Academic Press.

Cutting, J. E. and Rosner, B. S. 1974. Categories and boundaries in speech and music. *Perception and Psychophysics* 16, 564–70.

Dasen, P. R. 1972. Cross-cultural Piagetian research: a summary. *Journal of Cross-Cultural Psychology* 3, 23–9.

de Laguna, G. A. 1927. *Speech: its function and development*. Bloomington, Indiana: Indiana University Press.

Dennis, M and Whitaker, H. A. 1977. Hemispheric equipotentiality and language acquisition. In S. J. Segalowitz and F. A. Gruber (eds.) *Language Development and Neurological Theory*: New York: Academic Press.

Derwing, B. L. 1973. *Transformational Grammar as a Theory of Language Acquisition*. Cambridge University Press.

Deutsch, W. and Pechmann, T. 1978. Ihr, dir or mir? On the acquisition of pronouns in German children. *Cognition* 6, 155–68.

References

de Villiers, J. G. and de Villiers, P. A. 1978. *Language Acquisition*. Cambridge, Mass.: Harvard University Press.

de Villiers, P. A. and de Villiers, J. G. 1974. On this, that and the other: nonegocentrism in very young children. *Journal of Experimental Child Psychology* 18, 438–47.

Dewart, M. H. 1975. A psychological investigation of sentence comprehension by children. Doctoral dissertation, University College London

Dittmar, N. 1976. *Sociolinguistics: a critical survey of theory and application*. London: Edward Arnold.

Dodd, B. 1975. Children's understanding of their own phonological forms. *Quarterly Journal of Experimental Psychology* 27, 165–72.

Donaldson, M. 1978. *Children's Minds*. London: Fontana.

Donaldson, M. and Balfour, G. 1968. Less is more: a study of language comprehension in children. *British Journal of Psychology* 59, 461–72.

Donaldson, M. and Lloyd, P. 1974. Sentences and situations: children's judgments of match and mismatch. In F. Bresson (ed.) *Problèmes actuels en psycholinguistique*. Paris: Centre National de la Recherche Scientifique.

Donaldson, M. and McGarrigle, J. 1974. Some clues to the nature of semantic development. *Journal of Child Language* 1, 185–94.

Donaldson, M. and Wales, R. J. 1970. On the acquisition of some relational terms. In J. R. Hayes (ed.) *Cognition and the Development of Language*. New York: John Wiley.

Dore, J. 1975. Holophrases, speech acts and language universals. *Journal of Child Language* 2, 21–40.

Drummond, W. B. 1907. *An Introduction to Child-Study*. London: Edward Arnold.

Edwards, A. D. 1976a. *Language in Culture and Class*. London: Heinemann.

1976b. Speech codes and speech variants: social class and task differences in children's speech. *Journal of Child Language* 3, 247–65.

Edwards, D. 1973. Sensory motor intelligence and semantic relations in early child grammar. *Cognition* 2, 395–434.

1978. Social relations and early language. In A. Lock (ed.) *Action, Gesture and Symbol: the emergence of language*. London: Academic Press.

Edwards, M. L. 1974. Perception and production in child phonology: the testing of four hypotheses. *Journal of Child Language* 1, 205–19.

Eilers, R. E. and Oller, D. 1976. The role of speech discrimination in developmental sound substitutions. *Journal of Child Language* 3, 319–30.

Eilers, R. E., Oller, D. K. and Ellington, J. 1974. The acquisition of word-meaning for dimensional adjectives: the long and short of it. *Journal of Child Language* 1, 195–204.

Elliot, A. J. and Donaldson M. Forthcoming. Language. In S. Modgil and C. Modgil (eds.) *The Taming of Piaget: Crossfire and Cross-currents*.

Entus, A. K. 1977. Hemispheric asymmetry in processing of dichotically presented speech and non-speech stimuli by infants. In S. J. Segalowtiz and F. A. Gruber (eds.) *Language Development and Neurological Theory*. New York: Academic Press.

Estes, K. W. 1976. Nonverbal discrimination of more and fewer elements by children. *Journal of Experimental Child Psychology* 21, 393–405.

Farwell, C. B. 1973. The language spoken to children. *Papers and Reports on Child Language Development* 5, 31–62. Stanford University, Stanford, California.

Fay, D. 1978. Transformations as mental operations: a reply to Kuczaj. *Journal of Child Language* 5, 143–9.

Feldman, H., Goldin-Meadow, S. and Gleitman, L. 1978. Beyond Herodotus: the creation of language by linguistically deprived deaf children. In A. Lock (ed.) *Action, Gesture and Symbol: the emergence of language*. London: Academic Press.

Ferguson, C. A. 1975. Towards a characterisation of English foreigner talk. *Anthropological Linguistics* 17, 1–14.

1977. Baby talk as a simplified register. In C. E. Snow and C. A. Ferguson (eds.) *Talking to Children*. Cambridge University Press.

Ferguson, C. A. and Farwell, C. B. 1975. Words and sounds in early language acquisition. *Language* 51, 419–39.

Fillmore, C. J. 1968. The case for case. In E. Bach and R. T. Harms (eds.) *Universals in Linguistic Theory*. London: Holt, Rinehart and Winston.

1973. May we come in? *Semiotica* 9, 98–115.

Flavell, J. H. 1963. *The Developmental Psychology of Jean Piaget*. Princeton, NJ: Van Nostrand Reinhold.

Fodor, J. 1976. *The Language of Thought*. Hassocks, Sussex: The Harvester Press.

Fodor, J., Bever, T. and Garrett, M. 1974. *The Psychology of Language*. New York: McGraw–Hill.

Ford, W. and Olson, D. 1975. The elaboration of the noun phrase in children's description of objects. *Journal of Experimental Child Psychology* 19, 371–82.

Forster, K. I. and Olbrei, I. 1973. Semantic heuristics and syntactic analysis. *Cognition* 2, 319–47.

Fouts, R. S. 1973. Acquisition and testing of gestural signs in four young chimpanzees. *Science* 180, 978–80.

Fraser, C., Bellugi, U. and Brown, R. 1963. Control of grammar in imitation, comprehension and production. *Journal of Verbal Learning and Verbal Behavior* 2, 121–35.

Fromkin, V. A. 1973. *Speech Errors as Linguistic Evidence*. The Hague: Mouton.

Furrow, D., Nelson, K. and Benedict, H. 1979. Mothers' speech to children and syntactic development: some simple relationships. *Journal of Child Language* 6, 423–42.

Furth, H. G. 1966. *Thinking Without Language*. New York: Free Press.

Gardner, R. A. and Gardner, B. T. 1975. Evidence for sentence constituents in the early utterances of child and chimpanzee. *Journal of Experimental Psychology – General* 104, 244–67.

Garman, M. 1974. On the acquisition of two complex syntactic constructions in Tamil. *Journal of Child Language* 1, 65–76.

Garnica, O. K. 1973. The development of phonemic speech perception. In T. E. Moore (ed.) *Cognitive Development and the Acquisition of Language*. New York: Academic Press.

1977. Some prosodic and paralinguistic features of speech to young children. In C. E. Snow and C. A. Ferguson (eds.) *Talking to Children*. Cambridge University Press.

Garvey, C. 1975. Requests and responses in children's speech. *Journal of Child Language* 2, 41–63.

Gelman, R. and Gallistel, C. R. 1978. *The Child's Understanding of Number*. Cambridge, Mass.: Harvard University Press.

Gibson, E. J. and Levin, H. 1975. *The Psychology of Reading*. Cambridge, Mass.: MIT Press.

Gleason, J. Berko. 1973. Code switching in children's language. In T. E. Moore (ed.) *Cognitive Development and the Acquisition of Language*. New York: Academic Press.

Gleitman, L. R., Gleitman, H. and Shipley, E. F. 1972. The emergence of the child as grammarian. *Cognition* 1, 137–64.

Glucksberg, S., Hay, A. and Danks, J. H. 1976. Words in utterance contexts: young children do not confuse the meanings of same and different. *Child Development* 47, 737–41.

Goldman-Eisler, F. 1958. Speech production and the predictability of words in context. *Quarterly Journal of Experimental Psychology* 10, 96–106.

References

Gordon, P. 1978. Partial lexical entry and the semantic development of more and less. Undergraduate thesis, University of Stirling.

Greenfield, P. M. and Smith, J. H. 1976. *The Structure of Communication in Early Language Development*. New York, San Francisco and London: Academic Press.

Greenfield, P. M. and Zukow, P. G. 1978. Why do children say what they say when they say it? An experimental approach to the psychogenesis of presupposition. In K. E. Nelson (ed.) *Children's Language,* vol. 1. New York: Gardner Press.

Grice, H. P. 1975. Logic and conversation. In P. Cole and J. L. Morgan (eds.) *Syntax and Semantics*, vol. 3: *Speech Acts*. London: Academic Press.

Grieve, R., Hoogenraad, R. and Murray, D. 1977. On the child's use of lexis and syntax in understanding locative instructions. *Cognition* 5, 235–50.

Griffiths, P. D. 1974a. Review of M. Bowerman, *Early Syntactic Development: a cross-linguistic study with special reference to Finnish. Journal of Child Language* 1, 111–22.

1974b. *That there* deixis I: *that*. Unpublished manuscript, University of York.

Griffiths, P. D. and Atkinson, M. 1978. A 'door' to verbs. In N. Waterson and C. Snow (eds.) *The Development of Communication*. Chichester: John Wiley.

Griffiths, P. D., Atkinson, R. M. and Huxley, R. 1974. Project report. *Journal of Child Language*. 1, 157–8.

Gruber, J. S. 1967. Topicalisation in child language. *Foundations of Language* 3, 37–65.

Guess, D., Sailor, W. and Baer, D. M. 1974. To teach language to retarded children. In R. L. Schiefelbusch and L. L. Lloyd (eds.) *Language Perspectives: acquisition, retardation and intervention*. London and Basingstoke: Macmillan.

Halliday, M. A. K. 1975. *Learning How to Mean*: explorations in the development of language. London: Edward Arnold.

Harkness, S. 1977. Aspects of social environment and first language acquisition in rural Africa. In C. E. Snow and C. A. Ferguson (eds.) *Talking to Children*. Cambridge University Press.

Harris, M. 1976. The influence of reversibility and truncation on the interpretation of the passive voice by young children. *British Journal of Psychology* 67, 419–27.

Harris, P. L., Macrae, A. J. and Bassett, E. M. 1978. Disambiguation in young children. In R. N. Campbell and P. T. Smith (eds.) *Recent Advances in the Psychology of Language: language development and mother–child interaction*. New York and London: Plenum Press.

Henderson, D. 1970a. Social class differences in form–class usage among five-year-old children. In W. Brandis and D. Henderson (eds.) *Social Class, Language and Communication*. London: Routledge and Kegan Paul.

1970b. Contextual specificity, discretion and cognitive socialisation. *Sociology* 4, 311–38.

Higgins, E. T. 1976. Social class differences in verbal communicative accuracy: a question of 'which question?' *Psychological Bulletin* 83, 695–714.

Hill, W. F. 1980. *Learning: a survey of psychological interpretations*. Third edition. London: Methuen.

Hockett, C. F. 1960. The origin of speech. *Scientific American* 203, 88–96.

1968. *The State of the Art*. The Hague: Mouton.

Holden, M. H. and MacGintie, W. H. 1972. Children's conceptions of word boundaries in speech and print. *Journal of Educational Psychology* 63, 551–7.

Horgan, D. 1978. The development of the full passive. *Journal of Child Language* 5, 65–80.

Horton, K. B. 1974. Infant intervention and language learning. In R. L. Schiefelbusch and L. L. Lloyd (eds.) *Language Perspectives: acquisition, retardation and intervention*. London and Basingstoke: Macmillan.

Howe, C. J. 1976. The meanings of two-word utterances in the speech of young children. *Journal of Child Language* 3, 29–47.

Hughes, M. 1975. Egocentrism in pre-school children. Doctoral dissertation, University of Edinburgh.

Hurford, J. R. 1975. A child and the English question formation rule. *Journal of Child Language* 2, 299–301.

Huttenlocher, J. 1964. Children's language: word-phrase relationships. *Science* 143, 264–5.
   1974. The origins of language comprehension. In R. L. Solso (ed.) *Theories in Cognitive Psychology: the Loyola Symposium*. Potomac, Md: Lawrence Erlbaum.

Huttenlocher, J., Eisenberg, K. and Strauss, S. 1968. Comprehension: relation between perceived actor and logical subject. *Journal of Verbal Learning and Verbal Behaviour* 7, 527–30.

Huxley, R. 1966. Discussion of Klima and Bellugi. In J. Lyons and R. J. Wales (eds.) *Psycholinguistics Papers*. Edinburgh University Press.

Hymes, D. 1971. *On Communicative Competence*. Philadelphia: University of Pennsylvania Press.

Ianco-Worrall, A. D. 1972. Bilingualism and cognitive development. *Child Development* 43, 1390–400.

Imedadze, N. V. 1978. On the psychological nature of child speech formation under condition of exposure to two languages. In E. M. Hatch (ed.) *Second Language Acquisition: a book of readings*. Rowley: Newbury House. Reprinted from *International Journal of Psychology* 2, 129–32. 1967.

Ingram, D. 1972. Transitivity in child language. *Language* 47, 888–910.
   1974. Phonological rules in young children. *Journal of Child Language* 1, 49–64.
   1978. Sensori-motor intelligence and language development. In A. Lock (ed.) *Action, Gesture and Symbol*. London: Academic Press.

Jacobs, R. A. and Rosenbaum, P. S. 1968. *English Transformational Grammar*. Waltham, Mass.: Balisdell.

Jakobovits, L. A. and Miron, M. S. (eds.) 1967. *Readings in the Psychology of Language*. Englewood Cliffs, NJ.: Prentice-Hall.

Jakobson, R. 1960. Why 'mama' and 'papa'? In B. Kaplan and S. Wapner (eds.) *Perspectives in Psychological Theory*. New York: John Wiley.
   1963. Toward a linguistic typology of aphasic impairments. Paper presented to the Ciba Foundation Symposium on Disorders of Language.
   1968. *Child Language, Aphasia and Phonological Universals*, trans. A. R. Keiler. The Hague: Mouton. First published 1941 as *Kindersprache, Aphasie und allgemeine Lautgesetze*. Uppsala: Almqvist and Wiksell.

Jespersen, O. 1922. *Language, Its Nature, Development and Origin*. London: Allen and Unwin.

Johnston, J. R. and Slobin, D. I. 1979. The development of locative expressions in English, Italian, Serbo-Croatian and Turkish. *Journal of Child Language* 6, 529–45.

Jolly, A. 1972. *The Evolution of Primate Behaviour*. New York: Macmillan.

Jusczyk, P. W., Rosner, B. S., Cutting, J. E., Foard, C. F. and Smith, L. B. 1977. Categorical perception of nonspeech sounds by two-month old infants. *Perception and Psychophysics* 21, 50–4.

Karmiloff-Smith, A. 1977. More about the same: children's understanding of post-articles. *Journal of Child Language* 4, 377–94.
   1979. *A Functional Approach to Child Language: a study of determiners and reference*. Cambridge University Press.

Katz, J. J. and Bever, T. G. 1977. The fall and rise of empiricism. In T. G. Bever, J. J.

References

Katz and D. I. Langendoen (eds.) *An Integrated Theory of Linguistic Ability*. Hassocks, Sussex: The Harvester Press.

Katz, J. J. and Fodor, J. A. 1963 The structure of semantic theory. *Language* 39, 170–210.

Kellog, W. N. 1968. Communication and language in the home-raised chimpanzee. *Science* 162, 423–7.

Kess, J. F. 1979. Focus types and agent–patient word-order preference in Tagalog. *Journal of Child Language* 6, 359–64.

Kessel, F. S. 1970. *The Role of Syntax in Children's Comprehension from Ages Six to Twelve*. Monographs of the Society for Research in Child Development, serial no. 139, vol. 35, no. 6.

Kimura, D. 1964. Left right differences in the perception of melodies. *Quarterly Journal of Experimental Psychology* 16, 355–9.

1967. Functional asymmetry of the brain in dichotic listening. *Cortex* 3, 163–78.

Kiparsky, P. and Menn, L. 1977. On the acquisition of phonology. In J. Macnamara (ed.) *Language Learning and Thought*. New York: Academic Press.

Klatsky, R. L., Clark, E. V. and Macken, M. 1973. Asymmetries in the acquisition of polar adjectives: linguistic or conceptual? *Journal of Experimental Child Psychology* 16, 32–46.

Klima, E. S. and Bellugi, U. 1966. Syntactic regulation in the speech of children. In J. Lyons and R. J. Wales (eds.) *Psycholinguistics Papers*. Edinburgh University Press.

Krauss, R. M. and Glucksberg, S. 1969. The development of communication: competence as a function of age. *Child Development* 40, 255–66.

Kuczaj, S. 1976. Arguments against Hurford's 'Aux Copying Rule'. *Journal of Child Language* 3, 423–7.

Kuhl, P. K. 1979. Models and mechanisms in speech perception. *Brain, Behaviour and Evolution* 16, 374–408.

Kuhl, P. K. and Miller, J. D. 1975. Speech perception by the chinchilla: voiced–voiceless distinction in alveolar plosive consonants. *Science* 190, 69–72.

Labov, W. 1970. The study of language in its social context. *Studium Generale* 23, 30–87.

1972. The logic of non-standard English. In P. P. Giglioli (ed.) *Language and Social Context*. Harmondsworth: Penguin.

Lakoff, G. 1971. Presupposition and relative grammaticality. In D. D. Steinberg and L. A. Jakobovits (eds.) *Semantics*. Cambridge University Press.

1972. Hedges: a study in meaning criteria and the logic of fuzzy concepts. *Papers from the Eighth Regional Meeting of the Chicago Linguistic Society*. Chicago: Chicago Linguistic Society.

Lambert, W. A. 1977. The effects of bilingualism on the individual: cognitive and socio-cultural consequences. In P. A. Hornby (ed.) *Bilingualism: psychological, social and educational implications*. New York: Academic Press.

Lasky, R. E., Syrdal-Lasky, A. and Klein, R. E. 1975. VOT discrimination by four- to six-and-a-half-month old infants from Spanish environments. *Journal of Experimental Child Psychology* 20, 215–25.

Lawton, D. 1968. *Social Class, Language and Education*. London: Routledge and Kegan Paul.

Lenneberg, E. H. 1967. *Biological Foundations of Language*. New York: John Wiley.

1969. On explaining language. *Science* 164, 635–43.

Leopold, W. F. 1949. *Speech Development of a Bilingual Child: A Linguist's Record*. Evanston: Northwestern University Press.

1954. A child's learning of two languages. *Georgetown University Round Table on Languages and Linguistics* 7, 19–30. Reprinted in E. M. Hatch (ed.) *Second Language Acquisition: a book of readings*. Rowley: Newbury House, 1978.

Lieven, E. V. M. 1978. Conversations between mothers and young children: individual differences and their possible implication for the study of language learning. In N. Waterson and C. Snow (eds.) *The Development of Communication*. Chichester: John Wiley.

Light, P. H., Buckingham, N. and Robbins, A. H. 1979. The conservation task as an interactional setting. *British Journal of Educational Psychology* 49: 304–10.

Linden, E. 1974. *Apes, Men and Language*. Harmondsworth: Penguin.

Lloyd, B. 1972. *Perception and Cognition*. Harmondsworth: Penguin.

Lock, A. 1980. *The Guided Re-invention of Language*. London: Academic Press.

Lovaas, O. I. 1977. *The Autistic Child: language development through behaviour modification*. New York: Irvington Publishers Inc.

Lovell, K. and Dixon, E. M. 1967. The growth of the control of grammar in imitation, comprehension and production. *Journal of Child Psychology and Psychiatry* 8, 31–9.

Lyons, J. 1968. *Introduction to Theoretical Linguistics*. Cambridge University Press.

1970. *Chomsky*. London: Fontana 'Modern Masters'. Revised edition, 1977.

1975. Deixis as a source of reference. In E. Keenan (ed.) *Formal Semantics and Natural Language*. Cambridge University Press.

1977. *Semantics*. Cambridge University Press.

Macaulay, R. K. S. 1977. *Language, Social Class and Education*. Edinburgh University Press.

McCarthy, D. 1954. Language development in children. In L. Carmichael (ed.) *Manual of Child Psychology*. London: John Wiley.

McGarrigle, J. and Donaldson, M. 1974/5. Conservation accidents. *Cognition* 3, 341–50.

Macken, M. A. and Barton, D. 1980. The acquisition of the voicing contrast in English: the study of voice onset time in word-initial stop consonants. *Journal of Child Language* 7, 41–74.

Mackenzie, B. D. 1977. *Behaviourism and the Limits of Scientific Method*. London: Routledge and Kegan Paul.

Macnamara, J. 1972. Cognitive basis of language learning in infants. *Psychological Review* 79, 1–13.

McNeill, D. 1966a. Developmental psycholinguistics. In F. Smith and G. A. Miller (eds.) *The Genesis of Language*. Cambridge, Mass.: MIT Press.

1966b. The creation of language. *Discovery* 27, 34–8.

1970. *The Acquisition of Language: the study of developmental psycholinguistics*. New York: Harper and Row.

McNeill, D., Yukawa, R. and McNeill, N. B. 1971. The acquisition of direct and indirect objects in Japanese. *Child Development* 42, 237–49.

Macrae, A. J. 1976. Meaning relations in language development: a study of some converse pairs and directional opposites. Doctoral dissertation, University of Edinburgh.

1978. Natural descriptions and models of semantic development. Paper presented to the Child Language Seminar, University of York.

1979. Combining meanings in early language. In P. Fletcher and M. Garman (eds.) *Language Acquisition*. Cambridge University Press.

Maratsos, M. P. 1973. Decrease in the understanding of the word 'big' in preschool children. *Child Development* 44, 747–52.

1974a. How preschool children understand missing complement subjects. *Child Development* 45, 700–6.

1974b. When is a high thing the big one? *Developmental Psychology* 10, 367–75.

1976. *The Use of Definite and Indefinite Reference in Young Children*. Cambridge University Press.

References

Maratsos, M. P. and Kuczaj, S. 1978. Against the transformationalist account: a simpler analysis of auxiliary overmarkings. *Journal of Child Language* 5, 337–45.

Marshall, J. C. 1979. Language acquisition in a biological frame of reference. In P. Fletcher and M. Garman (eds.) *Language Acquisition*. Cambridge University Press.

Matthews, P. H. 1975. Review of R. Brown, *A First Language. Journal of Linguistics* 11, 322–43.

   1979. *Generative Grammar and Linguistic Competence*. London: George Allen and Unwin.

Mehler, J. and Bertoncini, J. 1979. Infants' perception of speech and other acoustic stimuli. In J. Morton and J. C. Marshall (eds.) *Psycholinguistics Series 2: Structures and Processes*. London: Paul Elek.

Menyuk, P. 1974. Early development of receptive language: from babbling to words. In R. L. Schiefelbusch and L. L. Lloyd (eds.) *Language Perspectives: acquisition, retardation and intervention*. London and Basingstoke: Macmillan.

   1977. *Language and Maturation*. Cambridge, Mass.: MIT Press.

Menzel, E. W. 1973. Leadership and communication in young chimpanzees. In E. W. Menzel (ed.) *Symposia of the Fourth International Congress of Primatology*, vol. 1: *Precultural Primate Behaviour*. Basel: Karger Press.

   1975. Natural language of young chimpanzees. *New Scientist* 65, 127–30.

   1978. Implications of chimpanzee language-training experiments for primate field research – and vice versa. In D. Chivers (ed.) *Recent Advances in Primatology*, vol. 1: *Primate Behaviour*. New York: Academic Press.

Messer, S. 1967. Implicit phonology in children. *Journal of Verbal Learning and Verbal Behavior* 6, 609–13.

Miller, W. and Ervin, S. 1964. The development of grammar in child language. In U. Bellugi and R. Brown (eds.) *The Acquisition of Language*. Chicago and London: University of Chicago Press.

Molfese, D. L. 1977. Infant cerebral asymmetry. In S. J. Segalowitz and F. A. Gruber (eds.) *Language Development and Neurological Theory*. New York: Academic Press.

Morehead, D. M. 1971. Processing of phonological sequences by young children and adults. *Child Development* 42, 279–89.

Morsbach, G. and Steel, P. M. 1976. 'John is easy to see' re-investigated. *Journal of Child Language* 3, 443–7.

Morse, P. A. 1979. The infancy of infant speech perception: the first decade of research. *Brain, Behavior and Evolution* 16, 351–73.

Morse, P. A. and Snowdon, C. T. 1975. An investigation of categorical speech discrimination by rhesus monkeys. *Perception and Psychophysics* 17, 9–16.

Moscovitch, M. 1977. The development of lateralisation of language function and its relation to cognitive and linguistic development: a review and some theoretical speculations. In S. J. Segalowitz and F. A. Gruber (eds.) *Language Development and Neurological Theory*. New York: Academic Press.

Nebes, R. D. 1974. Hemispheric specialisation in commissurotomised man. *Psychological Bulletin* 81, 1–14.

Nelson, K. 1973. *Structure and Strategy in Learning to Talk*. Monographs of the Society for Research in Child Development, serial no. 149, vol. 38.

   1974. Concept, word and sentence: interrelations in acquisition and development. *Psychological Review* 81, 267–85.

   1977. The conceptual basis for naming. In J. Macnamara (ed.) *Language Learning and Thought*. New York: Academic Press.

   1978. Semantic development and the development of semantic memory. In K. E. Nelson (ed.) *Children's Language*, vol. 1. New York: Gardner Press.

Newport, E. L., Gleitman, H. and Gleitman, L. R. 1977. Mother, I'd rather do it myself: some effects and non-effects of maternal speech style. In C. E. Snow and C. A. Ferguson (eds.) *Talking to Children*. Cambridge University Press.

Oatley, K. 1972. *Brain Mechanisms and Mind*. London: Thames and Hudson.

Olney, R. L. and Scholnick, E. K. 1978. An experimental investigation of adult perception of one-word utterances. *Journal of Child Language* 5, 131–42.

Olson, D. R. 1972. Language use for communicating, instructing and thinking. In J. B. Carroll and R. O. Freedle (eds.) *Language Comprehension and the Acquisition of Knowledge*. Washington: Winston.

1975. The languages of experience: on natural language and formal education. *Bulletin of the British Psychological Society* 28, 363–73.

Olson, D. R. and Filby, N. 1972. On the comprehension of active and passive sentences. *Cognitive Psychology* 3, 361–81.

Olson, D. R. and Nickerson, N. 1977. The contexts of comprehension: on children's understanding of the relations between active and passive sentences. *Journal of Experimental Child Psychology* 23, 402–14.

Palermo, D. S. 1973. More about less: a study of language comprehension. *Journal of Verbal Learning and Verbal Behavior* 12, 211–21.

1974. Still more about the comprehension of 'less'. *Development Psychology* 10, 827–9.

Parisi, D. 1974. What is behind child utterance? *Journal of Child Language* 1, 97–105.

Park, T. 1978. Plurals in child speech. *Journal of Child Language* 5, 237–50.

1979. Some facts on negation: Wode's four-stage developmental theory of negation revisited. *Journal of Child Language* 6, 147–51.

Piaget, J. 1926. *The Language and Thought of the Child*. London: Routledge and Kegan Paul.

1928. *Judgment and Reasoning in the Child*. London: Routledge and Kegan Paul.

1951. *Play, Dreams and Imitation in Childhood*. London: Routledge and Kegan Paul.

1952. *The Child's Conception of Number*. London: Routledge and Kegan Paul.

1962. *Comments on Vygotsky*. Cambridge, Mass.: Harvard University Press.

1977. *The Grasp of Consciousness*. London: Routledge and Kegan Paul.

1978. *Success and Understanding*. London: Routledge and Kegan Paul.

Piaget, J. and Inhelder, B. 1956. *The Child's Conception of Space*. London: Routledge and Kegan Paul.

1968. *The Psychology of the Child*. London: Routledge and Kegan Paul.

Piaget, J., Inhelder, B. and Szeminska, A. 1960. *The Child's Conception of Geometry*. London: Routledge and Kegan Paul.

Pike, R. and Olson, D. R. 1977. A question of *more* or *less*. *Child Development* 48, 579–86.

Pisoni, D. B. and Lazarus, J. H. 1974. Categorical and noncategorical modes of speech perception along the voicing continuum. *Journal of the Acoustical Society of America* 55, 328–33.

Plooij, F. X. 1978. Some basic traits of language in wild chimpanzees? In A. Lock (ed.) *Action, Gesture and Symbol: the emergence of language*. London: Academic Press.

Premack, D. 1971. Language in chimpanzee? *Science* 172, 808–22.

1976. *Intelligence in Ape and Man*. Hillsdale, NJ: Lawrence Erlbaum.

Premack, D. and Premack, A. J. 1974. Teaching visual language to apes and language-deficient persons. In R. L. Schiefelbusch and L. L. Lloyd (eds.) *Language Perspectives: aquisition, retardation and intervention*. London and Basingstoke: Macmillan.

Richards, M. M. 1976. Come and go reconsidered: children's use of deictic verbs in contrived situations. *Journal of Verbal Learning and Verbal Behavior* 15, 655–65.

Robinson, E. J. and Robinson, W. P. 1976. The young child's understanding of communication. *Developmental Psychology* 12, 328–33.

References

Rodgon, M. M. 1976. *Single-word Usage, Cognitive Development and the Beginning of Combinatorial Speech.* Cambridge University Press.

Rosch, E. H. 1973. On the internal structure of perceptual and semantic categories. In T. E. Moore (ed.) *Cognitive Development and the Acquisition of Language.* New York: Academic Press.

Rose, S. A. and Blank, M. 1974. The potency of context in children's cognition: an illustration through conservation. *Child Development* 45, 499–502.

Rumbaugh, D. M. 1977. *Language Learning by a Chimpanzee: the LANA project.* New York: Academic Press.

Sachs, J. and Devin, J. 1976. Young children's use of age-appropriate speech styles. *Journal of Child Language* 3, 81–98.

Scaife, M. and Bruner, J. S. 1975. The capacity for joint visual attention in the infant. *Nature* 253, 265–6.

Schaerlaekens, A. 1973a. *The Two-word Sentence in Child Language Development.* The Hague: Mouton.

1973b. A generative transformational model for child language acquisition. *Cognition* 2, 371–6.

Schiefelbusch, R. L. and Lloyd L. L. 1974. *Language Perspectives: acquisition, retardation and intervention.* London and Basingstoke: Macmillan.

Schlesinger, I. M. 1971. Production of utterances and language acquisition. In D. I. Slobin (ed.) *The Ontogenesis of Grammar.* New York: Academic Press.

1974. Relational concepts underlying language. In R. L. Schiefelbusch and L. L. Lloyd (eds.) *Language Perspectives: acquisition, retardation and intervention.* London and Basingstoke: Macmillan.

Searle, J. R. 1969. *Speech Acts: an essay in the philosophy of language.* Cambridge University Press.

Segalowitz, N. S. and Galang, R. G. 1978. Agent–patient word-order preference in the acquisition of Tagalog. *Journal of Child Language* 5, 47–64.

Seidenberg, M. S. and Petitto, L. A. 1979. Signing behaviour in apes: a critical review. *Cognition* 7, 177–215.

Seitz, S. and Stewart, C. 1975. Imitations and expansions: some developmental aspects of mother–child communications. *Developmental Psychology*, 11, 763–8.

Shatz, M. 1978. Children's comprehension of their mothers' question-directives. *Journal of Child Language* 5, 39–46.

Shatz, M. and Gelman, R. 1973. *The Development of Communication Skills: modifications in the speech of young children as a function of listener.* Monographs of the Society for Research in Child Development, serial no. 152, vol. 38.

Shipley, E. S., Smith, C. S. and Gleitman, L. R. 1969. A study in the acquisition of language: free responses to commands. *Language* 45, 322–42.

Siegel, L. S. 1977. The cognitive basis of the comprehension and production of relational terminology. *Journal of Experimental Child Psychology* 24, 40–52.

Sinclair, H. 1967. *Acquisition du langage et développement de la Pensée.* Paris: Dunod.

Sinclair, H. and Bronckart, J. P. 1972. SVO: a linguistic universal? A study in developmental psycholinguistics. *Journal of Experimental Child Psychology* 14, 329–48.

Sinclair, H. and Ferreiro, E. 1970. Etude génétique de la compréhension, production et répétition des phrases au mode passif. *Archives de Psychologie* 40, 1–42.

Sinha, C. G. and Walkerdine, V. 1978. Conservation: a problem in language, culture and thought. In N. Waterson and C. Snow (eds.) *The Development of Communication.* London: John Wiley.

Skinner, B. F. 1957. *Verbal Behavior.* New York: Appleton-Century-Crofts.

188

Slobin, D. I. 1966. Grammatical transformations in childhood and adulthood. *Journal of Verbal Learning and Verbal Behavior* 5, 219–27.

1968. Recall of full and truncated sentences in connected discourse. *Journal of Verbal Learning and Verbal Behavior* 7, 876–81.

1971. *Psycholinguistics.* Glenview, Ill.: Scott, Foresman.

1973. Cognitive prerequisites for the acquisition of grammar. In C. A. Ferguson and D. I. Slobin (eds.) *Studies of Child Language Development.* New York: Holt, Rinehart and Winston.

1975. On the nature of talk to children. In E. H. Lenneberg and E. Lenneberg (eds.) *Foundations of Language Development,* vol. 1, New York: Academic Press.

Smith, N. V. 1973. *The Acquisition of Phonology: a case study.* Cambridge University Press.

1975. Review of B. L. Derwing, *Transformational Grammar as a Theory Of Language Acquisition. Journal of Linguistics* 11, 261–70.

Forthcoming. An audit of developmental phonology. In T. Myers, J. D. Laver and J. M. Anderson (eds.) *The Cognitive Representation of Speech.* Amsterdam: North-Holland.

Snow, C. E. 1972. Mothers' speech to children learning language. *Child Development* 43, 549–65.

1977. The development of conversation between mothers and babies. *Journal of Child Language* 4, 1–22.

Snow, C. E. and Ferguson, C. A. (eds.) 1977. *Talking to Children: language input and acquisition.* Cambridge University Press.

Snow, C. E. and Hoefnagel-Höhle, M. 1978. The critical period for language acquisition: evidence from second language learning. *Child Development* 49, 1114–28.

Snowdon, C. T. 1979. Response of nonhuman animals to speech and to species-specific sounds. *Brain, Behavior and Evolution* 16, 409–29.

Staats, A. W. 1974. Behaviourism and cognitive theory in the study of language: a neopsycholinguistics. In R. L. Schiefelbusch and L. L. Lloyd (eds.) *Language Perspectives: acquisition, retardation and intervention.* London and Basingstoke: Macmillan.

1975. Review of A. Schaerlaekens, *The Two-Word Sentence in Child Language Development. Journal of Child Language* 2, 322–6.

Stark, R. E. 1979. Prespeech segmental feature development. In P. Fletcher and M. Garman (eds.) *Language Acquisition.* Cambridge University Press.

Steffensen, M. S. 1978. Satisfying inquisitive adults: some simple methods of answering *yes/no* questions. *Journal of Child Language* 5, 221–36.

Streeter, L. A. 1976. Language perception of two-month old infants shows effects of both innate mechanisms and experience. *Nature* 259, 39–41.

Strohner, H. and Nelson, K. E. 1974. The young child's development of sentence comprehension: influence of event probability, nonverbal context, syntactic form and strategies. *Child Development* 45, 567–76.

Sully, J. 1896. *Studies of Childhood.* London: Longmans.

Sylvester-Bradley, B. and Trevarthen, C. 1978. Baby talk as an adaptation to the infant's communication. In N. Waterson and C. Snow (eds.) *The Development of Communication.* Chichester: John Wiley.

Tanz, C. 1980. *Studies in the Acquisition of Deictic Terms.* Cambridge University Press.

Terrace, H. S., Petitto, L. A., Sanders, R. J. and Bever, T. G. 1979. Can an ape create a sentence? *Science* 206, 891–902.

Thomson, J. R. and Chapman, R. S. 1977. Who is 'Daddy' revisited: the status of two year olds' over-extended words in use and comprehension. *Journal of Child Language* 4, 359–75.

References

Townsend, D. J. 1974. Children's comprehension of comparative forms. *Journal of Experimental Child Psychology* 18, 293–303.

Tracy, F. 1893. The language of childhood. *American Journal of Psychology* 6, 107–38.

Trehub, S. E. and Abramovitch, R. 1978. Less is not more: further observations on nonlinguistic strategies. *Journal of Experimental Child Psychology* 25, 160–7.

Trevarthen, C. 1974. Conversations with a two-month old. *New Scientist* 62, 230–3.

Trudgill, P. 1974. *The Social Differentiation of English in Norwich*. Cambridge University Press.

Turner, E. A. and Rommetveit, R. 1967. The acquisition of sentence voice and reversibility. *Child Development* 38, 649–60.

1968. Focus of attention in recall of active and passive sentences. *Journal of Verbal Learning and Verbal Behavior* 7, 543–8.

Turner, G. J. 1973. Social class and children's language of control at age five and age seven. In *Class, Codes and Control*, vol. 2. London: Routledge and Kegan Paul.

Turner, J. 1975. *Cognitive Development*. London: Methuen.

Tyack, D. and Ingram, D. 1977. Children's production and comprehension of questions. *Journal of Child Language* 4, 211–24.

Varma, T. L. 1979. Stage I speech of a Hindi-speaking child. *Journal of Child Language* 6, 167–73.

Volterra, V. and Taeschner, T. 1978. The acquisition and development of language by bilingual children. *Journal of Child Language* 5, 311–26.

Vygotsky, L. S. 1962. *Thought and Language*. Cambridge, Mass.: MIT Press.

1978. *Mind in Society*. Cambridge, Mass.: Harvard University Press.

Wales, R. J. 1979. Deixis. In P. Fletcher and M. Garman (eds.) *Language Acquisition*. Cambridge University Press.

Wales, R. J. and Campbell, R. N. 1970. On the development of comparison and the comparison of development. In G. B. Flores d'Arcais and W. J. M. Levelt (eds.) *Advances in Psycholinguistics*. Amsterdam: North Holland.

Wales, R. J., Garman, M. and Griffiths, P. D. 1976. More or less the same: a markedly different view of children's comparative judgments in three cultures. In R. J. Wales and E. Walker (eds.) *New Approaches to Language Mechanisms*. Amsterdam, New York and Oxford: North-Holland.

Warden, D. 1976. The influence of context on children's use of identifying expressions and references. *British Journal of Psychology* 67, 101–12.

Waterson, N. 1971. Child phonology: a prosodic view. *Journal of Linguistics* 7, 179–211.

Webb, P. A. and Abrahamson, A. A. 1976. Stages of egocentrism in children's use of *this* and *that*: a different point of view. *Journal of Child Language* 3, 349–67.

Webb, R. A., Oliveri, M. E. and O'Keeffe, L. 1974. Investigation of the meaning of 'different' in the language of young children. *Child Development* 45, 984–91.

Weeks, T. 1971. Speech registers in young children. *Child Development* 42, 1119–31.

Weiner, S. L. 1974. On the development of 'more' and 'less'. *Journal of Experimental Child Psychology* 17, 271–87.

Weir, R. 1962. *Language in the Crib*. The Hague: Mouton.

Wells, G. 1974. Project report. *Journal of Child Language* 1, 158–62.

1981. *Learning through Interaction: the study of language development*. Cambridge University Press.

Wilcox, S. and Palermo, D. S. 1974/5. 'In', 'on' and 'under' revisited. *Cognition* 3, 245–54.

Wode, H. 1977. Four early stages in the development of L1 negation. *Journal of Child Language* 4, 87–102.

Wolff, J. G. 1973. *Language, Brain and Hearing*. London: Methuen.

INDEX

Index

critical period   10, 23–8
cultural variation   13, 47–8, 152–3, 167;
    see also language-specific factors

deaf   24, 32, 56–7
deixis   59, 89, 140–8; *see also* gesture;
    pointing
Derivational Theory of Complexity   105,
    111–12, 132
determiners   53, 136, 144–5; *see also*
    reference
dimensional terms   111–12, 114, 129–31
discontinuity in development   4–5, 63–4,
    84, 123–4
discourse features in experiments   112–13,
    136–7, 140
  in motherese   152, 158
discrimination
  of sounds   64–75
  semantic   132–4, 142–4
Dutch   26, 99, 103, 153–4

egocentric speech   39–42
egocentrism   39–42, 59, 124, 143–4,
    168–73
elicitation of adult speech by
    children   153–4, 158, 162–3, 170–1
environmental language   150; *see also*
    motherese
environment of learning   5–6, 9–10, 15,
    29–30, 35, 42, 66–7, 153, 163; *see also*
    communicative context; language-
    specific factors; motherese
errors, interpretation of   84, 87, 106–8,
    111–12
explanation: *see* awareness

family types, positional and
    personal   167–8
Finnish   98–9
foreigner talk   159–61
formal operations   42
French   53, 55, 144–5, 147–8; *see also*
    Sinclair, H.
frequency, interpretation of   83–4
fricatives   55, 66, 69, 70, 73
function
  of articles   144–5
  of holophrase   93
  of motherese   161–2
  see also origins of language

Garo   55, 174–5
gender   53–4
generalization   9, 31; *see also*
    overextension

genetic epistemology   43
Georgian   55
German   54, 106–7, 148, 174–5
gesture   22, 57, 64, 92; *see also* pointing
glides   63, 69
goal strategy   145–6
grammars
  of adult language   7–11
  of child language   37, 93–9
grammatical categories   20, 34, 51, 93, 98
grammatical judgements   13, 30, 94

Hebrew   56
hemispheric differences   23–8
Hindi   103
holophrase   49, 51, 57, 90–3, 101
Hungarian   54–5
Hypothesis testing   9–11, 85–9

illocutionary force   58, 93
imitation
  by the adult   160
  by the child   2, 81, 82, 84, 117, 170
  comprehension and production   117
individual differences   70, 89, 97–8, 153;
    see also intelligence; social class
induction   9–10
information-processing ability   11n, 27, 35
informativeness
  of child speech   58, 91–2, 171–3
  of speech codes   164–6
innateness   10–11, 28, 48, 52n, 66–7, 95,
    163
input   7–9, 15–17, 95, 149–63
instrumental
  case   55
  function   60–1
  passives   118
  relation   99
intelligence
  as measured by IQ tests   4, 10–11, 16,
    56, 154, 168
  as studied by Piaget   42–51
interactions
  between experimental factors   70, 75–7,
    108, 112–13
  social   15–16, 41, 45, 61, 152, 154, 158,
    161, 163
  see also context; strategies
interpersonal relationships: *see* interactions:
    social
intonation   21, 57, 61, 63, 93, 101, 142,
    151, 152, 161
Italian   54, 174–5

Jakobson, R.   63, 72–3, 151

192

Index